THE VIRTUAL LEARNING ORGAN

The Virtual Learning Organization

*Learning at the
corporate university workplace campus*

Edited by

GORDON PRESTOUNGRANGE
ERIC SANDELANDS
RICHARD TEARE

CONTINUUM
London and New York

Continuum

Wellington House	370 Lexington Avenue
125 Strand	New York
London WC2R 0BB	NY 10017–6503

First published 2000

British Library Cataloguing-in-Publication Data
A catalogue record for this book is available from the British Library.

ISBN   0 8264 4707 4

Typeset by Kenneth Burnley, Wirral, Cheshire
Printed and bound in Great Britain by Cromwell Press Ltd, Trowbridge, Wiltshire

Contents

Editors and contributors

Gordon, Baron of Prestoungrange, PhD, was a founding subscriber of the IMCA in 1964 and Principal of its qualification programmes from 1982 to 1996. He has worked with mid-career managers and in professional associations throughout his business life. Most recently he led IMCA through its transition to the world's first global Internet professional association for managers and tutored the first doctoral Cyber programmes to conclusion. He has worked in over twenty countries as a marketing and logistics professor from 1965 to 1982 with the UN and in Bradford, Tulsa, Western Australia, Queensland, Alberta and Cranfield Universities. He has also written more than thirty books, most recently *The Knowledge Game* and *Your Enterprise School of Management*. He was a founder director of MCB University Press in 1967 and founding editor of *Management Decision* and the *European Journal of Marketing*.

Eric Sandelands, DPhil, is a specialist in Internet-resourced learning. He is a Director of Internet Research and Development Centre, Head of Courseware at International Management Centres Association, Dean of the Americas for IMCA and Dean at the Canadian School of Management. He was previously Chairman of specialist publisher VUP International which publishes (with IMCA) the *Virtual University Journal*, *Continuing Professional Development* and the *Worldwide Hospitality and Tourism Trends* e-journals, among others. Previously he was Director of the Transformational Publishing Unit at MCB University Press before becoming Chief Executive Officer of its database publishing division, Anbar Electronic Intelligence.

Richard Teare, PhD, DLitt, FHCIMA, is Academic Chairman of IMCA and Principal and Granada Professor of the Association's US-based University of Action Learning. He has held professorial roles at three UK universities and worked for national and international hotel companies. Richard is a former

Chairman and non-executive director of the National Society for Quality through Teamwork in the UK, Editor of the *International Journal of Contemporary Hospitality Management*, an Associate Editor of the *Journal of Workplace Learning*, and Worldwide Research Director for the HCIMA's *Worldwide Hospitality & Tourism Trends*. He is a member of the Editorial Advisory Boards of seven international journals and has co-authored and edited nineteen books and more than 100 articles and book chapters.

*   *   *

Molly Ainslie has worked with the International Management Centres Association since its inception. Prior to this she worked in health care, hospitality, retail and financial services. In October 1996 Molly successfully led the team seeking ISO 9002 accreditation for IMCA's administrative procedures, Membership Services and its Internet site. In November 1998 she took up the position of Programmes Development Manager where she works on the development and delivery of Global Internet-based Master's and Doctoral programmes.

Kathy Biermann is the Regional Director of Training for Marriott International and leads the management development training programme for over 60 hotels in Continental Europe. Prior to this and to moving to Germany three years ago, she worked in various training and development roles with Marriott Management Services in the United States. Kathy graduated from Valparaiso University and holds a Master's Degree in Organizational Development from the American University in conjunction with National Training Laboratories. Kathy is currently developing academic alliances for the Marriott Virtual University in Europe.

Jennifer Bowerman is a writer and independent consultant in the field of management/executive development. She works closely with the Canadian School of Management to develop educational and business programmes based on action learning principles. Jennifer worked for 24 years with the Alberta provincial government in a variety of posts, most recently as an internal training consultant, and as an organizational learning specialist. She has designed and delivered a number of successful action learning programmes, and has published several articles in various journals and books. Jennifer is currently a doctoral student with the IMCA.

Jacqueline A. Cannon has worked in the hospitality industry for 24 years, initially in an operational role, including that of Deputy General Manager for the Whitbread Hotel Company. In 1992 she began to specialize in training and development and is currently a Human Resource Manager for Whitbread, based in Edinburgh. Jacqueline recently completed an Advanced Diploma in Virtual Training & Development during which she also took on the role of Deputy Set Adviser for the Marriott Virtual University prototype course. She is currently completing an MSc in Training & Development.

Anne Christie heads the Published Learning office of IMCA. She is Editor of several online journals including *Management Literature in Review* and the *International Journal of Action Learning*. Anne is working with colleagues to create and develop an online career development Web portal on behalf of IMCA which will be the home of the Action Learning Institute (ALI). ALI's focus on action learning as a route to professional development will incorporate a host of online facilities including career advice, online discussions and conferences, action learning programmes, news and articles.

Hadyn Ingram, MPhil, DPhil, is Director of Corporate Development at IRDC and proprietor of a hotel in Salisbury. He is a third-generation publican, having been the licensee of a large west London pub for fifteen years after training in hotel management. He has held lecturing posts at the Universities of Bournemouth and Surrey and he writes on the subjects of hotel management, properties management and strategy. Hadyn is currently a Professor of IMCA and of its University of Action Learning, responsible for the management and tutoring of a number of MBA virtual courses with large organizations.

Jane Neil is the Regional Director of Training for Marriott International, based in the UK. During the past sixteen years her career has focused on human resource management, service quality, training and organizational development. Most recently she has been involved in the early development of the Marriott Virtual University, completing an Advanced Diploma in Virtual Training & Development and leading the UK prototype programme as its Set Adviser. Jane is currently completing an MSc in Training & Development as a core team member for MVU.

Jim O'Hern was, until recently, Vice President, International Training & Organization Development, Marriott Lodging International. In this role he led the development of the Marriott Virtual University during 1998/99. He also managed operations training, management development, executive education and university alliances for more than 230 Marriott hotels in 52 countries outside the continental US and Canada. Jim is now Vice President of Learning Resources for Marriott and, among other qualifications, he holds a Master's degree in Human and Organization Development.

Carol Oliver is currently Director of Partner & Accreditation Relations for the International Management Centres Association and its US-based University of Action Learning. Prior to this Carol led the Customer Services team and the Multinational Registry for IMCA. In this capacity she worked closely with the Association's membership services and accrediting bodies. Carol is Managing Director of the Internet Research & Development Centre and a core team member of the Partner Development Group for the IMCA.

Sarah Powell is a business journalist and editor who has written widely about subjects ranging from education and careers to general management. Initially Sarah worked in London and Brussels where she specialized in EU issues. In Brussels she also worked as a consultant for an EU monitoring unit, advising international businesses on the potential impact of European trends and legislation. Since moving to Bradford, Sarah has contributed to a number of MCB publications.

David Towler, DPhil, FIPD, FRSA, is IMCA's Dean of Action Learning and Continuing Management Development. Based in West Yorkshire, he specializes in developing and evaluating work-based learning. This includes standards development, competence-based learning, management development, action learning, learning organizations and lifelong learning. He works with individuals and organizations from a variety of cultures throughout the world including North America, the UK, Europe, the Middle East and the Far East. His doctoral work focused on the management of network organizations.

Catherine Waddle is the Human Resource Manager for the Leeds Marriott Hotel, operated by the Whitbread Hotel Company. In this capacity she has managed the human resources function for 220 Associates since May 1997. Catherine recently completed an Advanced Diploma in Virtual Training & Development, during which time she was also the Programme Manager for the UK prototype. She is currently working towards her MSc in Training & Development. Prior to working for Whitbread, Catherine was a Personnel Manager with Sainsbury's for four years.

Peter Watson, MSc, FCA, is Professor of Accounting and Financial Management at IMCA. He has also been the David Sutton Research Fellow of the Association (1997–1999) and undertook research into the feasibility of private investment in higher education in the UK. This culminated in the development of an innovative Internet site known as the International Business Network, or IBN. Future developments should allow the site to progress to greater levels of interaction between users and information sources. Peter is also Chairman of a heavy leather tanner, and was previously Executive Pro-Vice Chancellor of the privately funded University of Buckingham.

Julian G. C. Wills, PhD, FGS, is the Director of the Global Centre for Credit Mapping and Accreditation of Prior Experience and Learning at the International Management Centres Association. The Global Centre has responsibility for developing and implementing policy relating to the accreditation of prior experience and learning for the Association and its US-based University of Action Learning. Julian is an experienced research and writer, having previously worked in the field of environmental engineering.

Mathew Wills is a chartered accountant and Finance Director of IRDC. He is also Finance Director of IMC (Internet Action Learning) Ltd. Mathew is a specialist in Internet systems design and he is currently Project Manager for IMCA's Site 2000 Internet Project and the development of a community Portal for the international hospitality and tourism industry, with the Hotel & Catering International Management Association and Ingenta Ltd. Mathew was previously Vice President of Anbar Electronic Intelligence at MCB University Press.

Preface

Towards a twenty-first-century prospectus for learning at work

This book seeks to explore and establish the framework around which global organizations might embed their own corporate virtual university. Why would they want to do this? The simple answer is to enable individual learners and the organization as a whole to leverage the benefits of action learning at work. The experiences, processes and accredited framework needed are drawn from the International Management Centres Association (IMCA) and its recently established global Internet University of Action Learning. IMCA is the leading global professional association for career and management development through action learning. It offers independently accredited programmes to industry and to individual learners via its Action Learning Institute. The Association's goals and structures are outlined in the Appendix and online at: www.i-m-c.org.

The book is divided into three parts: Design Issues, Practical Examples and Outputs and Impacts. Each in its own way seeks to 'ground' the concepts and realities of operating a complete, global infrastructure for accredited training and learning with organizations around the globe.

Part 1: Design Issues

The opening chapter considers the rationale and underpinning for workplace learning and the 'added value' of the Internet for learning at work – anywhere and at any time. Gordon Prestoungrange contends that customer orientation and motivation is the key to creating an effective learning organization. Chapter 2 examines the barriers to entering the accredited learning marketplace and Peter Watson reviews the ways in which publicly funded higher education 'controls' access to learning. He considers the alternatives and implications for privately funded 'alternative' workplace structures for learning. How then can corporations design the kind of learning experience that they truly need to compete in the twenty-first century? In Chapter 3, Gordon Prestoungrange re-visits and updates the concept of an Enterprise School of Management (ESM), this being the organization's own business school, founded upon the issues and challenges that it is seeking to confront. In so doing, Gordon considers how the organization might harness its true potential for learning. If the enterprise itself is the key to success in learning at work, what value should be placed on the information resources that are used to support this endeavour? In Chapter 4, Peter Watson reviews the factors determining information values and how they impact on the economics of the virtual university, with particular reference to the financial benefits that arise from the global Internet resourcing of all learning resources (including accreditation and concurrent certification with regional university partners). Finally in Part 1, Richard Teare provides a design framework for a corporate virtual university. If the enterprise is to utilize its own learning resources and 'internalize' the structures, processes, experience and knowledge needed to run its own virtual university, how can and should this be implemented? The purpose of Chapter 5 is to explain the basis of the model and the 'critical path' developed by the IMCA, with reference to the stages of internalization and the key activities involved.

Part 2: Practical Examples
If a theory for designing and implementing a corporate virtual university is to mean anything in practice, it must be based on experience of testing, refining and evaluating prior work – this is the very essence of good theory. Some of the truly ground-breaking work at the start of the Internet revolution was undertaken by MCB University Press, under the leadership of Gordon Prestoungrange. In Chapter 6 Sarah Powell reflects on the processes used and the outcomes derived from piloting the ESM concept with the world's largest publisher of academic and professional management journals.

Much of this work was taken up and extended by the IMCA, which was charged with facilitating the ESM design process. In Chapter 7, Gordon Prestoungrange and Carol Oliver review the processes used and progress to date in the creation of an alternative paradigm for managerial learning in the workplace. Gordon and Carol outline IMCA's progress as a multinational association and its mechanisms for self-reflection and improvement, including its metamorphosis from a business school to a career development association. They also identify the 'value added' role of virtual and face-to-face Annual Professional Congress events in the evaluation of experiences and learning from around the globe. What do learners (or Associates) think of the IMCA model and processes for virtual learning? In Chapter 8, Jennifer Bowerman provides a learner perspective on the processes and values that can be attributed to learning at work. Jennifer relates the challenges of senior managerial work to the possibilities for effecting improvements via the process of researching, exploring and writing a practitioner doctorate. The opportunities for 'strategizing at work' are related to her own experiences of global Doctoral Set study.

If corporations are serious about establishing their own virtual university, they must come to terms with the dynamics of online action learning. In Chapter 9, Eric Sandelands reflects on the lessons and outcomes of scoping and designing global, Internet only, Doctoral and Master's level action learning tutor groups (or Sets). In part, these outcomes provided the foundation upon which the Marriott Virtual University (MVU) was designed and launched, working with Marriott International's senior human resources and training team from around the world. Eric provides an account of the starting point for this work in the form of an innovative Diploma in Virtual Training and Development and the advances in understanding that occurred as a consequence. Building on this theme, Kathy Biermann, Jacqueline Cannon, Hadyn Ingram, Jane Neil and Catherine Waddle offer a client perspective on how to internalize action learning. They relate the experiences of prototyping an MVU programme in the UK with students (or Associates) from the Whitbread Hotel Company to the challenges and benefits of work-based learning. In so doing, Chapter 10 seeks to model the process of establishing and managing Set-based learning from a corporate viewpoint. This includes the roles of the in-company Set Adviser, Programme Manager and supporting Internet, mentoring and project client relationships. Finally in Part 2, Richard Teare and Jim O'Hern consider the challenges for service leaders as they set out an agenda for the virtual learning organization. Here they reflect on the key questions for designing tomorrow's learning organization with reference to the Marriott Virtual University. The chapter depicts a sequence of 'change factors', 'enablers' and 'impacts' that provide a reference point framework for learning and for focusing on business outcomes. If these are the key deliverables, what kind of learning process is needed to ensure that managerial and organizational activity is properly aligned? The twenty-first-century solution to accredited training and learning is likely to be a very different creation and they foresee Internet-resourced action learning as the centre piece.

Part 3: Outputs and Impacts

What are the impacts and implications of IMCA's experiences in designing and implementing virtual learning environments? Part 3 seeks to address the processes needed to sustain and continuously improve the services and support given to workplace learners.

In Chapter 12, Gordon Prestoungrange and Molly Ainslie review IMCA's experiences and progress in using 'just-in-time' quality assurance processes, and in pioneering the use of ISO 9002 protocols with Internet-resourced learning. Among other benefits emerging have been self-improvement models, designed with customers, that enhance the value of the learning process – both for learners and in terms of the credibility of the process itself. Action learning is essentially output-driven, and in Chapter 13 Julian Wills explains the concept and application of credit mapping as a means of validating work-based training using action learning outcomes.

Julian establishes the context for linking training and learning outcomes via credit mapping and explains how integration is achieved by evaluating the outcomes of training as an integral part of certifiable achievement. He also relates the 'period of study time' to prior learning and sets out how accelerated learning can be achieved at MBA level by accrediting prior learning. This draws upon a self-evaluation of own managerial learning, a self-critical portfolio of learning (that evidences the realities of prior achievement) and 'entry point' challenges (in the form of a learning template for the programme of study) via an own-organization monograph with career development.

If the output from a programme of in-company learning is to be valued, one of the essential evaluative measures is the return on investment yield from individual and shared organizational learning. In Chapter 14, Gordon Prestoungrange and Carol Oliver identify the benefits of action learning for client organizations and their learners, with specific reference to the 'value added' of Internet-resourced learning. This, as we have seen, enables a closer relationship with the workplace to be maintained with less 'time out' from work. The concept of a 'knowledge worker' and the contribution that they might make to the intellectual capital of a business has become a hot topic in recent years. The IMCA approach to knowledge management focuses upon the harvesting of learning outcomes and recycling them as knowledge for the benefit and application of learners and their sponsoring organizations. In Chapter 15, Anne Christie and Eric Sandelands explain this approach to published learning and outline its future potential as a knowledge management service provided by the University of Action Learning to its client corporate virtual university customers. If the benefits of action learning are to be fully realized, it is essential to ensure that learners are afforded the opportunity to implement the outcomes of their work. David Towler identifies the ways in which the momentum achieved during a certified period of learning might be maintained with reference to mechanisms for learning renewal (at one-year and thereafter five-yearly intervals). His manifesto for career-long development in Chapter 16 is based on a philosophy of learning renewal. Here, David presents a frame-work for self-assessment and renewal in relation to career-long development and he concludes by identifying the implications for both self-driven and action Set-related study. Finally, in Chapter 17, Mathew Wills explores the future context of Internet-resourced learning. He reviews its potential in terms of current and future capabilities and the opportunities for enhancing and enriching the learning environment via interactive libraries, communities of interest, courseware and the integration of broadcast media as envisaged by digital television operators. Mathew's insights on how to build a university campus without walls reflect IMCA's vision of a global Internet University for Action Learning – now a reality at the start of the twenty-first century.

It is our firm belief that the virtual learning organization really is set to become the core enabler for transformational change and renewal at the heart of corporate life. In this, action learning will be the key to sustaining career-long learning in the workplace with the International Management Centres Association.

We should like to thank our colleagues and clients for contributing to this book and for sharing their learning with us. We should also like to thank Anne Christie, Nina Hugill and Vicky Reevell from IMCA's Published Learning team for their excellent work in collating the book, Charles Margerison for writing the Foreword, David Barker at Continuum, and copy editor and book designer, Kenneth Burnley. Finally, thank you to Avril, Claire and Rachel for your love and support.

GORDON PRESTOUNGRANGE, ERIC SANDELANDS, RICHARD TEARE
Buckingham, January 2000

Foreword

Great changes occur when people see things in new ways; but it takes courage to challenge the *status quo*, as Galileo did when he proclaimed his views about our world as he saw it. In his day he was branded as a heretic and suffered for telling the truth. Today we take for granted that which in his day was so controversial. This book challenges many of the obvious things about how we can improve our work and organizations. There may be a tendency to reject it, like Galileo's work was, because it does not fit easily into the framework to which we have been conditioned. But stand back and ask, 'Why not?' A number of years ago people scoffed when McDonald's initiated Hamburger University. Today, many more organizations are establishing their own corporate universities and this book shows how this is being achieved, particularly though the work of the International Management Centres Association (IMCA). As a professional association dedicated to career development, it has members in 44 countries and it is taking the lead in changing the way people are developing their careers.

The focus of IMCA's activity is action learning. It is yet another example of turning things upside down and challenging the traditional ways. We have been taught at school that we have to learn first before we can do things. Not so, said Reg Revans, a founder of the action learning approach. In particular, for adults, action is the main source of learning, but it is rarely well organized. Revans was the founding President of the International Management Centres Association and he made it clear that adults should first and foremost study the jobs they do at their place of work, not at some business school or college. He showed how it could be done, by getting managers of coal mines to visit each other's mines and learn with and from each other. He also demonstrated how it could be done in hospitals, by getting nurses, doctors and administrators together to show how they could work together more effectively. He showed how it could be done in private enterprise companies and in government departments. But no university at the time would take him seriously, until the International Management

Centres Association gave spirit and structure to action learning. As Einstein, with whom Revans had worked, observed: it takes an unusual mind to see the obvious. That is what IMCA does. It helps people at work to see what is under their noses, by seriously studying how to improve their jobs.

The book contains examples of action learning at work, yet it is easy to read them and to forget them. That is not the point. The question is: are you learning from action in the way that the contributors to this book have done, or are you locked in a time warp, doing things in the same old way?

Here are some straightforward questions you can use to evaluate how much you know about the work that you do:

- Have you a list of questions about your job, which you are now studying?
- Are you sharing those questions with other colleagues, and asking their advice on a regular, planned basis and writing up the issues arising?
- Are you helping colleagues identify questions about their jobs, and how they can study them, and writing up the learning points?

No doubt you work on projects, and regularly discuss your progress – and theirs – with colleagues. But do you go beyond the casual chat, so as to reach an in-depth understanding of the issues, as required in action learning? This is what the IMCA enables you to do. There are three key activities required of all who qualify for membership. It involves writing and sharing with others the following:

1. Describing the work you do and the action you take.
2. Identifying the learning you have derived from such experience.
3. Implementing the learning and recording the results.

The IMCA brings together communities of people, from different industries and professions, who want to learn with and from others. The Association is the world's largest professional body devoted to career improvement through action learning. There are currently twelve constituent member offices around the globe:

- Holland.
- South Africa.
- Finland.
- Canada.
- Britain.
- Singapore.
- Australia.
- Hong Kong.

- Vanuatu.
- Malaysia.
- New Zealand.
- Papua New Guinea.

All of the Association's members are engaged in practical action learning, combined with a wider understanding and review of how it compares with what is written in the literature about such issues.

This book records some fine examples of action learning in practice. It shows what can be done by ordinary people, acting and learning in extra-ordinary ways. In so doing, they are able to gain awards at Certificate, Diploma, Bachelor, Master and Doctoral action learning membership levels of the Association.

The Association is also a global organization through its virtual learning, centred on the Web, and face to face in over 40 countries around the globe. This is reflected in the way in which people from different countries and regions are now interacting to share and compare with each other in order to improve their performance and that of their organization.

I commend the book to you with the simple question: what will you do to do likewise?

DR CHARLES MARGERISON
Founding President of the Action Learning Institute
(http://www.action-learning.org)
International Management Centres Association
(http://www.i-m-c.org.)

Part 1
Design Issues

Chapter 1

Customer orientation and motivation

The key to effective learning organizations

GORDON PRESTOUNGRANGE

Organizations *per se* learn in discrete steps. Their culture (the systems that determine and sustain them) move on when knowing and caring individuals within any organization have the power to change such systems. This is not, as some suggest, a 'continuous' process of change or improvement. Organizations cannot communicate or adapt themselves on a continuous basis. Typically it occurs on a time cycle with a frequency derived either from external pressures or from a self-disciplined internal approach – annual/triennial reviews for example. In the interim, if the people at work in the culture are wise and well led, incremental adaptations/interpretations are made on an ongoing basis. The cultural norm does not change, but it is intelligently applied to circumstances. The accumulation of sufficient extra-normal interpretations will surely be a signal to the wise for change to be explored. Knowledgeable carers need to be empowered.

It is accordingly vital that all organizations that wish to be effective in their learning should continually listen out for the extra-normal. They must not have systems which are so rigid that deviations from the norm are not entertained, or are derided or ridiculed. And they must not have placemen as cultural guardians who are insufficiently aware of the extra-normal to be able to see or hear it when it makes itself manifest.

In competitive marketplaces for goods and services, these required learning disciplines are greatly assisted by the diverse behaviours of other providers. Customers become sophisticated, readily make comparisons, venture feedback and vote with their feet. While it is often suggested that such marketplaces trivialize the offerings available, they also have at the same time a power to do the precise opposite. Given effective communication of the value-added benefits of a non-trivialized marketplace, all manner of improvements and subtleties that reflect customers' wishes will be added to the basic service proffered. It is always unwise to deem one's customers foolish or trivial. If at times they seem to behave that way, there will surely be good reason which, as providers, we need to understand with alacrity.

But there is a tried and well-tested way in which organizations can hold back these external pressures on them to learn how better to meet the wishes of their customers. They can seek to limit supply and create entry barriers so high that few, if any, can surmount them. This is commonly known as a 'cartel' in industry, and is normally deemed to be against the interests of the customer – unless the cartel's inspiration is society itself through the instrumentality of the state. In a phrase, competition is deliberately excluded from the marketplace except among those who accept the rules of the cartel. For a societal cartel, these rules will normally be enshrined in the law of the land.

In many countries for instance, corporations must have their annual accounts audited by an individual from a short list of organizations approved by the state. And they, in turn, write the rules as to how it will be done. In most countries around the world society does likewise for higher education. For whatever reason – and in the contemporary world it is normally because that is the inherited culture – the state limits the number of institutions allowed to offer degree programmes and invites them to write rules and procedures for their own conduct within that cartel. It normally goes further, and establishes and sets as a barrier to entry the requirement convincing those already in the cartel that a new entrant should be permitted.

The justification for such an approach is to keep charlatans out, to provide an acceptable standard of quality, and, *en passant*, to control the overall direction of national educational strategy. Clearly, society believes or implies by this approach that it knows better than the customer. The customers left to their own devices are expected to make an inappropriate decision. And whilst this is in order for the purchase of homes, health care, motor cars or holidays, it is not for higher education.

The weakness of the approach clearly lies in the trust it places on those within the cartel to pursue the best interests of customers when they are truly at their mercy. A reasonable measure of how well that trust is perceived to be exercised can be found in the extent of contracting out/not contracting in that is present where alternatives can be found despite the cartel's apparent supremacy.

New vectors of dissent

Customers for higher education have always had one very expensive option available – to travel outside the society where one lives to gain what is felt to be best. And many millions of individuals do that every day of every week across the world.

A second major opportunity for self-determination for 400 years and more has been the private purchase of books, magazines and, more recently, radio, TV and video higher educational programmes. Their content and approaches have been conceived and delivered in a wide variety of contexts around the world.

But the greatest contemporary vector for dissent has been workplace learning led and funded by employers, of which the arrival of corporate universities is just the latest manifestation. Workplace learning has been high on the agenda of employers around the world for some 40 years or more. In the US such provision receives more funding than the higher education sector itself. Many other countries have growth rates in workplace learning programmes that provide further evidence that the state-created and state-supported cartel is woefully failing to meet needs or is simply disinclined to do so.

After fifteen years seeking to develop university participation in customer-focused lifelong learning, the Royal Society of Arts' Fellow, Sir Christopher Ball[1] concluded that the universities have failed to respond.

Yet even if it was correct that workplace learning was growing apace in a customer-oriented fashion, it seemed until most recently that the universities' role as guardians of, and wise guide to, the body of knowledge was assured. The university library remained the great centre for scholarly access to the body of knowledge. But now the Internet has swept this assumption away. There is nothing now to hold back the emergence of a global competitive marketplace in higher education, funded by and driven from outside the state, except the customers themselves and their conditioning.

The conditioned customer

One of the greatest paradoxes of a cartelized life is its certainty. Right or maybe wrong, it goes on from year to year. Change will be slow. Change will be at the pace determined by the cartel. Customers will be denied choice but bedazzled with the aura of self-serving merchandising. Customers denied choices are as a consequence undiscriminating. If there is nothing to choose between them, what is the point in seeking to be choosy! And as undiscriminating customers they are indeed prone to fall for trivialization of the services offered. In several countries, league tables of the universities are published that purport to guide customers in making choices. Yet the validity for such tables lies in the disaggregation of those elements that impact on the learning of the individuals attending them rather than on the 'overall' rating that creates positions in the league.

Corporate universities have the ability to break through such conditioning by giving credibility of their own, derived from the legitimacy and inherent motivation arising from the organizations where we work. The fact that 'our' organization, where we are content, and often enthusiastic to work, espouses a pattern of learning, is good enough for us. And for each one of us as individuals, the Internet offers the opportunity to enrol at universities the world over, and to gain not only that freedom to enrol where and how we might wish, but also the additional benefits of learning with others from diverse contexts around the world.

Customer orientation's pre-requisites

For most of us in higher education, a prerequisite is something that the supplier/university requires of us. In customer orientation mode it is exactly the reverse. The supplier must understand how an individual can be motivated to want to learn, not make a selection from a long queue of hopefuls on the basis of prior grades. The benefits must be articulated in ways that will compete for attention and time in the myriad activities that already fill the individual's waking life, and in ways that will win time and fees to pay the supplier appropriately. Soft benefits such as 'education is a good thing', or even hard, self-serving benefits such as 'denial of entry' without given qualifications will not suffice. Customers look for a return on their investment of time and money. Both have competing uses, and the supplier has to justify both for the service offered.

Customers look for a learning process that is appropriate for their self-actualization. Few, if any, are looking for a return to chalk and talk. Most have life and workplace experiences that must be interpreted and built upon for self-actualization to be effected: and those experiences will differ greatly. Furthermore, that difference in itself can be a major fillip to learning.

As such, a normative curriculum can be nothing more than a reference point; and even that can be a dangerous imposition. To suggest that a normative curriculum and control of inputs by hour or quantum can deliver quality is clearly an assertion not based on the rubric that 'quality is fitness for customer's purpose'.

But none of these comments are unknown to the educationalists working in the cartel's institutions. They are daily taught and learnt, and regularly substantiated by a mountain of research evidence. So the conundrum is, why does the evidence not drive the behaviours of the institutions *qua* institutions? Why does Sir Christopher Ball despair of the institutions prescribed as society's trusted elite? Why do corporate universities cease to patronize them and resolve to do it their own way? Are they all perverse, indeed wrong-headed? Surely not.

The reality seems to be that the external pressures for organizational learning are weak or non-existent as we understand them. The individuals who know and care do not have the power or the motivation to do anything about it. And the state sustains the cartel because it too does not have the knowledge or the caring or indeed the power in the timeframes its politicians address to do anything about it. And within the organizations, the interminable internal processes of annual/triennial review do not pose the questions as customers would pose them. Rather, they seek to establish how well the faculty members have sustained the normative phenomenon, and they regard quality as accomplishment against their own criteria, not those of the customer.

Clues for those who listen
We have already drawn attention to the major vectors of dissent, to how one can opt out altogether. But within, as the wise pay attention to the articulated dissent, the scope for re-design is readily apparent. This can be well illustrated by what are here characterized as clues. They are all taken from the field of adult learning among workplace practitioners, professionals, managers and senior leaders attending formal off-the-job learning activities.

Clue 1: 'I learnt more in the bar than in the classroom'
This feedback is widely found and widely acknowledged in adult education. It is normally treated in two ways. First the faculty team is exhorted to teach better in competition with the bar: to make the classroom a more intriguing place; to vary the pace and the activities. Faculty who cannot score well on a rating scheme are replaced by others who can. Assuming classroom time is right, these steps are likely to improve effectiveness.

The second approach is to seek to comprehend what goes on in the bar that the customer found so valuable, more valuable than the faculty member could muster in the classroom. It normally has little to do with the beers available on draught, and almost everything to do with the pattern of ideas exchange. Research analyses show that there are two clear strands. The first is to compare one's own problems and approaches with those of others in similar roles but quite different contexts. The second is to learn from and receive guidance from individuals who have clear credibility in the field of knowledge in action rather than simply in the field of knowledge *per se*.

Provided there is no normative curriculum that the provider is determined to convey, even test for recall, on the table, and that the agenda is to assist the individuals concerned to learn and to learn how to move their organization along, the focus can be straightforward. How can the classroom's and the bar's activities find equi-marginal learning returns? How can the two locations be seen as a continuum rather than discrete? Only the customer can unite the two as the customer seeks to acquire and make use of the learning opportunity available.

Clue 2: 'The pace of the programme was too slow'
Practitioners arriving for an educational experience from a busy world of day-to-day working often wistfully recall the leisured pace of life as a student. The gaps between receiving an educational assignment and completing it were euphemistically termed 'reflection'. So presumably were the

gaps between submitting an assignment and receiving feedback. In practice, many other extra-curricula activities filled the time, some extremely active and few of them reflective.

In the place of work these are measured as efficiencies. They are optimized against standards derived from careful analysis. The phenomenon of reflection would be treasured, but equally expected to be accountable. But more important than the contrast in work and lifestyles is the reality of the learning styles most likely to be encountered. Research has repeatedly and not surprisingly shown that faculty members in higher education prefer reflection and theorizing as their ways to learn. Unless they were so, they would find their tenures there insufferable. The typical practitioner is in practice because that is a preferable place to be. Learning is more active and pragmatic than reflective and theoretical.

In a customer-oriented learning process it is simple to see that a successful supplier will be one who deploys learning approaches that are most compatible with those of the learner. If these are the precise opposite of those of the faculty member, the faculty member has to be capable of adjusting the approach. Failure to do so results in a faculty fail, not a student fail – unless of course the faculty member is judge and jury in the cause.

When practitioners report that the pace is too slow, the most normal observation from faculty is that the whole point of the programme is to get them to reflect and not to spend their life shooting from the hip. The evidence that giving extra time to a busy person leads to reflection is not well substantiated. Rather they look for something else to do in lieu of reflection. They are all long conditioned to working in teams, and with support staffs and colleagues on whom they rely, rather than working solo. There may be a clue there, perhaps, to ways to achieve the required reflective processes. These might generate alternatives for thorough exploration before over-hasty action. Is the mission to contradict the reality of the lives of the customers of higher education or to explore that reality and facilitate its more effective conduct, as well as articulating alternatives?

Clue 3: 'Thank goodness that's over. I can forget about that now'
One of the more fascinating assignments to receive from practitioners in workplace learning situations is their answer to: 'What did you do with the things you learnt on your previous major learning event – Bachelor/Master etc.?'

The great majority report that, as far as they can discern, much of what they learnt has been irrelevant for their life since, or is now so out of date that they would be a danger if they used it. Now such reporting may or may not be bad news. After all, they certainly learnt how to learn when they needed to meet whatever testing requirements were presented to them. But the fascination from their feedback is of a different nature. It can form a powerful basis for inviting them as customers to articulate what they expect of the learning experience to come.

Is such a level of subsequent irrelevance a good or a bad or an inevitable thing? Can they, by looking forward, divine a better, more constructive learning experience? Would they rather learn in teams? How much of a normative structure do they want proposed and delivered by a knowing faculty, and how much do they wish to drive their learning agenda?

Most recently, chastened by the confessed extent of their failure to deliver on their good implementational intentions, practitioners argued that it might be appropriate to substitute the implementation of a follow-on learning process for colleagues in their organization for a dissertation or thesis *per se*. In one now-famous example, in the emergent field of virtual training and development, the practitioners literally put themselves through the learning experience to help themselves understand the experience others would soon have at their instigation. The evaluation of what happened and what should best be structured for the next cohorts was itself the assignment or measure of what had been learnt and embedded in the culture for the future. There was no normative curriculum here: there was focused reflection. And there was much pragmatism in the learning. There was lots of action and pace.

Clue 4: 'Saliency, Just in Time and Right First Time'

Perhaps the most subtle feedback that customer orientation affords is oblique. In the complex world of adult life, where lifelong and workplace learning are omnipresent but bustling for priority among myriad other opportunities, the final clue comes from the way practitioners behave, the way they prioritize their work and manage their time – longitudinally.

Saliency, the extent to which an issue or concern is top of mind as opposed to lurking, is a common enough phenomenon. To be effective in a learning context, saliency has to be accomplished and sustained. Yet, as with any service, there will always be moments of truth that can be used as critical triggers. What are these? How can they be educed, shared, managed, reinforced? Truly, they are unlikely to be the seasons of a medieval academic calendar. They will have their own situationally derived determinism. For senior managers for instance, a linkage to corporate planning cycles within an organization can be powerful. The visioning and scenario writing phases, break-out sessions and competitor impact evaluations all have powerful saliency already which can be harnessed.

The learning cycle has its own saliencies too. Start-up sessions are of very great significance, setting expectations. The scheduling of sessions and assignments can be readily synchronized to suit the customer rather than imposed by the supplier. The venues can be rotated to reinforce the shared learning with colleagues within and beyond any given group and, importantly, to develop the social and self-actualization dimensions of the process.

And saliency is close to urgency. Life is busy for most. There are many deadlines to meet, and whilst many will take pride in beating deadlines by a day or so, few will have a work style that beats them by weeks. Furthermore, and perhaps most significantly of all, there is a requirement at such deadlines to be right first time. Yet 'right' seldom means for the pragmatist what it means for the reflector. For the pragmatist, 'right' typically implies high-level satisficing, not polished perfection. Not for the pragmatists are concepts of 100 per cent service levels, which are known to be far more expensive to provide than any likely benefit arising. Not for the pragmatist tidying up after the event so the outcome looks fine for a casual future reader. If the extra mile is required, some far higher outcome than tidying up is required. Experience shows that publication of the substance is far more likely to drive and motivate the adult forward to greater learning, beyond the initial satisficing.

Acceptance of such customer behaviours as the ones to which suppliers need to respond, transforms all patterns of logistical support and service. As time for the final assignments draws near, high levels of deviant behaviour appear. Each individual coming from his or her own context has wholly different pressures acting upon them. The goal is shared – to complete on time for graduation or presentation or for *viva voce* defences. But the complexity of the contexts is the reality. Customer services surely respond.

Mediocracy and democracy on the Internet
As has already been opined, there can be little room for doubt that the Internet offers customers who know how to make use of it a much wider array of choices in higher education. In terms of programme access, only language is likely to bar admission, and with current trends in translations even this will pale. In terms of sheer knowledge access, the arrival of online databases has both accorded universal access and at the same time drastically minimized the expense incurred. Millions of articles, thousands of books by chapter are now available to individuals at any location with a phone line, a modem and a credit card. The wait of weeks or months, even if the existence of the item concerned was known, is a thing of the past.

And so the new challenge is one of data overload. From dependency on library access and faculty guidance, the world of knowledge is instantly accessible and we now seek guidance on how to make sense of it all. And the new intermediary will be what is termed 'info-mediation'. It is a combination of imaginative search engines posited on well-classified/key worded original documents and structured databases of knowledge. The customer who has taken charge of the agenda for learning can readily seek and find what is known in that field and do so effectively and efficiently. The control of knowledge bases *per se* has been democratized.

But more than that, the ability to join the knowledge game and publish has been greatly expanded too. The limiting processes of finite library space and budget, acquiring a narrow range of so-called high quality journals, whose authors were drawn from the cartel within the field of knowledge concerned, has also been fractured, if not yet broken. Ease of access through info-mediation and intranet systems will mean that far more individuals in lifelong and workplace learning will have ready access to knowledge. The expectation must be that, despite their busy lives, they will make greater use of it. Adam Smith's classic dictum, 'sales are only limited by the *extent* of the market', will prevail.

Reform if you would preserve
As is argued throughout this book, the age of lifelong learning is upon us, not just as an imperative arising from the rate of change, but also as the deliberate wish of the better educated generations we have in society today. The driving force in lifelong learning is not the acquisition of knowledge *per se* as it is amongst youngsters, but rather self-actualization of individuals themselves through the organizations where they work and live. That can scarcely be accomplished through a normative curriculum or through any model of higher education provision based on the 'faculty knows most – and best'.

If our current institutions of higher education are to survive far into the twenty-first century they must reform apace. The advent of corporate universities and Internet access has already shown the way. A new phenomenon of info-mediation replacing the professoriat of old is emerging. The state, which currently sustains the anachronistic patterns by its legalized cartel, will continue its drive for greater fee support as opposed to a free social service. In short, they must become learning organizations themselves if they wish to maintain a role as organizations where others learn. Like most organizations faced with discontinuities and paradigm shifts of this magnitude, however, they are ill-prepared and wrongly resourced and staffed. The challenge for leadership goes largely unaddressed because of the archaic structures of decision-making they have inherited in society. What is taught to others in their classrooms is unknown and/or ignored in their own governance.

Customers are shrewd and normally wise. In every event they are the sole end and purpose of the activity and the justification for a continued existence. They must be cultivated and given choices so that they may better assist the processes of educational design to meet their needs.

12

**Design
Issues**

Note
1. Ball, Sir C., Remarks made on 23 June 1999 at Conference on Lifelong Learning, Cassell and Lifelong Learning Foundation.

Chapter 2

Barriers to entry[1]

*Implications for private finance initiatives
in university provision*

PETER WATSON

Introduction

The purpose of this chapter is to investigate the difficulties facing initiatives
to invest private finance in higher education. The emphasis is on privately
funded delivery rather than investing through publicly funded institutions.

In the UK, the largest proportion of higher education is funded by the
taxpayer. Most universities rely on government to fund much of undergraduate education through one route or another. Existing providers are also, in
effect, in control of market entry so that it is difficult for new providers to
establish themselves in the marketplace. As a result, the opportunities for
direct private investment are limited.

Technological change does offer opportunities for challenging existing
suppliers by competing with them on price as well as on the quality of the
service provided. This will result from the ability to deliver the library and
lecture services electronically to the home. The possibility of large-scale
provision of such services opens avenues for reducing both average and
marginal costs of delivery. This in turn gives a partially virtual university the
chance to offer high quality tuition services at low cost. The potential for
delivery to students at times and places of their choosing opens up the possibilities for a radical shift in the organization of workplace learning, with
the opportunity to accredit much existing workplace provision on a basis
comparable with other higher education provision.

The chapter first proposes a way of subdividing the product of universities
into five separate components. It then applies Porter's (1980) competitor
analysis structure to higher education. On the basis of this analysis it
examines the possibility of replicating current university institutions under
prevailing conditions and concludes that this is not feasible in the UK,
though other markets, the US in particular, may offer different and more
attractive opportunities. The changes in technology in information provision
do allow greater scope than has existed hitherto, particularly in knowledge
transmission, and the chapter goes on to investigate some of these.

The university 'product'
Looking carefully at universities, their outputs can be grouped under five main headings:

1. Research.
2. Knowledge transmission through libraries, computer networks, lectures and tutorials.
3. Assessment of learning through examinations and other means.
4. Hotel, conference and recreational facilities.
5. A network of future contacts.

Competitor analysis
When trying to identify opportunities for private investment in UK higher education, the major difficulty is the extremely high protective barrier that surrounds existing universities. Michael Porter's Competitive Strategy (*op. cit.*) seems a natural approach to analysing the competitiveness of the university business. John Daniel has used the same methods in his *Mega-Universities and Knowledge Media* (1996), though he writes from a position inside the stockade which takes the protective barrier for granted. Before using this analysis, it seemed that the most significant protective factor was the heavy subsidy the sector received. However, that is far from being the only barrier to be surmounted by new entrants. Applying Porter, the following picture emerges:

Barriers to entry
- Significant economies of scale, particularly in relation to management and systems.
- Reputation: there is considerable loyalty to key brands, in some cases built over hundreds of years – for example, the names of 'Oxford' and 'Cambridge' define quality in the UK context.
- Significant capital requirements in developing a campus, made doubly difficult for newcomers by the charitable status which all universities enjoy.
- Other cost disadvantages in the form of up-front investment in syllabus, systems and marketing.
- Access to distribution channels effectively prohibited for new entrants by the Education Reform Act 1988.
- Government policy of heavy subsidies makes it impossible for new entrants to compete on price.

Sources of power in the market for suppliers
- There is no concentration in the market for suppliers. The main input is manpower. There is a regular flow of substitute supplies in this market

produced by the universities themselves.
- There is weak unionization.
- The current suppliers of manpower have some control over the flow of substitutes through the examination system.
- The major source of supplier power is through the participation by academics in institutional management. This, however, is likely to work as a force that reinforces the protective barriers surrounding the market.
- Recent policies on quality assurance have actually strengthened these powers as individuals espoused to the cultural assumptions of the main providers have effectively captured the institutions concerned with quality assurance. Academics have one other source of power, and that is through their significant participation in the quangos that control the financial allocations to the university sector.

Sources of power in the output market
- The real customers of the university market, that is the students, have very little power. Unlike most markets, the universities are in a position to exclude those customers who are seen as being unhelpful. This matters to the customers because of the major potential impact on their lifetime prospects. If they do not graduate, job prospects are substantially more limited.
- The real customers of the universities do not even have the power to influence a particular supplier's revenues by changing to an alternative supplier.
- There is one other extremely powerful customer, namely the government, which pays for approximately half of the costs of the industry.

Threats of substitute products
- There is relatively little threat from substitute suppliers. A small minority of UK students chooses to study overseas. Costs of doing so are greater than studying at home, and competitors on the European mainland offer a lower quality of provision. There are few private suppliers and their market position is weak because of the relatively high prices they have to charge. Their position has been further weakened, both by constraints on the provision of grant funding for students studying outside the state sector, and by measures taken to strengthen the licensing arrangements for operating in the sector. This has put the control of such processes even more effectively in the hands of existing suppliers.
- There is a small but flourishing market in the supply of professional education, but for the most part the customers of that market will already have to have purchased a degree before they commence their professional education.

- The knowledge supplied by the primary market for higher education can be obtained from textbooks and self-study, but as this would not supply a certificate of authentication of the product, this is of limited value to the purchaser who also has to purchase the product of the universities. The textbook publishers have an interesting symbiotic relationship with the universities.

Jockeying for position
- There are over 100 suppliers of broadly the same size. However, for their principal output, undergraduate students, the level of sales revenue is effectively fixed in most years. The jockeying for position between providers therefore takes the form of reputation building in order to attract better customers.
- Industry growth comes in fits and starts, dependent significantly on government policy. Future growth is likely to be relatively slow because of funding constraints.
- Customers tend to make a single major purchase, and it is difficult to switch once they have selected their provider. However, even if they do switch, the short-term impact on the provider's revenue is minimal and there is a behaviour code that discourages such switching, even prior to purchase. There are some signs that the ability to switch will become easier in future with the arrival of CAT (credit accumulation and transfer) schemes.
- The industry does have high short-term fixed costs, and the product, as a service, cannot be stored. However, because of the predetermined sales quotas, this is normally only a problem for marginal producers who can usually cope with it by adjusting their customer specifications by taking students with lower examination grades.
- Capacity increments are relatively modest in the light of overall market size.
- There are high exit barriers because of the relatively specialist nature of many university assets, but again the management of the overall market mitigates the effect of this factor. There is also considerable protection for producers against the threat of insolvency that reduces the imperative for competition.
- There is some diversity of rival strategies, but the effect of this is limited by the impact of the tacit agreement which, effectively, the suppliers of labour negotiate with the government
- There are two sub-markets in which there is significant competitive activity: the markets for overseas students, and for research. The overseas student market is characterized by fierce competition on selling expenses, in order to build volume, and this further increases the costs of entering the university market. The market for research is

largely an artificial creation. It results from the insistence of the suppliers of labour that teaching can only be supplied jointly with research. The ensuing competition for a fixed amount of government funding has two impacts. It increases the salaries of those who are judged by their peers to produce excellent research, and it provides a profitable business for a number of successful academic journal producers.

It is worth noting that the competitive analysis of the university sector differs from country to country. For other leading countries in Western Europe, the position is, if anything, bleaker than that set out for the UK. The USA, on the other hand, is a different picture altogether. There, the principle of paying for university education is well established. The federal and the state governments get involved in providing subsidies, both directly to institutions, mainly through the state universities, and to individual students. There is more competition for students between universities, and also a greater openness to new market entrants, though local variations in a variety of governmental regulations make this more difficult than it might appear at first sight. But the leading private institutions, which charge very substantial fees, have established reputations for which students or their families will pay if they are able. There is a very significant market for higher education delivered in English in Far Eastern markets. At present those students whose families can afford the cost go to universities in the USA, UK and Australia.

The analysis suggests that there are two dominant power sources in the UK university market: the government, and the suppliers of academic labour whose power is reinforced by their significant involvement in university management. In their relations with the government, there is an element of co-operation between different universities through the Committee of Vice-Chancellors and Principals (CVCP) to try to influence the overall allocation of funds. There is some tacit fragmentation in this process, as groups of universities which regard themselves as having a set of interests in common with, but different from, the university sector as a whole, co-operate to lobby on issues of particular interest. There is very little competition on price, for the obvious reason that price reductions would reduce employment in the sector, and the effective supplier control rules that out. Outmoded methods of production are, therefore, not only tolerated but encouraged. The industry as a whole is therefore still organized on what is largely a craft basis, to supply what is increasingly a mass market.

The main form of competition is market focus through brand building to attract better customers. Again, this is entirely predictable, as the result is to improve working conditions for those employed in institutions that are successful in this respect. Though there is a rhetoric that encourages diversity of provision within the system, there is no strong evidence of significant competition through product differentiation. In fact the quality control arrangements effectively discourage this form of competition.

Competitive strategy under present conditions

Set out like this, it is difficult to see how anyone could withstand the pressures of starting up in this particular marketplace. The number of non-subsidized suppliers, or of suppliers outside the main network of government suppliers, has been minimal. Those that have been successful have previously developed the highest reputations as niche suppliers of a specific academic product, for example arts and music. Even so, this is not a winning strategy except for the very best, and a number of similar suppliers have been placed under very heavy and even intolerable competitive pressure by reduction or removal of partial subsidies, for example schools of dance or agriculture. Those that have sought to differentiate their product in different ways, for example the University of Buckingham with its two-year degrees and old-style tutorial support, or IMC with its emphasis on action learning, have discovered that the capacity of the existing system to protect itself through licensing arrangements or quality control, coupled with the time it takes to build reputation even for a genuinely different product, have made the road equally hard. The question of reputation is critical. For university students, the perceived reputation of the product plays a dominant part in their choice of supplier. The intrinsic quality of the service offered is often less important than the quality of the other customers of a given institution. In a final twist, academics employed by institutions set up to compete with existing providers keep half an eye on their future employment prospects in with those other suppliers, with consequent effects on their willingness to innovate.

Given such a market analysis, which has not changed in its essence for many years, it might seem foolhardy even to think of trying to enter the marketplace. So why should one try? In the case of both Buckingham and IMC, there was a perception held by their respective founders that the inefficiencies of existing providers (though they would not have put it quite like that), what the economists would call the 'x' inefficiencies of a monopolistic or heavily protected marketplace, were not only giving students a raw deal, but provided market opportunities to compete by offering a product which better met the students' needs, albeit at a higher price. Those arguments still stand, even though it is doubtful whether the strategy of founding a new institution is viable. The reason for this lies in the difficulty of building reputation sufficiently quickly to overcome the price disadvantage imposed by the heavy subsidies received by existing institutions. So if a direct assault on this heavily fortified marketplace is out, what alternative strategies might there be to encroach on the market which would have a reasonable chance of success?

Changes in technology

There is one development in the marketplace that does provide possibilities for developing a strategy for competing successfully with existing universities. This is the very rapid technological change that is taking place in the field of information production, storage and retrieval.

Many writers examine the opportunities which developments in information technology provide for the universities. These originate principally from the significant reduction in both the marginal and the average costs of producing, storing and distributing information, which the Internet is bringing about. Over many years the environment in which universities operate has been subtly changing. Not only is information technology beginning to allow students to gain access in their own homes to knowledge which previously was only available in university libraries, but also the Internet is allowing opportunities for scholars to congregate electronically. The need for groups to come together to learn will never disappear, but the imperatives of time and place are much less important than they were. There is room for greater flexibility in the provision of education. This fits happily with the seen need for lifetime and workplace learning, which will only be met successfully if education is able to supply the legitimate requirements of a very different clientele from that to which it has been accustomed previously.

Much of the literature on the impact of the electronic revolution[2] perceives it as an adjunct to present systems, at least in the short to medium term, and is therefore seen as increasing rather than reducing costs. For example, the literature on electronic journals suggests that the need for electronic as well as paper copy makes the process more expensive. There are, however, some examples of the use of electronic databases changing the underlying processes fundamentally. For example, Ginsparg's (1996) pre-publication database in theoretical physics makes the subsequent paper journals virtually redundant, but for the authentication they add through peer review. It is easy to see that paper output is not even necessary for this. The real benefits from information technology will come from what has come to be called process re-engineering, or what Gordon Wills (1998) calls the Internet dividend.

The main impact of these changes is likely to be on the processes of knowledge transmission, that is education and research. This chapter concentrates on knowledge transmission, as it seems, as explained below, that the research business is already well catered for. Traditional universities have clustered round libraries, and the acquisition of knowledge or understanding has involved substantial use of libraries, supported by tutorials, and formal lectures. As HE has extended its reach, the library has assumed less importance, in reality if not in the rhetoric, and formal lectures, and particularly textbooks setting out the required knowledge for particular disciplines, have assumed greater importance. As these changes have taken place, university education has tended to become less a process of learning and more a process of acquiring pre-packaged knowledge.

There are two specific developments emerging as a result of the lower costs of storing and disseminating information that are likely to affect this process. First, it is becoming economically viable to provide online libraries from which material can be accessed and transmitted in digital form. Second, it is technically feasible, and it will soon be economically viable, to provide online video material of lectures.

It is thus possible for a student at home to be given access to all the *knowledge* required to study a particular subject or discipline. *Knowledge* is italicized to make it clear that education involves far more than just knowledge itself. However, as suggested, the costs of knowledge transmission are a significant fraction of the costs of HE. The opportunity of reducing these costs provides scope for readjusting the balance of education more towards learning.

The degree of control which universities and university teachers have been able to gain over their marketplace has been explained earlier. In the UK, government policy has exacerbated this problem. However, the original basis for this control was probably the university libraries. Only these could afford to maintain complete collections of major scholarly works. Universities exercised considerable power by being able to control access to these collections. The electronic revolution has emphatically eroded this particular control, and potentially scholarly materials can now be made available more or less anywhere at any time and at a modest cost. The university's role as gatekeeper of its library collection is being eliminated. Residence will no longer be necessary to ensure proximity to library collections. The whole of the rationale of the current system and structures is being stripped away. This will, incidentally, have a much greater impact in the UK than the US where the developments in the mass market for higher education had already seen the libraries' role diminishing and a resulting opening up of the marketplace.

Competitive opportunities

If technology does offer fresh competitive opportunities, how can these be approached? There are three possible routes for entering the market. First, setting up a new institution for the specific purpose. Second, acquiring an existing provider. Third, looking to compete directly with only part of the output of a traditional university. The earlier discussion has suggested strongly that there are considerable difficulties when it comes to setting up an entirely new university institution, particularly one that has the specific purpose to undermine certain facets of existing processes of delivery.

In a strictly commercial environment, many companies would attempt to enter the market by means of an acquisition. Such considerations do not apply to universities in the same way as for a commercial activity. Further vertical integration is not feasible because of the fragmented markets of both suppliers and customers. In any case, as existing suppliers in the marketplace are charitable corporations, effectively controlled by their key workforce, there is not an obvious reason for thinking that market entry by acquisition is feasible at all. But is there a reason for thinking that some form of horizontal integration could bring benefits to companies in related marketplaces, for example publishing, telecommunications or television? And if so, is there any weak point at which the universities might be both vulnerable to strategic attack, and slow to respond against attack for cultural or other reasons?

With this in mind, we can now return to the simple model of university outputs, to see whether there are any of these individually which might be open to potential competition. In other words, it may be possible to compete with part of what a university produces, rather than by replicating it as an entire institution. So:

- *Research.* Independent research institutes exist, funded either by charitable contributions or corporate contracts. They face a problem in that academics can choose to provide their time free of charge out of their subsidized salaries. Universities are therefore in a position to resist competition through the use of cross-subsidies. Widespread commercial opportunities probably do not exist or are already being exploited. Conventional wisdom is in any case that most research has to be state funded because it is not a sound commercial proposition. Given the level of subsidies already involved, it might be argued that this is a self-fulfilling prophesy!
- *Knowledge transmission through libraries, computer networks, lectures and tutorials.* The difficulty previously for anyone competing in this area is that universities generally offer similar services on a no-charge or heavily subsidized basis. There are examples where the quality of provision is so poor that private suppliers can earn a return by supplementing the state-funded provision. While such arrangements are inherently unstable, they can provide good returns to private providers. In Germany private tuition organizations coexist with large public universities and also provide opportunities for part-time supplementation of low public sector academic salaries. Such opportunities may develop in the UK. Furthermore, textbook publishing and academic journals are thriving examples of a similarly symbiotic/parasitic relationship between public and private providers. There are also areas of professional education and training that the government has chosen not to subsidize directly and in which universities have only started competing

relatively recently. The advent of partial tuition fees will correct the balance somewhat. Different considerations may also apply to part-time students and adults pursuing lifelong learning.

- *Assessment of learning through examinations.* This really does seem to be the core business of universities, and is heavily protected by the licensing arrangements. Unlicensed providers cannot even trade in the UK. NVQs provide some opportunity for engagement in this area but reputational issues mean that it is likely to be relevant only in special situations. However, would-be market entrants do need to gain access to a secure basis for awarding their qualifications.

- *Hotel, conference and recreational facilities.* There are limited market opportunities here. Universities rarely provide fully for residential or recreational needs. Investment of private capital is being encouraged through the PFI, but opportunities are limited, and in the case of the PFI applied to educational facilities, repayments come from the current income of universities and this is likely to mean cutting other costs. The use of cross-subsidies to deter unwanted competition is also a risk here. The increasing proportion of mature students together with workplace learning are likely to undermine demand for space in residential universities.

- *A network of future contacts.* It is difficult to see this as offering significant opportunities for private investment.

Of these opportunities for private investment, the only one that seems to provide significant new opportunities is in the provision of teaching and library services. Other areas only offer limited specialized opportunities, for most of which there are already specialized providers. The provision of teaching services is an area of vulnerability for UK universities for three reasons. First, quality has been steadily falling despite quality assurance and its associated rhetoric. Apart from the inherent difficulties involved in improving quality by what are fundamentally top-down processes, the reasons for this are a matter of simple calculation: there are more students than ever and no more academic staff. Those there are have to spend more of their time keeping up with the research selectivity exercise. Second, the main focus of universities has tended to be school-leavers even though half the intake is of mature students. Quality assurance tends to reinforce this. It may well be that mature students are more interested in the content and process of educational courses than school-leavers. More important, as the University of Phoenix in the USA has illustrated, they place different values on the service attributes delivered, particularly time and convenience. Third, the business of preparing individually crafted lectures in over 100 institutions across the country is a mode of production that can no longer be justified in a mass market. Figures are difficult to come by and will need justification, but say as an example, an academic's time, as a long-term average, is divided as follows: preparing and giving lectures 30 per cent; research 30 per cent; tutorials 10 per cent; assessment 10 per cent; and participation in institutional management 20 per cent. Textbooks, which are based in any case on the lectures of particular teachers, already summarize much of what is delivered in lectures. There is still a good case for presenting the material in a form other than the printed word, whether on audiotape or on screen. But there really is no good reason as to why a video presentation should not accompany the textbook. The effect of this would be to make most lectures redundant.

Why doesn't this happen already? In fact it does to a limited extent. The Open University produces its own supported texts. Much of the material produced is excellent. However, OU productions have tended to be expensive, and they also produce a size of unit that is incompatible with course lengths at most other universities. Further, the video aspect has tended to be broadcast within normal television schedules. With the possibility of Internet delivery, there is no longer any need for such scheduling. The fact that such products have not taken off probably has much to do with the inherent conservatism of current producers, coupled with the cosy relationship which exists between textbook publishers and academics. In the UK, figures from the book trade (1997) suggest that in 1996 sales of academic and professional books were £689 million and that 53,199 new titles were produced, a very significant marketplace.

One organization that has tried to break into this market is the Open Learning Foundation (OLF). OLF is a charitable body founded by a number of the new universities specifically to produce core course material in a way that avoids unnecessary duplication of effort. To date it has achieved a turnover of £1 million per annum, and produced materials most notably in the fields of business studies (where it has the material for a full degree course), health and nursing, and social work. OLF materials for a business degree cost £15 to £20 per course consisting of twenty CAT points, eighteen courses or 360 CAT points constituting a full degree. At this price the expected volume is in the region of 2,000 copies per annum.

It is noteworthy that most of the UK distance learning material is produced at either pre-degree or postgraduate level. There is very little material at undergraduate level, probably a result of the concentration of subsidies on undergraduate education. At postgraduate level, there are a number of established suppliers of MBAs, for example, Heriot Watt through the Edinburgh Business School and Financial Times Management, Henley Management Centre, and the Open University Business School. Prices tend to be high; for example, the OU Business School charges £8,200[3] for a full MBA by distance learning. This is a 180-unit programme. The minimum course length is 30 units, and the average price works out at £45 per CAT unit.

The nature of the market for textbooks is such that current suppliers have a reputation for being slow to innovate. This should not be surprising. Academics need textbook publishers to help them add to their publication list and get promoted. Textbook publishers are not in a concentrated supply market so their own power is limited. They benefit from the low costs they pay to academics for writing the book in the first place, and academics also help their sales by recommending textbooks. A textbook publisher would have to think hard before jeopardizing such relationships.

However, textbook publishers themselves would appear to be vulnerable to technological change. The analysis is much the same as that which applies to the publishing of academic journals. It is possible for any academic to make lecture notes available on the Internet. A trip round the Net reveals that an increasing number of academics already have their own home pages containing both teaching and research material. The advantages to academics of so doing are to reduce the costs borne by their students and to increase their own publicity by allowing free access to their material. Further, it allows hypertext linkages to other course materials, and even to videos at the appropriate point of their own lectures. The disadvantages would be the loss of royalty income (fairly minimal anyway), and the loss of the *imprimatur* of a reputable publisher. The benefit of the book on the list of publications is somewhat illusory, as it would be unlikely to count in the research selectivity exercise.

If such developments persist, only the best textbooks, those that offer significantly more than individually crafted Internet sites, will retain sales. The development of personal sites will run counter to what might be expected as a result of the new technology. It will happen because UK universities have no effective control over how academics spend their time, and because they, the academics, will see the additional work as being relatively minor in comparison with their accumulated investment of time in preparing the lectures in the first place.

What steps should publishers be contemplating in the face of these developments? Textbook publishers do add value in the shape of their business processes bringing products to market, editorial skills and *imprimatur* or reputation. John Kay points out that the effect of the IT revolution on publishing is likely to be similar to the invention of printing where the reduced costs of production led to an increase in the diversity of printed materials both in terms of scope and language. As has already been suggested, trips around the Internet show that is already happening. In time, there will be a role for a limited number of highly reputable publishers to produce travel guides for would-be students interlinked to and providing information about the quality of the various sources they are accessing. This is the role that Anbar, the management publication database, has clearly identified and is looking to fill. There should be room in the market for a few high quality guides to basic knowledge in a given subject, available on the Internet; these will provide links to other supporting textual, audio and video material. Such providers will also have an interest in enhancing the quality of the underlying material, both in terms of its writing and its presentation. They will also be concerned with the quality of Internet access through what are effectively library sites. Which providers will move first to develop the high quality materials in these areas?

Pricing

Probably the most interesting question about electronically delivered print and video material is its price. Like any information good, its production is characterized by high initial costs and very low costs of replication. Despite the interim phase of higher costs, which results from the supply of both electronic and paper copy, the long-term effect of the electronic revolution is undoubtedly to drive down the marginal cost of delivery.[4] Price therefore depends very significantly on the volume of sales that can be achieved in relation to a given level of initial investment in the preparation of the material, as explained in Chapter 4.

There is one area of potential difficulty. The costs of gaining access to library material could be a significant deterrent in the short to medium term. Present UK students make free use of libraries. If access to journals were to be supplied on a commercial basis, costs would depend very much on the developments in that market. Indications have been suggested above which could mean that it was possible to obtain access to articles either directly from an academic's home page, or perhaps from low-cost pre-publication databases. However, both university libraries and journal publishers have an interest in prolonging their power to exist or to earn revenues on a similar basis to the present. How successful they will be in delaying the introduction of very low-cost online electronic print material is very much an open question.

It is, understandably, a source of some irritation to academics that publishers of both journals and textbooks seem to enjoy significant commercial success at their expense. It is worth a little thought to understand why this has come about. In simple terms, normal commercial considerations are extremely distorted by the levels of government subsidy. There is no shortage of individuals ready and willing to write textbooks. So far as scholarly publications are concerned, the pressure to publish means that there is little shortage of potential copy. Indeed, journals are in a position to charge authors for the cost of considering their work. The shortage in the market is space in journals, not material to fill them. It is therefore no surprise that most authors receive little direct reward for their efforts. While there is such a surfeit of material competing for publication, there is little prospect that the direct rewards to authors will bear much relation to the cost of producing articles measured in terms of the time spent.

This factor does introduce an element of instability into the relationships in the marketplace, leading to a suspicion that change may well take place sooner rather than later. The proliferation of authors is such that any change is unlikely to increase their material rewards. However, the balance of power between authors and publishers will be changed fundamentally by the authors' ability to distribute publications directly to the marketplace through the Internet. If the value added by the publisher is insufficient to compensate the author for the restrictions on access which would result, an author would self-publish.

The implications of this are that neither libraries nor publishers will be in a position to strangle the market, and that the price of access to the information *per se* will be low. The costs of network access, whatever they are, will be the major cost of accessing digital material.

Tentative proposal

So far as this study is concerned, the area identified as offering a possible commercial opportunity for investing in higher education is in supplying high quality courseware for courses with significant student numbers. Business studies and engineering are the largest subject groupings at UK universities, with over 100,000 students each at any time. Of these two, business studies at undergraduate level would appear to offer the most potential. This is because it is somewhat less fragmented than engineering, and requires less by way of laboratory space, and has the greatest number of students.

There are two potential ways of opening up this market: first, directly via the textbook market to individual students; and second, through business and commercial customers. The difficulty with the first approach is that it is virtually a frontal assault on the existing customers of universities. As such, this line of attack would almost certainly attract maximum retaliation from universities. This could be achieved through lecturers not only not recommending purchase of the material produced, but also actively undermining its credibility. Further, the textbook market would not necessarily be an easy channel through which to launch a new and innovative product. There would be very high costs for marketing and publicity to secure the necessary initial sales volumes. Questions of display, comparability to existing texts and so on would make it more difficult to establish perceptions of a genuinely new, more versatile and superior product. In addition, if the courseware also involved purchase of an existing text, discrimination from existing texts would be even more difficult to establish. The additional cost of the courseware as compared to textbooks would be a deterrent to students, who are not well off as a group, even though it did deliver greater value for money.

The second approach, which would involve the corporate market, has rather more to recommend it. First, companies are disillusioned with much of the existing product. Second, there is potential market expansion if companies see the product as meeting their education and training needs for existing employees who would not necessarily go to university. Third, companies could find it attractive to have input into the content of the product. Fourth, it would be beneficial if the product could link in with material produced by companies for their own educational programmes. Fifth, if the product were combined with a formal scheme of accreditation of prior learning, it would not only be seen as fair in recognizing the value of similar work, but it would also reduce the costs to the customer. Sixth, as a market this is aimed more at mature students. It is possible, as it is not envisaged that the provider of the courseware would deliver more than a fraction of the academic support, that other universities would see use of the courseware as a way of building corporate business.

In the corporate market, price would probably not be as crucial as in the textbook-related marketplace. At this stage, little research has been done on potential volume. For courses with a sales volume of 5,000 students, a target price range of £75 to £100 for courseware and texts could be envisaged. This is the maximum price contemplated for the individual market. In the corporate market it would not be unreasonable to think of doubling this price to a range of between £150 and £200 per course. At this price, if the courseware can also be sold in smaller modules, a selling price of £20 to £25 per module, representing fifteen hours of study, would appear to be very attractive indeed in relation to the costs of commercial courses or indeed self-study briefing material, even if the courseware material had to be supplemented by tutorial support.

The intention is to deliver the main product over the Internet, and it remains to be decided whether non-Internet versions would be produced. The development of company and industry fora would be an essential part of the product to allow ease of support within the company. It would be crucial to achieve and sustain a high quality product.

Conclusion
The intention of this chapter has been to outline the strategic considerations of investing in higher education. On the one hand, it is a well-protected market with high barriers to entry. However, the technological changes in the production, storage and dissemination of information have a significant potential impact on the existing processes of higher education. The destabilizing effects of these may well present significant opportunities for competing successfully with part of the output of existing producers. It is not easy to recognize quite which direction future developments will take. There is undoubtedly a potential for a reduction in the costs of information.

Hitherto, both libraries and publishers have been natural points of restriction on the output and availability of information. Both will now become vulnerable to the possibility of self-publication by academics. This is happening to an extent already through personal Web pages where early drafts of articles can be posted to attract comment.

The consequent proliferation of information provides new opportunities for services that use independent experts either to provide advice on the quality of particular material, or to provide structured access to materials available. The latter opportunity is the one highlighted in this chapter. It envisages high quality travel guides for the Internet providing clear explanations of the basic knowledge in specific areas, with direct links to supporting materials embedded into the text.

For this to work as a proposal there are really two essentials. The first is to provide the materials at a low enough price to make it an attractive purchase to a large number of potential users. The second is to develop delivery mechanisms and means of marketing which actually bring the product to a sufficient number of purchasers. There is a significant challenge in this. However, there is also a large opportunity for the bold investor who gets it right and can crack the marketing problem. If successful it would put very substantial pressure, particularly on academic publishers, and eventually on universities.

Notes
1. This chapter was written on the basis of work undertaken as David Sutton Research Fellow of IMC. Thank you to Gordon Prestoungrange for his help in the genesis of this piece. Any errors are my responsibility.
2. See for example the comments of S. Harmad (1997) 'The paper house of cards (and why it's taking so long to collapse', *Ariadne*, http:/www.ariadne.ac.uk/issue8/harmad/.
3. Open University website, http://www.open.ac.uk/, based on £1,490 for a 30-unit course.
4. See for example A. Odlyzko (1997) 'The economics of electronic journals', *First Monday*, http://www.firstmonday.dk/issues/issue2_8/odlyzko/index.html.

References
Daniel, J. S. (1996) *Mega-Universities and Knowledge Media: Technology Strategies for Higher Education*, London, Kogan Page, pp. 68–9.

Ginsparg, P. (1996) 'Winners and losers in the global research village', *Unesco Conference Paris*, http://xxx.lanl.gov/blurb/pg96unesco.html.

Porter, M. E. (1980) *Competitive Strategy: Techniques for Analysing Industries and Competitors*, New York, The Free Press.

Wills, G. (1998) 'E-postcard 20 – the Internet dividend', http://www.imc.org.uk/imc/occpaper/postcards/posted24.htm.

Chapter 3

Sustaining learning capture in unstable workplaces

GORDON PRESTOUNGRANGE

The proposition was advanced in 1993 by Wills that enterprises could and should institutionalize their continuous action learning processes within a framework he called an Enterprise School of Management, or ESM. Since that time he, and many more working with him or in total ignorance of his proposal, have carried such ideas into practice around the world. In this chapter we will reprise the main line of analysis and highlight the major successes and constraints that have arisen and how they are being overcome. The unexpected yet spectacular impact of the emergence of the Internet since the ideas were originally advanced will also be discussed.

What is an ESM?
The notion of an Enterprise School of Management is built on the assertion that 'managers learn best at work'. The most frequently quoted phrase from Wills is his opening line: 'The enterprise where we work is far and away the most significant business school that managers ever attend.' What he implied was that no amount of study of textbooks or theories or other people's case experiences written up as teaching aids can replace learning by doing *provided that* the doing is captured, reviewed and integrated into the enterprise's learnt systems. He argues that a learning organization is one where the feedback from actions taken and evaluated is continually used as the basis to update and amend the 'way we do things around here'. A successful learning organization is one that learns at least as fast, and preferably faster, than change is making old systems and procedures obsolete.

To capture what is learnt from doing is the challenge. Wills argues that much of the learning is not even distilled sensibly, and even less is captured in systems and procedures. *Intra*preneurs spend much time being sponsored or protected by a mentor as they go around the edges of systems and procedures. *Entre*preneurs have normally opted out of the enterprise to be able to proceed with changes and new ideas without the unending frustration of yesterday's systems and procedures.

The ESM's purpose is to offer an official, institutionalized process framework which legitimizes the distillation of improved systems and procedures from action in the field of play. Systems for the enterprise belong to all who operate them, and Wills proposed that the Principal of the ESM should be the senior operations management executive or director.

Much of this line of argument is analogous with the ISO 9000 approaches to continuous quality improvement of systems and practices. Its difference is in seeing the ESM's activities as changing systems and procedures as a logical consequence of real action rather than a process of monitoring variances. The ESM as presented by Wills is closer to the theories of double and treble loop learning, but goes further. He wants to see it implemented by having the top operations executives right in the midst of the process. They already direct the action; now they are invited to direct the learning and its capture.

If and when such an acceptance exists, the curriculum at the programmes of learning within an ESM are wholly derived from the challenges facing the enterprise. Normative notions of what should be taught or learnt, such as a traditional business school would propound, are irrelevant. The curriculum arises from the challenges which are best expressed as questions. Faced with this uncertain situation (not a puzzle to which an answer is already known), what should we do next? There are no right answers, only workable action lines that can be resourced and tested and learnt from and used as the base for the next level of questioning.

What has been happening?
The ESM was acknowledged in a private communication by Charles Handy with the author as the definitive justification of action learning, the blueprint for its use within the enterprise: and so it has proved. And as in all fine questioning sequences, it has gained its own momentum and metamorphoses.

From our own originating institution, International Management Centres Association (IMCA), it has been conducted with five successive cohorts of health care leaders from myriad professional disciplines to help create St Helier as one of the best managed Health Care Trusts in the UK. It has been deployed within five successive cohorts of quality leaders in the French multinational electronics enterprise, SEMA. It has been used (as we describe elsewhere) to assist the world's leading academic publisher of management journals, MCB University Press, to come of age as an enterprise and to scale the heights and plumb the depths of uncertainty as it seeks to metamorphose itself from paper based/high price/low volume activities to e-publishing/low unit price/global access via wholly different channels of distribution.

Within IMCA itself we have taken our own medicine to address the transformation of global delivery of action learning programmes to corporate clients and individuals in 44 countries from face-to-face small Sets to one of global CyberSets with face-to-face sessions of the Associates/students' own volition – by embracing change and the new technologies of the Internet just as MCB University Press has done.

In each and every case it was driven, and still is being driven, by self-confident operations management, with a continuity of leadership over a period of five years and more. The workplace leadership has been unstable in a massively changing and uncertain external environment. For health care it has been the government's evolving policy frameworks and an escalating demand within constrained budgets; for electronics engineering, academic publishing and global action learning education it has been the impact of undreamed-of technological and consequent marketplace transformations.

The second major component of what has been happening (and it is far bigger than IMCA's participation) has been the emergence of corporate universities. These have been well chronicled and championed by Meister (1998). What is significant here is that every one of these institutional frameworks seeks to address a part of the ESM's agenda: the curriculum must be what the corporation or enterprise perceives as the learning challenges – not what is deemed requisite by another, normally state-funded, self-serving academic elite (see Chapter 2). Whether they have addressed, especially but not exclusively, literacy in the basic workforce as Motorola U or Nissan U in South Africa have done; or customer service skills sets as Unipart U and McDonald's U do; or high level development of aeronautical engineers as at British Aerospace U – they have all been consistent. They determine the curriculum and the budgetary allocations made to their own priorities. What took place in many fields of advanced and industrial research from the 1950s to the 1970s across the world is now taking place in terms of adult learning. The state-funded universities have allowed themselves through their myopia to lose out on the greatest and best-funded marketplace for learning in the twenty-first century.

The corporate university is, however, much less ambitious than an ESM. Its agenda is more modest, more traditional, although its branding is bolder. It normally seeks to develop the individual on the assumption that the individual will, as night follows day, be able to impact the enterprise at large. It is a more elegantly formed version of regular company training activities rather than a well-conceived revolution in learning organization development.

What lessons are to hand thus far?
There are two critical issues that have emerged thus far in enabling the ESM to flourish. The first, which has already been referred to, is continuity of leadership within any given enterprise. The second is the instruments and practices by which learning is captured for the enterprise and then incorporated into its culture, its learnt systems.

Continuity of leadership

Most large-scale enterprises are complex, having a multitude of sub-cultures; and the affairs of the subcultures ebb and flow. Most significant leaders rely on new fashions or fads in management, addressing well-tried and well-tested needs, to act as a fillip for delivering sustained motivation and enthusiasm in their workplace. Many leadership roles are held for relatively short periods of time as a result of promotions, career changes within and outside the enterprise, or in unfortunate times to downsizing or restructuring. Insofar as the momentum and support for an ESM, even when institutionalized, is associated with a departing or departed leader, there is always the temptation for the incoming leader to make an impact by doing things in his or her way.

It is not necessarily inappropriate, one should add, for successful leadership that this should be so. To proceed with confidence in a leadership role is normally vital, and the sources of inner and outer confidence will seldom come from what one's predecessor did or championed: they will come from one's own distinctive other experiences. Accordingly any leadership change that seeks to do things differently, as opposed to carry things forward in similar fashion, will put the ESM in jeopardy. And once it loses its leader's support it can be expected to face crisis.

The origin of the exploration at IMCA that engendered the concept of the ESM was a search to see how an institutionalized framework might survive changes of leadership. In this respect the emergent conclusion that can be offered is that in those circumstances where the future is most uncertain, and the benefits are likely to be greatest, the stability of leadership is most vulnerable unless it stems from a subculture that is and can be expected to continue in a relatively stable way when the macro picture changes in response to greater uncertainties. This would appear to be the case for both St Helier and SEMA; or, as in the cases of MCB University Press and IMCA, where the enterprise concerned is privately owned either by shareholding owner directors committed to the longer term or the members themselves of a professional association.

Other major ESM initiatives by IMCA, as with Allied Irish Banks (Britain), with Maybank and Malaysia Airlines in Malaysia, did not endure beyond the leadership change, despite their clearly demonstrable success in terms of ROI (return on investment) and evolved cultures. The biggest ESM of all, with National Sorghum Breweries in South Africa, was also unable to survive the collapse of its acceptance among dissenting senior managers despite the demonstrable fact that its contribution to black managerial empowerment was inestimable. The ESM initiative with Metal Box was unable to survive its merger with Carnaud of France.

The second critical issue has been the extent to which the managers directly participating in an ESM are able to articulate to colleagues and follow through on implementation of appropriate changes. As is shown elsewhere, the follow-through on major single projects has been good, and the ROI, on average, spectacular. Yet paradoxically, while this was happening, the reported concerns of managers very much included a lack of support in the workplace for what they sought to accomplish. Fellow managers and bosses, not directly involved with the action learning protocols and in all events very busy with significant other tasks, did not identify as much as those who were participating would have hoped. They were often apathetic and sometimes obstructive.

Here the initial thrust, which is still continued, is to involve fellow managers in the derivation of projects and issues for the curriculum, and to invite fellow learners to each location in turn to allow colleagues to meet with and understand the broader background. Steering Groups of topmost executives are also established to ensure earliest buy-in which, of course, is at the very heart of the ESM model. Most lately, working with British Airports Authority (BAA) it was proposed and has been energetically pursued ever since that all work undertaken should be distilled for quite specific feedback into the enterprise, to the ears and offices of the leaders concerned, by the tutorial staffs. The tutors in financial management, for instance, are mandated to work with the managers on the programme to prepare, through mutually agreed drafts, a proposal for action, Action Lines. This output is the first, and in many ways the most crucial, outcome of what is known as 'Project Harvest' (imc.org.uk/imc/harvest/publish.htm). Each individual manager's own recommendations are made and acted upon as appropriate in their discrete context; but the tutor's contribution, on behalf of IMCA and all the managers together, is intended as the 'cultural adjustment/learnt systems change' Action Lines. The notion is of course a tough one for the tutors, and sometimes even tougher for the senior executives, particularly as follow-up checks are pursued by IMCA and the managers concerned through an evaluative learning instrument known as the A+ (Action Plus) Review.

The second and more visible aspect of 'Project Harvest' has been the introduction of requirements to publish articles both on the literature and knowledge unearthed and interpreted in the enterprise's own context, but also on the gestalt implications of each manager's inquiry and actions. These are not only useful in their own right to those elsewhere in the organization, but also to the wider managerial professional community of IMCA.

Finally and most lately, IMCA has resolved to encourage two new initiatives. The first is to set trios/small groups to work on its own professional qualification programmes to provide critical mass and balance in the initiatives undertaken, and even more significantly to enhance the probability of acculturation arising and Action Lines being implemented. The second is to offer the option on all programmes to take as the basis for the major action learning project the design and conduct of an action learning programme among one's peers and subordinates, thereby firmly communicating the meaning of the ESM and gaining even broader support for acculturation and Action Lines.

It can be seen in all these respects that the organizational realities of the enterprise are increasingly determining the learning structures and designs adopted. This is truly discomforting for many tutors. Many wish for a known and stable context in which to work. Yet the reality of the managers' workplace is that it is frequently unstable and there is no real alternative if one wishes to be relevant and work on the field of action, but to respond to the realities that are there. And if the ESM is to be a success, the enterprise needs to ensure that the design and curriculum includes the delivery of effective outcomes as well as meaningful outputs.

The bitter-sweet role of the Internet

To all who have been actively exploring the Internet these past five years it is clear that it has the ability to transform the effectiveness of a number of mainstream learning elements, e.g. more comprehensive, more easily searchable and routinely updated knowledge resources globally available without despatch and transit delays. It also enables the mobile manager to stay in touch with colleagues at a distance in a discussion forum/environment, and to meet virtually with colleagues normally out of reach altogether.

Working with global organizations, where the sun never sets on their operational staffs, a-synchronous communications via the Internet, and increasingly as necessary with video linkages too, the opportunities for sharing are not only increased exponentially but new opportunities are created. Where the sheer expense involved in meeting or the time involved in travel and the accompanying disorientation of jetlag would have ruled out meeting and sharing except by synchronized phone systems, extensive multiple participant communication has been enabled.

Even where the enterprise does hold three-, six- or twelve-monthly review meetings face to face, these can be conducted in a better prepared and shared virtual environment *prior* to the face-to-face sessions. Everyone can be well down the line of discussions already and the agenda-in-action rather than the agenda-de-nouveau can be the focus when face-to-face or synchronized telephone contact is finally made.

These approaches have enabled the unstable/uncertain/fluctuating workplace environment to live with that instability while still pursuing activities that would normally have been ruled out.

The Internet has, of course, also democratized the access to information and the opportunities for participation in discussions to all levels that are authorized or determined to join a discussion forum in whatever way. That is good news but also potentially debilitating. It is bitter-sweet. The opportunity at all levels to challenge and question and to look-in critically as others seek to learn their way through to an outcome, can communicate to the inexperienced watcher an apparent confusion which is truly no more than anticipatory debate. If widespread access accords time and space to doubting Thomases, too much nervous energy goes into arguing the case rather than trying it out. Leadership becomes the art of extended politics rather than a responsibility to make things happen in the longer-term interest and receive the brickbats.

New skills are required, however, to gain the sweet rewards. The access normally gives rise to data overload, with either too much knowledge to absorb or too many discussion forum elements posted. The frustration of having so many virtual opportunities to participate, not just in one or two conferences a year, but one or two every day of the year, is mind-blowing. The creation of capture systems, search engines and personalized travellers only makes matters worse. The benefit of a tutorial helper being available 24 hours a day, seven days a week, sounds ideal, but in the out-turn it means too much of everything. So we do have to learn to be wise, to wise up. We have to learn how to be highly selective, how to niche markets.

There is also felt to be a trend to trivialize issues in the ebb and flow of discussion. The circulation of jokes is a widespread phenomenon, but that is not a symptom of trivialization, rather the desire for some relief in the unemotional world of virtual wordage. It is uncertain whether it is the case that trivialization occurs, however. Rather, the issue may well be that such chatter and discussion as is enabled to take place whets the appetite for more profound discussion, and the individuals are not often ready or able to reach that level. In other words, the customary 'revolution of rising expectations' is present with us all here on the Internet. If this hypothesis indeed holds true, it is erroneous to accuse the Internet of trivialization; we must turn our attention to how to get the more profound elements to flourish. This requires a level of commitment as in face-to-face situations in life, to go much further. That requires a common commitment to the likely outcomes or a very substantial supportiveness of one for the other.

This begins to explain why virtual groups of individuals have a strong, even enhanced desire to meet face to face. They start to seek one another out because the issues they have explored at the seemingly superficial level on the Internet in the discussion forums cry out for more substantial (and also of course for the tactile/emotional) benefits of personal encounter. We feel we know one another well, but not well enough. The understood and accepted cost of face-to-face meetings is seen to have a superior or enhanced benefit. It is not simply that distance adds enchantment; it conveys the feeling that something more can well be added if only . . . if only indeed.

It is in such contexts as these, therefore, that we can understand that virtually trailed face-to-face conferences and workshops encourage larger attendance. It is a phenomenon present now both with providers who have moved from former face-to-face paradigms to use the Internet *and* for those who formerly used a distance education paradigm.

But let us not lose sight of the next quest on the Internet as we explore how the Internet enhances the perceived benefits of face to face. We have not yet seen the creation of successful high level conferring on the Internet; rather it is serving predominantly like the telephone as a conversational medium. To undertake high level conferring requires a different media mix, which presently involves online and offline working. To undertake this mode of interaction requires a strong mutual commitment. It is certainly asynchronous; yet, with the arrival in the next several years of linked video, this too might be expected to change in the same way as presence at a conference enables rapt attention and considered response, even prior reading and contributed debate.

The secret is most likely to lie in providing a clear role for Individual B in making comment of Individual A, which either contains its own rewards or reciprocal assistance and critique. We have come to call it 'shoulder tapping' as an initial approach, singling out a given individual to take the lead and then requiring specific individuals to respond. It is a common enough technique at face-to-face conferences where the chair will often deliberately 'place' questions in the audience to get discussion going after any given presentation. The difference here is that every individual is chair to his or her own ideas and must learn and practise the requisite skills.

Instability rules

There are some who believe that unstable workplaces can simply be wished away in learning design. On the contrary, they are in fact themselves a major field for learning, to which all too little attention has been given. Adult life is notoriously unstable for all, and the controlled or make-believe world of childhood or adolescence is not available. If learning is to flourish, providers have to accept that designs must be robust to the buffeting they will receive, and build in response and recovery tactics to handle it.

As in all service industries, there will be moments of truth that can be managed objectively and with high profile behaviours expected. But much of the in-between times, when most of the learning is taking place and when most of the experiences happen, on which the learning will be based, are untidy and subject to high levels of instability.

One of those moments of truth is the moment of capture itself, of realization that something is well worth writing down and doing that very thing; or sharing in a conference or in a discussion forum. I am doing that very thing here and now, writing this chapter of this book. In learning, we must frequently use 'assignments' to give the moment greater emphasis. We call for reports or discussion papers, as much to clarify what the writer knows but has not distilled, as for the benefit of the recipient. The more fragmented and disjointed adult life becomes, the more we need such reference points or touchstones. But they must be well crafted to achieve the required outcomes. A very great deal of thought needs to be focused on them, but when it has been done that way, the capture is mighty, as is demonstrated later in the chapter devoted to the workings of MCB University Press as an Enterprise School of Management in face of the revolution in electronic publishing.

References
Meister, J. C. (1998) *Corporate Universities: Lessons in Building a First Class Workforce*, 2nd ed., McGraw Hill.
Wills, G. (1993) *Your Enterprise School of Management*, MCB University Press.

Chapter 4

Assessing the value of information resources[1]

Implications for the virtual university

PETER WATSON

Introduction

Historically, universities were places where scholars congregated. An excellent library was an essential concomitant. Serious students needed access to both scholars and books, and to achieve this, had to be in residence close by. This allowed them to belong to networks that also included other students. They could achieve reputation, through recognition in the circle in which they moved, for the knowledge they gained.

Modern universities for the most part still follow this age-old pattern. They are places to which students come to gain access both to scholars and books in order to acquire knowledge. The university offers opportunities for networking with other students. It typically provides places where students and scholars can meet, and is likely to be involved in the property business in supplying places where students can live while they are in residence. Universities also offer their scholars substantial encouragement, and patronage, to increase knowledge through research. Finally, because there has been a huge increase in the number of students, and personal reputation is not a sufficient basis for recognition of the knowledge gained by a student, universities offer an elaborate system of certification to perform this function.

As Gordon Wills (1997) has pointed out, the library has been one of the underlying imperatives of the way in which the great universities have developed. Until recently, specialist books have been expensive, and the overall costs of maintaining a complete collection for a particular subject have been large in relation to the actual level of usage. For this reason, the best libraries have tended to attract the best scholars and best students to take up residence close by. Economies of scale have been a force against distributing the supply of university-level education to places and times convenient to students. Students have been required to attend at the place and the time required by the university. What the great universities have done, the lesser have tended to emulate, though on the whole it is highly questionable whether the quality of the libraries they offered would justify this. Nevertheless, the economics of UK universities are currently driven by the need to ensure that a sufficient number of students join a course to justify the costs of preparing and delivering lectures which encapsulate the subject matter of a particular topic.

As many have pointed out, the arrival of unimagined economies in the cost of storing and distributing information offers huge potential in the field of education. For university education in particular, where ability to gain access to established knowledge is important, it is technically possible to allow students to access the bulk of the body of knowledge from their own homes. This could include video presentations by skilled lecturers and presenters in place of lectures. The virtual university is in a position to compete with traditional universities in the supply of both libraries and lectures. This has the potential to transform higher education so that it can be vastly more flexible in meeting the needs of students as to the time and place of delivery. The economics of delivery will come to be driven by the size of tutorial groups, rather than by the requirement for economic lecture sizes.

Libraries are in essence stores of information made accessible to users. This paper examines the economics involved in the supply of information, to see how costs are likely to change when such services are capable of being provided electronically, and how third parties might supply information currently available through university libraries. It also discusses how registry systems could be provided in a similar way.

The nature of information
At this stage it is probably appropriate to provide some explanation as to what is meant by information. The Chambers Dictionary is not very helpful. It defines information in terms of knowledge, and knowledge in terms of information. Kenneth Boulding (1966) more helpfully explains the generation of information on the basis of two processes, printing and organizing. The process of printing involves the creation of a copy of existing information. The process of organizing involves the development or recording either of new information, or of new understanding of existing information, through synthesis or learning.

The outcomes of both these processes would normally take the form of a written or print record. The content of such records may be distinguished between new raw data recording events, new interpretations, and copies of old data or interpretations. There are further distinctions to be drawn between information which is in some way published on the public record, and can therefore be accessed by any individual without having to pay a direct price; information for which a fee is charged for access; and information which is private to an individual or organization. Finally, economists distinguish between information relevant to trading in particular market places, and other information. This distinction is important because of the greater importance of timeliness in market information. The different categories of information are represented in Figure 4.1. This shows a box or three-dimensional drawing that may also be visualized as a pile of bricks. The horizontal divisions represent whether the information is private, priced or public, and the vertical divisions on the front face, whether the information is new data, new interpretations, or old data or interpretations. The bricks forming the front half of the pile represent the various categories of other, i.e. non-market, information, and the bricks at the rear represent the categories of market information. Altogether, there are eighteen categories of information. This is only intended as a loose categorization, and it will be apparent that not all information fits neatly into a single box or category.

The purpose of the diagram is to demonstrate two points. The first is the variety of types of information. The implication of this is that it may be difficult to come to general conclusions which apply to all categories of information. The second is that there are likely to be substitutes for many specific sources of particular information. For example, a copy of any published information in the UK or USA has to be deposited in the British Library, or the Library of Congress respectively, and is therefore publicly available at no price, even though it is also supplied at a price through other distribution routes. One of the effects of the information revolution has been to increase the ease of access to much publicly available information. The availability of close, and low-cost, substitutes is a particularly important consideration with respect to the provision of priced Internet services.

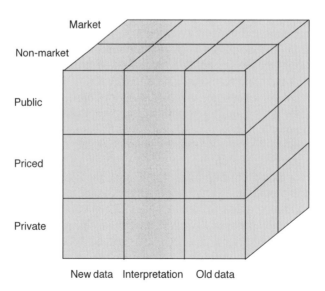

Figure 4.1
Categories of
information

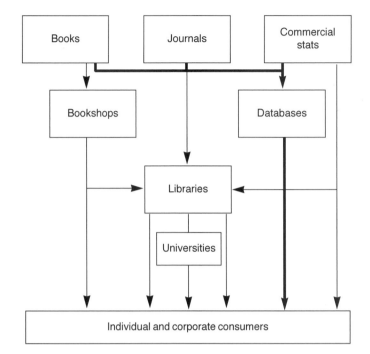

Figure 4.2
Information
industry structure

Overall structure of the information industry

It will also be helpful to have in mind a picture to categorize the various organizations involved in producing, storing and distributing or disseminating information. The overall structure is shown in Figure 4.2. Historically there were three main ways in which print information, other than private information, was distributed to end users: books, including those produced by government; journals, magazines and newspapers; and commercial and government reports and statistics. For simplicity, the related media of television and radio are omitted from the diagram. The distribution channels vary from retail outlets, or libraries, to direct mailing, to end users of limited circulation commercial reports. Higher education is part of the wider business of generating, storing and transmitting information (van Alstyne, 1998). Universities have special roles both in generating much of the new published information, and in introducing successive groups of students to the information in their chosen subject areas, and many have specialist libraries attached.

Bold arrows on the diagram above show the new routes for transmitting information direct to end users that are opened up by the information revolution. Technically it is now possible for the originator of the information to hold a single digital copy that may be directly accessed electronically by users. For academics, personal Web pages perform this function. Using search engines, users locate, access and download copies of information through the World Wide Web. In doing so they circumvent the services offered by the intermediaries in the current distribution chains: the publishers, book wholesalers, book retailers, journal distributors and libraries. Such intermediaries are involved in producing and distributing additional copies of information. In bypassing the current distribution chain, considerable chunks of cost are avoided. These costs are replaced by the costs of the telecommunication links utilized, and the time spent by individuals in searching, sifting, organizing and evaluating information.

Information agents

It would still be reasonable to expect forms of intermediation between information sources and end users[2] as suggested in Figure 4.3. These are referred to as agents because they act for either the providers or the users of information and negotiate with the other. Existing intermediaries may well find that part of their current role continues. It would appear, however, that there will be substantial changes in the roles required. The new roles will fall broadly into two categories. The first will allow savings in telecommunication costs by collecting copies of most frequently accessed information sources on sites distributed according to patterns of usage. These data 'warehouses' will be the digital equivalent of the library in their role as distributed stores of information. The second will assist end users by understanding their information needs and providing that information in a way which is both convenient and readily understood.

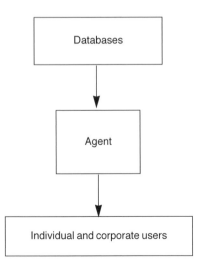

Figure 4.3
Information agents

Costs of providing information

The main proposition underlying this paper is that the information revolution opens opportunities for reducing costs of storing and transmitting information. This in turn opens possibilities for supplying information to many more individuals at a total cost that makes it worthwhile for them to purchase.

The production of an information good is characterized by high initial costs and very low costs of replication. Publishers refer to the initial costs as first copy costs, and in this it is important to remember the costs of what Boulding (*op. cit.*) would describe as organizing the information. Despite an interim phase in which there may be higher costs resulting from the supply of both electronic and paper copy, the long-term effect of the electronic revolution is believed to be a significant reduction in the marginal and average costs of delivery, as a result of both technical advances and simplification in the distribution chain. It may, however, increase the amount of the initial investment required to produce the stored electronic copy. Only part of this cost is directly related to the volume of usage. The provision of sufficient network capacity to allow acceptable access for the projected users is loosely related to the number of users. However, it would be reasonable to suppose that there would be some natural economies of scale – cable capacity as a proportion of the diameter of a cable would be an obvious example of this.

The average cost per unit delivered depends very significantly on the volume of sales that can be achieved in relation to a given level of initial investment in the preparation of the material. There are two ways of keeping initial costs per unit down: first by being efficient in the initial preparation of materials by using pre-existing material where possible; and second by ensuring that the sales volume is as large as possible. Judging the initial price to achieve the required sales volume is tactically challenging. Advice on approaches to this varies. At one extreme it is possible to start with a niche product where the customers are prepared to pay the price, whatever it is. At the other extreme lies the strategy of giving away initial product to establish reputation and volume before reverting to a relatively low price justifiable by the high volume of sales that have been achieved.[3] Provided not too many producers have used the same strategy, a dominant market position may be achieved.

Figure 4.4 demonstrates how the unit cost falls as the initial fixed cost is divided over an increasing volume of sales. The implication of this is that it is likely that the supply curve for information goods slopes downward from left to right for much of its range as a result of the falling average cost per unit as volume increases. There is a possibility of two or more points at which the market would be in equilibrium, the extremes of which could be a relatively high price for an exclusive service for a limited number of customers, and a significantly lower price for a mass market.

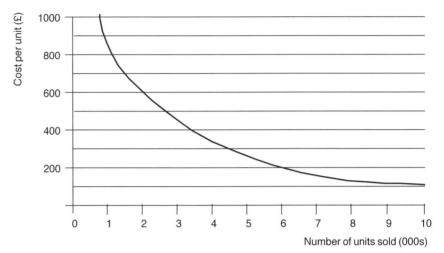

Figure 4.4
Effect of volume:
example of an
upfront investment
of £1 million

Demand for information

The reduction in the average and marginal costs per unit resulting from the information revolution opens up the possibility of supplying customers on parts of the demand curve which were previously unattainable, at least at prices which would yield any return to the supplier. It seems likely that demand will be highly elastic with respect to price along the newly accessible stretch of the demand curve. The main reason for this would be the existence of close substitutes for the information provided, as suggested above. This means that the demand for an information service will be particularly sensitive to its price, unless it supplies new information. As a result of this, and the nature of the supply curve, it is reasonable to expect that price reductions would lead to short-run increases in both revenue and profit in the relevant range of the demand curve.

The pattern of development of mass markets seems to involve a move from low-cost uniform products towards products designed to exploit specific niches representing the particular needs of groups of similar customers. This appears to be relevant to the market for information. It follows from an understanding that the information market is not based on the aggregate demand for a single uniform product, but on an aggregation of individual needs, all of which are slightly different, depending, among other things, on the prior knowledge of the individual concerned. In this way it differs from the standard economic analysis of supply and demand which is based on a homogeneous product.

A further consideration is that the price paid for access to an information source is only one component of total cost to the consumer, the other component being the transaction costs borne by consumers. Substitute sources for the information must also be judged in terms of both the price charged for the source of information, and the transaction costs borne by the user.

The price sensitivity may also be exacerbated by the relatively small and uncertain extent of the perceived benefits of the information, together with the sensitivity of those perceptions to changes in the ease of access to the information involved. There is also a possibility that perceptions would be influenced by the choices of other consumers. The more who join the band-wagon, the more apparent its attractions may seem.

Therefore, what is important in judging demand, is understanding not only the value that the consumer attaches to the information itself, but also the personal costs involved in obtaining and using the information. The theoretical analysis of supply and demand is based on having a product to sell. The properties of the product are, conventionally, well defined, and assumed to be understood by both the buyers and the sellers. There are markets in which it is apparent that the sellers have a better understanding of what the product is than do the buyers. In this market for information, the seller may also be ignorant as to the exact nature of what the buyer is pur-chasing and why. By definition, the seller does not know the personal calculations that the buyer is making, and can only infer on the basis of actual experience. Further, it is a matter not only of inferring the demand curve for the given product, but also of discovering what the purchaser is buying, and why, to the extent allowed by the information collected, and using this knowledge to refine the elements of the service provided. In order to understand this better, it is necessary to investigate further the factors that determine the value a user places on a source of information.

The value of information

What is the value of a copy of an information source that is in the public domain? At this point it is important to distinguish between the value of information to the owner of a particular copy of it, and its value to the user. Formally, the information has no value to its owner because it can be obtained elsewhere free of charge. This follows from the standard defini-tions of value to owner, or deprival value (see for example writers such as Baxter (1975)). The deprival value of information owned by an individual is the lower of its replacement cost, and the higher of its value in use or its resale value. When the information is available in a public library, its limiting value is zero, subject to the transaction costs which different users incur. The only exception to this is when a patent gives its owner exclusive use of the patented discovery for a specified period of years.

Once information is in the public domain, its originators, or owners of the copyright, are also not in a position to extract any specific returns by selling it as information *per se*. This follows from the same analysis above in that any individual can gain access to the information in a public library. There is also a passing resemblance to the efficient markets hypothesis of theoretical finance. This suggests that all publicly available information, in this case market information, is already incorporated into the price of any security, so no one can gain as a result of possessing the information – in other words, the value of the information in use is also zero. For example, the price of market security data twenty minutes old is low or zero (Grapper, 1998), and this is available through the Internet at no cost.

Information may, nevertheless, be perceived by individuals as having some personal value which still justifies them paying a price, or incurring costs, to obtain it. If individuals acquire information, having not previously possessed it, they may see it as enabling them to take courses of action that are personally more valuable. However, if the efficient markets hypothesis is to be believed, this would normally be in relation to real economic decisions rather than market security transactions.

A person who possesses a copy or copyright of the information may be able to provide it in ways that save the recipient transaction costs; for example, the convenience of accessing a source close at hand with its consequent savings in time. Individuals may even purchase their own copy of information for similar reasons.

The owners of an electronic database are subject to similar considerations. Applying the concepts of deprival value, access to it can only be sold if the buyer of the access believes that the total costs incurred are justified by the personal value gained from the information obtained, and are less than the total costs of alternative means of obtaining the same information. Demand is not directly derived from the utility of the information to the consumer, but is also dependent on the costs of access to other copies of the same information, unless the alternative means of obtaining the information all cost more than the value of the information. Sometimes the information may be unique, in which case the main determinant of demand and price is the aggregate of the individuals' demand functions derived from the value added from possession of the knowledge. This is the basis on which restricted access private reports are sold. In other cases, the database may have attributes that other copies of the same data do not have. For example, the owner of the original copyright may be able to make uses of the data which other suppliers would be unable to because of copyright restrictions, and is in a position to limit the number of copies, possibly increasing revenues as a result, provided demand is inelastic. Nevertheless, any value that those additional attributes may have is still derived from the same components, namely the value added to the users of the information reduced by any costs incurred in gaining the information. This is because copyright of published material requires that a copy be lodged in a copyright library, and the information is therefore in the public domain.

The value of the information contained in a database is thus determined from the future revenue flows that can be earned from its sale, and not from any intrinsic value its contents have as information. If the demand function for the information in a database is elastic with respect to price, this implies that lower prices will lead to maximizing revenue in the short run. There will be exceptions to this in specialized niches where there is a single supplier or where timeliness or some other service feature is highly valued by the user of the information.

The longer-term implications of this are that if there are a number of competing suppliers all offering similar services, the price will be driven down towards zero. Fishburn *et al.* (1997), for example, explain the reasons for this. The conclusion is that the price of information in such marketplaces will approach zero. Recent decisions by Sun and Microsoft to provide core business software products free of charge over the Internet are examples of this thinking in practice.

This would not seem to offer a long-term business proposition and the implication, in the absence of a regulatory intervention, is a single natural monopoly supplier in such a marketplace, a result which follows from the nature of the cost function of information supply. However, for suppliers who learned to differentiate their products to meet the specific needs of particular groups, there would be greater returns to be earned (Kehoe, 1999). The nature of the potential differentiation may be understood better by examining the provision of information as if it were a service.

Information as a service
The provider of an information service can supply the basic information required in an almost infinite variety of ways. These range from a library or database service allowing the user access to search for the required information, to a personal service which supplies a specific requirement for a particular customer. The information service is best thought of in two parts. The first of these is the raw data, or information itself, which may be obtained from many different sources unless it is unique, and the second is an agent meeting the requirements of the purchaser, not only for the actual information, but the other attributes provided by the service and valued by customers. These include reliability or accuracy, its selection or authoritativeness, the responsiveness of the service in terms of timeliness, the helpfulness in dealing with queries, and the tangible form in which the information is delivered. As has been explained, the 'principal' requiring the information service is often capable of meeting an information need through public sources but would incur costs in so doing, both in terms of time and travel, and in compromising some of the qualities provided in the agency service. Thus the nature of the price paid to the agent means that it is best thought of as incurred to obtain a bundle of service characteristics, rather than a single product. Similarly, the decision to make use of the agent to acquire the information will depend on how successfully the agent

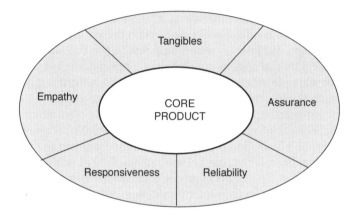

Figure 4.5
Service dimensions

delivers against a number of dimensions measuring the different aspects of the service delivered. The principal may judge this against the costs avoided in not having to acquire the information through alternative routes.

The other attributes of an information service correspond closely with the service dimensions included in the SERVQUAL (Parasuraman *et al.*, 1986) measures of service quality. The dimensions, which are illustrated in Figure 4.5, are the core product, reliability, responsiveness, empathy, assurance, and the tangible characteristics of the product. The information counterparts are the information itself, its accuracy and completeness, its timeliness, the helpfulness of responses to questions, the authoritativeness of the information, and the tangible form of the product.

The price a user will pay for the service attributes of the information delivery are closely related to the costs of using substitute sources of information. It has been suggested that the decision to make use of substitutes will depend on the comparative levels of total cost, including particularly costs of travelling to the location where the information can be accessed, and of searching and evaluating the information. These, in turn, relate to perceptions of the service's responsiveness, reliability, helpfulness and authoritativeness, and how the service organizes and presents the information. Applying a service mentality ensures that the various factors involved in the users' decisions are measured and considered to ensure that the service is continually developed and adjusted to fit the needs of the user. The precise factors involved will depend on the users. For example, security traders would attach a high value to timeliness and reliability.

For any service-based business, customer retention is a key consideration. There are two reasons for this. The first relates to word-of-mouth recommendation, the most powerful means of acquiring new customers. A dissatisfied former customer is a far more powerful negative influence than a satisfied present customer is a positive influence. Reducing the number of unhappy ex-customers, by ensuring their continued loyalty, therefore has a disproportionate influence on the effectiveness of word of mouth as a marketing tool. The second is that new customers are far more costly than existing customers, perhaps as much as five times more costly (Hart *et al.*, 1990). A new customer involves costs in the selling and conversion process, recording and payment, and help in learning the ropes. By and large these costs are either lower or non-existent for established customers.

The nature of service provision therefore involves a process of continuous development and adjustment. In essence, the customers' satisfaction is measured against expectations of service levels. As expectations will be modified in the light of experience, it is reasonable to expect them to adjust over time to expect different levels of service quality. The service company strives continuously to keep ahead. A successful company is likely to have a good knowledge of its customer base and have developed accurate ways of measuring and recording such information. This would constitute the Internet equivalent of point-of-sales information. This is arguably the most important, and least easily copied, source of competitive advantage.

When the service delivered involves information, there is a further interesting twist to the process of development or adjustment. The information users must be expected to learn as a result of their use of the information source. Learning will involve not only the information itself but also the sources from which it is derived. As a result, individuals making use of the service may be expected to see reduced personal costs of making use of substitutes, for example by making direct access to the original source of a particular piece of information. This has the effect of cutting out the middle man. Therefore, long-term customer retention will also involve modifying the product over time to anticipate the learning of the customers. Modification will involve introduction of new, related information, as well as different interpretation of current information.

It is possible to observe similar processes of product modification in many competitive mass markets. It is a particularly important consideration with a product for which the demand curve is highly elastic. The gradual upgrading of successive versions of a car model is perhaps the most obvious instance.

The new technology is also affecting other related markets such as entertainment through television, telecommunications, retailing and financial services. The impact is similar in that the new means of delivery largely have the ability to reduce the transaction costs of the recipients of the services.

Pricing structures for information provision
A question that faces information providers is whether to charge users on the basis of the information that they actually access, or through a fixed

subscription regardless of use. This is a variant of the problem of whether a consumer prefers to pay a fixed subscription rather than a cost per use. Well-organized and easily navigable information sources may also allow users to discover the existence of information of which they were previously unaware.

The reduction of the costs of storing and disseminating information is likely to lead to an increase in the number of sources of published information. The reason for this, as has already been suggested in Chapter 2, is that all it will take to publish in future will be a Web page. Many academics already have their own, and there are growing numbers of examples of electronic publishing, often at very low cost. The corollary of this, however, will be that most of the specific information will have a very low value. This is simply the working of the basic laws of supply and demand. There will be a few exceptions to this rule, mainly academics with exceptional reputations for whom consumers will readily pay a price for what they perceive to be the authoritative quality of the information, which will mean that they can avoid spending time assessing the quality of alternative sources themselves.

For the rest of the available information, the opportunities for authors to make much money will be limited.

Implications for the virtual university

This analysis has some important implications for the virtual university. Perhaps the most significant is that the basic library or information service is unlikely to be dedicated to a single university institution. The economic logic for an electronic library service is for it to be shared between a number of universities, and also for it to be open to other users. This follows from the cost structure of such a service with reducing average costs per unit as the number of subscribers to the service increases. A virtual university is therefore likely to subcontract its library services rather than regard them as a part of its core business. It is perfectly possible to do this in a way which allows the service to be branded as being part of a particular institution, and new technology makes this possible at minimal cost.

Similar considerations also apply to the other information system that all universities employ, namely the registry system. This is a set of records that allows the progress of each student to be followed and monitored through a course of study. At present such systems tend to be proprietary to each university, but the availability of systems operating through the Internet is likely to lead to subcontracting of such services, again with a resulting reduction in costs. Some such services may well also offer certification and examination. In a mass market, there really seems to be no good reason why, in areas of relatively standard knowledge, there should not be external examining bodies on the same model as the 'A' level school-leaving examinations in the UK.

What does this leave for the virtual university? As others have pointed out, it allows it to concentrate on the core business of tutorial contact with the student. This is probably the most satisfying part of the university teacher's involvement, in stark contrast to the necessary but somewhat arid administrative involvement in examinations and such like. It is the function which is gradually being squeezed out, particularly in the state-funded and controlled universities in the UK where comparability and the consequent levelling down has assumed far more importance than any attempt to improve real quality of provision.

The very real possibility is that what has come to be known as the virtual university will allow the separation of university provision into those parts where the economic driving force dictates large-scale and necessarily impersonal provision, and those parts that involve direct contact with individual students by dedicated teachers. Because expansion of higher education in to mass markets has put pressure on costs, the need to reduce costs of fixed provision by increasing the volume has been the dominating force. However, the real scale economies will only be achieved when universities cease to regard themselves as having to provide all basic services themselves.

It is always difficult in the face of social and technical change to foresee precisely the direction in which future events will be affected. The arrival of the printing press was seen as a potential tool for the Catholic Church to increase its hold over the population by reducing the cost of producing standard religious publications (Kay, 1997). The actual effect was a surge in the reproduction of vernacular materials that loosened the church's hold permanently. The reduction of the fixed cost of printing had the effect of allowing individuals access to a wider variety of materials. Rather than strengthening existing institutions by reducing their costs, it weakened them by making it easier for others to compete.

It is argued here that the effect of reductions in the cost of storing and distributing information will have a similar effect on traditional terrestrial universities. The change in the distribution channels for print materials, coupled with the use of the same distribution channels for video materials, will allow much greater flexibility in meeting the specific needs of individuals. The end result will not be to provide the same product as universities presently provide at lower costs, but a wider variety of products more tailored to individual needs. The virtual university may be in the forefront of this change as a positive subverter of present practices. It will not make it popular with existing suppliers, though that does not matter if it succeeds in making itself popular with its customers.

Notes

1. This chapter was written on the basis of work undertaken as David Sutton, Research Fellow of IMC. Thanks to Gordon Prestoungrange for his help in the genesis of this piece. Any errors are my responsibility.
2. See for example W. P. Lougee (1997) 'Agent architecture and service markets for digital libraries', Ticer International Summer School, Tilburg, Netherlands, http://www-personal.umich.edu/~wlougee/TICER97/agents/.
3. See for example L. Downes and C. Mei (1998) *Unleashing the Killer Ape*, Boston, MA, Harvard Business School Press.

References

Baxter, W. T. (1975) *Accounting Values and Inflation*, Maidenhead, McGraw Hill.

Boulding, K. E. (1966) 'The economics of knowledge and the knowledge of economics', in D. M. Lamberton (ed.) (1971) *Economics of Information and Knowledge*, London, Penguin Books.

Fishburn, P. C., Odlynko, A. M. and Siders, R. C. (1997) 'Fixed fee versus unit pricing for information goods: competition, equilibrium and price wars', *First Monday*, Vol. 2 No. 7, http://www.firstmonday.dk/.

Grapper, J. (1998) 'What price information', *Financial Times*, 20 July, London.

Hart, C. W. L., Heskett, J. L. and Earl Sasser Jr, W. (1990) 'The profitable art of service recovery', *Harvard Business Review*, July–August, pp. 148–56.

Kay, J. (1997) 'Revising the revolution', *The Bookseller*, 8 August, pp. 20–1.

Kehoe, L. (1999) 'Software on tap', *Financial Times*, 1 September, London.

Parasuraman, A., Zeithaml, V. A. and Berry, L. L. (1986) 'SERVQUAL, a multiple-item scale for measuring customer perceptions of service quality', *Journal of Retailing*, Spring.

van Alstyne, M. W., 'Higher education's information challenge', in J. W. Meyerson (ed.) (1998) *New Thinking in Higher Education: Creating a Context for Change*, Anker Publishing Co.

Wills, G. (1997) 'E-postcards from the other side. Faxback 2', in G. Wills (ed.) (1997) *Engendering Democratic Action*, Bradford, MCB University Press.

Chapter 5

Modelling the virtual university

RICHARD TEARE

Is your organization ready for the millennium?
The business literature contains much anecdotal evidence about the difficulty of trading in the Internet age. Indicators of corporate survival vary: for
example, the average life of a UK business was once thought to be around 50
years, yet in the US, some 40 per cent of the Fortune 500 listed companies
simply ceased to exist during the period from the mid-1980s to the mid-
1990s. Is it getting harder to just survive – let alone prosper? The weight of
evidence would suggest so. CEO of General Electric US, Jack Welch, made
this chilling prediction: 'Drive change or it will drive you.' If staying abreast
of change means sustaining a kind of perpetual forward motion, then how
do you do this without creating chaos?

The purpose here is to advance the case for establishing a corporate
virtual university (CVU) that adopts the issues and challenges for organizational development as its dynamic curricula. Its goal is simply to connect the
career-long learning capabilities of the organization's human resource to
the change agenda. The CVU can accredit this process too and quantify its
outcomes using Internet-resourced workplace or action learning to draw
out the questions that give purpose and direction to business learning.

The case for business learning
Why design a corporate virtual university? The purpose here is to outline
the propositions that would enable the organization to drive its own investment in business learning:

- *Training and learning can be used to accelerate change and development.*
  A sense of purpose, interest and commitment to employee (or Associate)
  learning and development must be extended from what is commonly
  viewed as the remit of human resources, training and organizational
  development specialists to a shared agenda with 'buy in' from all
  managers. How can this transformation be achieved? It requires the

active involvement of senior executives in the process of translating key challenges for business learning and the specific business skills needed to address them. If the strategic goals for the enterprise are aligned and integrated with the pathways for training and learning, then 'value added' for each and every Associate and for the enterprise as a whole will be created.

- *Internet technology can be used to provide learner support – any time and in any place.* The strategic importance of the Internet for transacting business (e-commerce) and global communications (e-mail) can also deliver all the necessary learning resources and support direct to the point of use in the workplace. Total learner support can be customized via online courseware, libraries (searchable databases), forums (meeting places) and all the managerial and administrative functions needed to sustain momentum in learning at work. The ability to disseminate new material within the company overnight is now the expected norm. So with Internet-based learning, Associates can complete courses 'just in time' to apply new knowledge to new tasks.
- *Radical learning solutions can be crafted from a CVU structure.* The goal is to create a truly market-driven educational system, interlinked with external training and learning providers for inputs and accreditation. But if it is to 'add value' these providers must respect the enterprise's own agenda and the nature of its dynamic curriculum.

The rise of the 'corporate university', especially in the USA, is attributed to the rapid pace of change and the need to ensure that learning is firmly aligned with business needs:

> Rather than simply sending high potential managers to external executive education programmes, these organizations are developing focused large-scale customized action learning programmes with measurable results. These hands-on, application-driven programmes are based on actual business challenges facing an organization and give participants an opportunity to actively discuss, diagnose, and recommend solutions to real-life business challenges. (Meister, 1998, p. 15)

Exhibit 1 (page 64) lists some of the main questions and responses relating to the concept of a corporate virtual university and its 'fit' with organizational development.

The workplace agenda
How can learning to learn be embedded in such a way that it becomes a natural part of the way in which Associates think and behave on the job?

Table 5.1 profiles the changes needed in the approach to learning and delivery, but the right conditions must exist if the transition is to work. There are a number of characteristic features of organizations that might readily take the next step towards establishing their own CVU.

1. *Emphasis on team structures for learning* – in flatter, more flexible organizations, individual effectiveness increasingly equates with well-developed communication and collaboration skills. A key to unlocking this potential is shared learning and networking so that 'best practice' ideas are widely disseminated across the organization.
2. *Interest in maximizing personal capability and creativity* – 'working smarter' means that Associates need to work out for themselves how they might best improve and streamline their own working patterns. As a starting point, it requires the ability to develop own problem-solving skills and the ability to analyse situations, ask questions and suggest improvements. This approach causes learners to dig well below conventional 'surface' reasoning to produce innovative solutions to the more complex, unanticipated problems that twenty-first-century businesses will face.
3. *Willingness to sponsor career self-management* – as more responsive organizational structures become the norm, Associates will have to be better equipped to interpret information, apply it to their work, and make good business decisions. This, in turn, affects the kind of education and training that Associates need. The issue is not simply training Associates to learn more skills but rather introducing them to an entirely new way of thinking and working so that they can perform broader roles in the workplace.

Corporate learning features	*Current realities*	*Future realities*
Site of learning	Building-centred	Internet-resourced, on demand
Content	Upgrading technical skills	Portfolio of workplace skills
Method	Mainly learn by listening	Learn by doing and reviewing
Audiences	Individuals	Team/Action learning Set
Frequency	Time constrained, discontinuous	Continuous, active learning
Goal	Build individual skills 'off the job'	Solve business issues 'on the job'

Table 5.1
Changing the
emphasis from
standardized
training to
customized career-
long learning

Adapted from
Meister, 1998, p. 22

It can be argued that 'inspirational leadership' will eclipse 'managing' as the key to developing a shared mind-set in twenty-first-century organizations. In this scenario, all Associates are encouraged to be active change agents (rather than passive recipients of instructions). The imperative then is leadership development which focuses upon identifying and developing exceptional people who are capable of moving the organization through 're-invention' phases – rapidly.

How do we make our CVU happen?

Should we use a traditional or a work-related system for design, delivery and accreditation?
The business marketplace is now advancing on the traditional domains of higher education because continuous learning in the workplace is more necessary than ever before. Yet tighter corporate training budgets, rapid technological advancement, and the ever constant drive to sustain competitive advantage contribute to a real sense of corporate tension. This is driving the emergence of a new learning model where corporations become the customers and the suppliers of education. In other words, we are certainly heading for a market-driven education system for business learning, and the most significant benefit of this paradigm shift is that it puts the organization firmly in control of the learning process. So how can the organization demonstrate the credibility of its CVU?

The most obvious way of accrediting the CVU learning process is to work with a traditional university. It will have designs for business learning, tutors to deliver and manage them and a quality assurance system that recognizes and tests the acquisition of 'new' learning. However, there are drawbacks. Its courses will reflect standard academic designs, with little true scope for customization, and the 'static' systems and procedures used for quality assurance cannot be readily adapted to meet the needs of customers.

In sum, the traditional way is familiar and respected, but it is 'product', not customer, focused, and 'static' in terms of its relevance to fast-paced change. Further, if the CVU adopts this route to accreditation, it will have to cede control of its learning goals and ambitions to an accreditation system that was conceived for a wholly different purpose – to maintain the *status quo* and preserve academic standards that may have little relevance to the workplace. A new 'dynamic' approach is needed if the CVU is to prosper, together with a system for accrediting learning at work that is relevant to the enterprise, puts the needs of adult learners first and adopts 'fitness for purpose' as the basis of its quality assurance process.

The International Management Centres Association (IMCA) has worked with more than 2,000 organizations in 44 countries over a period of some 36 years. Its action learning programmes were inspired by the vision of Reg Revans, a prominent and founding exponent of action learning. An action learning approach combines the study of learning resources and literature with the real-life challenge of specific business situations – a two-pronged approach which provides a rich learning experience of immediate relevance, underpinning specific corporate goals and development visions. IMCA combines Revans' philosophy of action learning with two key learning organization philosophies: Senge's five core disciplines, and triple loop learning (an adaptation of Kolb's learning cycle), the goal being to link action learning, individual career-long learning, and organizational learning.

IMCA's programmes are independently accredited by the Distance Education Training Council (USA) and the British Accreditation Council (UK) with Internet-based registry and quality assurance systems that are fully ISO 9002 compliant. The accreditation and quality assurance procedures used are at least as robust as those used in traditional learning. They are also 'dynamic' in that they use ISO variance monitoring procedures to check and adjust the learning process in real time as the programme progresses. The procedures are transparent, can be inspected at any time by the external examiner appointed to examine associates in the learning Set (typically twelve to sixteen people) and respect the needs of adult learners who must customize their own learning process so that it is meaningful to them. The Association also works in selected areas with traditional universities, and all of its mainstream programmes have been approved for this purpose. This is a helpful benchmark, but when working concurrently with a traditional university it means operating two systems of accreditation in parallel ('static' and 'dynamic') – a difficult, costly and time-consuming task. In response, the Association has incorporated its own global Internet University as the 'hub' for its membership awards.

How can the Association help us to create our CVU?
The IMCA's global network is founded upon its work with industry. Many companies around the world have embraced action learning, achieving real and often remarkable results. National Sorghum Breweries (South Africa), Malaysia Airline Systems, Fina Petroleum, BAA Airports, Marriott Hotels, Seagram Europe, International Distillers & Vintners (IDV), Australia Post, Allied Irish Bank, Jones Lang Wootton, Ernst & Young, NatWest Bank, ICI, Pilkington, Shell, Cummins Engines, St John Ambulance, Maybank, St Helier Hospital Trust, to name a few, can attest to the significant benefits of IMCA's action learning approach.

The Association's engagement in workplace learning over the years is firmly underpinned by the belief that 'The enterprise where we work is far and away the most significant business school that managers ever attend . . .'

IMCA's CVU programme seeks to equip a partner organization to educate and develop its key people within an accredited corporate virtual university framework. This unique approach builds on the individual manager's in-depth knowledge of company and culture, while encouraging breadth of vision through contact with IMCA faculty members, and learning Associates from other companies, as appropriate.

How does the Association's CVU programme work?
The CVU learning programme benefits all company stakeholders: corporate development has bottom line impact; programmes respond to senior management's business priorities; organizations benefit from managers' extended skills and experience, from the knowledge gained and 'banked' during learning programmes, and from the results of workplace projects; learning motivates Associates, bringing them visible success in terms of managerial empowerment and progression, and considerable personal satisfaction – and enhanced reputation – on completion of successful projects.

Tutoring, mentoring and course learning materials are provided via the Internet for ease of access, communications and learning. Associates share their information and ideas, teamworking being a basic tenet of action learning. The global reach of the Internet means managers from a variety of organizations across the world can learn with and from one another, which considerably enhances the learning experience, encourages exchange of views and aids personal networking. Within their own organizations, learning Associates are encouraged to promote wide use of new knowledge gained, building up a 'library' of experience which will offer invaluable background information for the future. IMCA provides the training necessary to enable senior managers to direct the learning process, sharing their specific expertise with learning Associates and contributing to the corporate knowledge base.

Summary: Five key features of the Association's CVU programme
- Learning is tailored to meet organizational imperatives, focusing firmly on your business agenda and workplace challenges.
- Learning is determined by the issues, realities and best practice of today, and the potential challenges of tomorrow, a focus promoting cultural change and innovation.
- Learning is clearly able to demonstrate a worthwhile return on investment, increasing managers' value to the organization, and offering measurable improvements to the bottom line.
- Learning via Internet-based resources and communications transforms

cost bases and ensures comprehensive access to knowledge worldwide.

- Personal career development is integral to the process and learners gain valuable professional qualifications from the IMCA and its global accreditation structures.

How do I sell the benefits of this approach?

The IMCA provides a complete qualification structure of action learning courses, and Associates normally use the learning process to gain accredited business qualifications at all levels up to doctorate. In recognition of the constraints of workplace commitments, learning Associates can pursue a modular learning approach, building up credits towards qualifications. This enables them to study at their own pace while remaining part of the management team. After graduation, continuous learning support encourages work towards A+Enhancement through the implementation and evaluation of project proposals, while career-long learning is fostered through a system of five-yearly renewal of Association membership. The learning process can also be strongly inspirational to others in the organization, fostering cultural change and innovation, and thus be a powerful stimulant to the organization as a whole.

STEP 2: DESIGN AND IMPLEMENT YOUR OWN CVU

How do we justify the investment?

The Association's CVU programme is designed to enable the client organization to 'internalize' the managerial and administrative functions needed for accredited action learning. The significance of this cannot be understated. For possibly the first time, this enables the organization to craft, manage and control its own global university structure and use the Internet to deliver all the learning resources needed to sustain active learning – direct to the workplace. The triple benefits of: *internalization* (for lower cost and 'best fit' customization), *Internet-based systems* (for maximum workplace convenience and minimum 'time out') and *accredited learning* (based on 'fitness for purpose') means that there are no barriers or constraints to encouraging, supporting and recognizing excellence in business learning. Furthermore, because the emphasis in action learning is on finding and implementing real solutions to problems and challenges, it is possible to quantify the return on investment by tracking the outcomes of the learning process. Associates are challenged to apply their learning via assignments that are *always* real workplace projects, and it is the *application* of experience, shared learning and new knowledge (not the ability to recall information) that is examined by continuous assessment and oral examination.

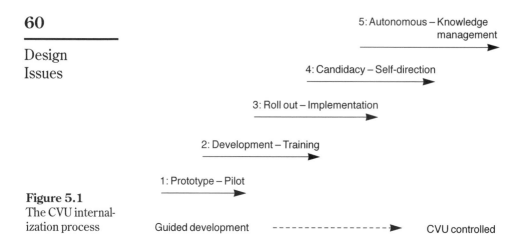

Figure 5.1
The CVU internal-
ization process

Where do we start?

A five-stage internalization process is shown in Figure 5.1. This aims to achieve some early 'wins' (at Stage 1: Prototype) so that the core team can sell the case for scaling-up the investment at Stages 2: Development (an intensive skills and knowledge transfer process) and 3: Roll out. Thereafter, the CVU is empowered and equipped to run its own courses, initially with support at Stage 4: Candidacy and then on its own at Stage 5: Autonomous. While a five-stage approach may seem rather long, it aims to reflect the different points of emphasis as the programme progresses. The stages necessarily overlap and the timings are determined by the client's own state of readiness to proceed. It is possible to progress through all five stages in two years, but to achieve this, a stable core CVU team is needed with board level support for time (for focused effort on the internalization process) and funding (to scale up the process). By Stage 3: Roll out, the CVU will be able to run cost-effective, fully customized and accredited learning programmes. Further, as the scale of implementation increases, the unit cost decreases and the CVU's strategic value will rise as the in-built process for knowledge management attains high profile. It also possible to maximize the return on investment by establishing a profit centre operation and extending access to the CVU's courses to the organization's customers and supply chain.

The internalization process builds on first principles and enables a CVU core team of human resource, training and operations personnel to build on their own skills and experience in personal and organizational development. The activities at each stage adopt an integrated, progressive approach to addressing the main disciplines or themes needed to manage the CVU as depicted in Figure 5.2. The nine themes are: project development, learning

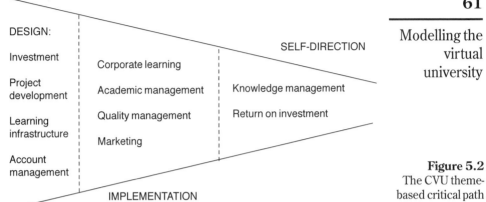

DESIGN:

Investment

Project
development

Learning
infrastructure

Account
management

Corporate learning

Academic management

Quality management

Marketing

SELF-DIRECTION

Knowledge management

Return on investment

IMPLEMENTATION

Figure 5.2
The CVU theme-
based critical path

infrastructure, academic management, quality management, account management, corporate learning, investment, marketing and knowledge management. A CVU theme-based generic 'blueprint' of activities can be found at Exhibit 2 (page 66).

How do we keep the internalization process on track?
The core CVU team will in most cases be drawn from different geographical regions and/or functions and so it is essential to set out the key objectives for each stage and the means of evaluating progress via a checklist of the activities that need to be addressed. The main objectives of each stage are as follows:

- *Prototype (1)* – to customize and implement a pilot course (such as an MBA for senior managers) that demonstrates from the outset the potential of the action learning approach. Second, to work with members of a CVU core team on a straightforward method for recognizing and accrediting the organization's own training courses. A credit mapping template is used for this purpose. Third, to begin work on customizing a generic blueprint for the CVU, so that it fully reflects the organization's business culture and ways of working.
- *Development (2)* – to transfer the skills and knowledge needed to run the CVU to its core team, via a progressive series of training courses, in preparation for the Roll out stage.
- *Roll out (3)* – to implement the CVU with core team members as course leaders (Set Advisers), course administrators (Programme Managers) and its own Dean and sub-Deans with overall responsibility for the conduct of programmes, registry, quality assurance and ongoing CVU training and development. These activities are fully supported by experienced faculty members of the IMCA.

- *Candidacy (4)* – to adjust and finalize plans for completing the internalization process so that the CVU can manage its own affairs as a constituent member of the Association.
- *Autonomous (5)* – to focus on medium- to long-term plans for wider scale implementation (possibly involving customer and supply organizations) and on establishing and utilizing the CVU's internalized procedures for knowledge management and for tracking return on investment via its own programme of evaluative action research.

How will the 'knowledge transfer' needed to run a CVU be achieved?
The core CVU team of twelve to sixteen (some of whom will have been involved in the pilot course (Prototype stage)) undertake a 'train the trainer' process. This work constitutes the main focus of the Development stage and, on completion, the team will have been equipped to continue the knowledge transfer at a pace and in a way that suits the organization. As this is the single most demanding phase, those who successfully complete the training and related assignments will be awarded a Diploma in Virtual Training & Development. The training process and related certification is profiled in Figure 5.3 and the assignment schedule and related key questions in Exhibit 3 (page 70).

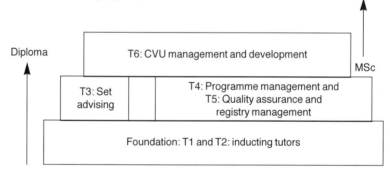

Figure 5.3
Development
stage knowledge
transfer: training
and certification

DIPLOMA IN VIRTUAL TRAINING & DEVELOPMENT (DIP. VTD)
To facilitate the knowledge transfer, a series of online resource templates is used:

       CVU Process Flow Chart
       Published Learning Action Guide
D: VU Training & Development
P1:   Piloting a Programme
M1: Mentors
C1:   Credit Mapping
T1:   Inducting Tutors

T2:   Inducting Tutors
T3:   Set Advising or
T4:   Programme Management
T5:   Quality Assurance and Registry Management (Pre-requisite is T4:
       Programme Management)

On completion of the Diploma, team members will be able to: undertake the
credit mapping of internal and external training courses; design and run
courses for CVU mentors and recruitment, selection and 'orientation'
sessions for Associates; induct new tutors and undertake and/or train
others to function as a Set Adviser (Course Manager) or Programme
Manager (Course Administrator).

   A second, continuous phase of training for team members responsible for
CVU Management (as the Dean or Sub-Dean or specialist development
role) leads to the award of a Master of Science (MSc) in Training & Development. To be eligible for this award, team members must have completed
the Dip. VTD training and related assignments.

DIPLOMA IN VIRTUAL TRAINING & DEVELOPMENT (DIP. VTD) TO
MASTER OF SCIENCE IN TRAINING & DEVELOPMENT (MSc)
Additional online resource template:

T6:   CVU Management and Development

On completion of the MSc, team members will be able to: undertake all managerial, administrative and technical functions specified at Diploma level
(Set Advising, Programme Management, Quality Assurance & Registry
Management) and assume all the roles and responsibilities of CVU Management and Development as CVU Dean, sub-Dean or specialist trainer.

Summary

'Where there is no vision, the people perish' (Proverbs 29:18).

The purpose of this paper is to advance the case for establishing a corporate
virtual university for organizational learning and development in the
Internet age. There are three main propositions:

1. Training and learning can be used to accelerate change and development.
2. Internet technology can be used to provide learner support – any time
   and in any place.
3. Radical learning solutions can be crafted from a CVU structure.

The IMCA's CVU programme is designed to enable the client organization to 'internalize' the managerial and administrative functions needed for accredited action learning. The significance of this cannot be under-stated as this enables the organization to craft, manage and control its own global university structure and use the Internet to deliver all the learning resources needed to sustain active learning – direct to the workplace. The triple benefits of: *internalization* (for lower cost and 'best fit' customization), *Internet-based systems* (for maximum workplace convenience and minimum 'time out') and *accredited learning* (based on 'fitness for purpose') mean that there are no barriers or constraints to encouraging, supporting and recognizing excellence in business learning. Furthermore, because the emphasis in action learning is on finding and implementing real solutions to problems and challenges, it is possible to quantify the return on investment by tracking the outcomes of the learning process.

If your goal is to be 'an employer of choice' and to embed active learning for career-long development, then the ability to design, implement and manage this process – and drive change (rather than letting it drive you!) – is a vital 'win' for the business. If you are interested in career and management development through action learning, then contact the International Management Centres Association at: http://www.imc.org.uk/imc for details of how to establish your corporate virtual university.

References

Meister, J. C. (1998) *Corporate Universities: Lessons in Building a World-Class Workforce*, New York, McGraw-Hill.

Teare, R., Davies, D. and Sandelands, E. (1998) *The Virtual University: An Action Paradigm and Process for Workplace Learning*, London and New York, Cassell.

Wills, G. (1998) *The Knowledge Game: The Revolution in Learning and Communication in the Workplace*, London and New York, Cassell.

Exhibit 1
Building a case for establishing a corporate virtual university: key questions and answers

Adapted from Meister, 1998, pp. 267–72

Questions	Responses
What is a CVU?	The strategic umbrella for developing employees and potential customers, and suppliers, aligned with the organization's business goals, using Internet delivery and workplace or action learning methodologies.
Why call this learning initiative a 'university'?	Because learning is becoming a core requirement for all employees and it is essential to provide a cohesive brand identity for the organization's total learning enterprise.
How is it different from a training department?	A training organization tends to be reactive, decentralized, and serves a wide audience with an array of open enrolment programmes. A CVU is the centralized umbrella for strategically relevant learning solutions for each and every tier of employees within the organization.

Who delivers the learning programmes in the CVU?	A wide array of learning partners is likely to provide delivery services. These range from trainers, business unit managers, university faculty, consultants to the executive management. The key managerial and administrative functions are internalized and run by the organizational development specialists.
What are the key CVU drivers?	The main reasons for establishing a CVU are to:

What are the key CVU drivers?

The main reasons for establishing a CVU are to:
- inter-link learning and development to key business goals;
- create an integrated framework for career-long learning, training and development;
- energize the organization and embed a culture of learning and improvement;
- improve the flexibility and transferability of employees across the organization.

What are the critical success factors for a CVU?

- The involvement of senior management from the outset.
- The creation of a funding model to spread the cost of participation to the full range of customers – internally and externally.
- Focus on workplace learning systems for delivery and learning.
- Inter-link external providers of training and learning services with the CVU architecture – wherever they are supportive, but not in cases where they might be obstructive.
- Build in a process of evaluation to track the return on investment.

Why might a CVU fail?

One or more of the following factors will contribute to failure:
- Absence or failure of senior management commitment to the CVU model.
- Lack of consensus among the broader managerial community on the need for a CVU.
- Insufficient focus on linkages and subsequent integration of the CVU learning programmes and the organization's business goals.
- Failure to create organizational profile for the CVU.
- Inability to demonstrate a return on investment (in learning benefits and in financial terms) of the CVU.

What is the typical operating budget for a CPU?

- US organizations average 2.2 per cent of payroll.

Exhibit 2
CVU theme-based
generic blueprint
of activities

Components	Key tasks	Stage of activity
		1 2 3 4 5
Key stages	Key: 1 = Prototype; 2 = Development; 3 = Roll out; 4 = Candidacy; 5 = Autonomous Corporate Virtual University (CVU)	
Emphasis	Key: Main focus [M] On-going activity [On]	M On

PROJECT DEVELOPMENT:

Components	Key tasks	1	2	3	4	5
Establish a business case	Value-based analysis of Internet-resourced action learning, managed by the client as a CVU (lower cost, better fit).					
(1) Prototype: Form the project team	Explain staged 'critical path' internalization and need for a blueprint. Client project leader customizes the blueprint (as MSc or MPhil). Establish a steering committee for this and the pilot work.	1	2	3	4	5
(1) Prototype: Run a pilot programme	e.g. accelerated MBA. Aim to maintain focus and momentum for maximum visibility, success and benefits selling.	1	2	3	4	5
(1) Prototype: Identify mentors	Connect with client's own arrangements for coaching and mentoring – activity managed by client project team member.	1	2	3	4	5
(1) Prototype: Pilot credit mapping	Work with client project team members to credit map a suite of training courses for a CMS award – use standard template.	1	2	**3**	4	5
(1) Prototype:		1	2	3	4	5

LEARNING INFRASTRUCTURE:

Components	Key tasks	1	2	3	4	5
Introduce learning diagnostics	Use: team and personal learning styles, aptitude profiling, career review analysis and Accreditation of Prior Experience and Learning (APEL) courseware, supported by action learning articles.					
(1) Prototype: Provide Web access for pilot programme	Set up standard Web Forum and meeting place with courseware and library access.	1	**2**	3	4	5
(1) Prototype: Customize Web access	Agree protocols for managing the Web learning site: passwords, confidentiality and knowledge management.	**1**	2	3	4	5
(3) Roll out:		1	2	**3**	4	5

Components	Key tasks	Stage of activity
		1 | 2 | 3 | 4 | 5

ACADEMIC MANAGEMENT:

Build
implementation
team — Explain accreditation (DETC, BAC, ISO 9002) to core team and the aims of the Diploma in Virtual Training & Development re: internalizing skills for Tutors, Set Advisers, Programme Managers, Registry services and CVU Mgt.

M   O
            n

(2) Development:
Faculty training — Run training re: recruitment, induction, appraisal and refreshment of tutors.

| 1 | **2** | 3 | 4 | 5 |

(2) Development:
Set Advising — Run training re: Set Advising role, programme start-ups, assignments, marking and feedback to Associates, client-centred coaching and mentor development.

| 1 | **2** | 3 | 4 | 5 |

(2) Development:
Roll out
co-ordination — CVU Dean (and sub-Deans) establishes an infrastructure for regionally based registry management and co-ordination. This may include appointing one or more CVU academic co-ordinators.

| 1 | **2** | 3 | 4 | 5 |

(3) Roll out:
Other learning
providers — Connect existing training and learning suppliers (as appropriate) to CVU infrastructure via credit mapping and tutor inputs – CVU core team to run faculty inductions.

| 1 | 2 | **3** | 4 | 5 |

(3) Roll out:

| 1 | 2 | **3** | 4 | 5 |

QUALITY MANAGEMENT:

Programme
management — Run training re: entry requirements; aptitude profiling and learning diagnostics; assignment handling; payments to faculty and other disbursals, minutes of formal meetings (Set, Project Panel, Steering Group); external examining roles and ISO 9002 compliant procedures.

(2) Development:
Information
services and
support — Run training re: information systems and procedures for CVU registry, membership services and ISO 9002 quality assurance.

| 1 | **2** | 3 | 4 | 5 |

(2) Development:
CVU
management — Run training re: roles and responsibilities of the CVU Dean (and regionally based sub-Deans (as appropriate)).

| 1 | **2** | 3 | 4 | 5 |

(2) Development:

| 1 | **2** | 3 | 4 | 5 |

Components	Key tasks	Stage of activity
		1 | 2 | 3 | 4 | 5
ACCOUNT MANAGEMENT:		
Relationship management	Establish communication and decision-making channels for action planning/project management at all subsequent stages, based on the Enterprise School of Management fee structure.	M ... O n
(1) Prototype: Partnership with the IMCA	IMCA Partner relations team to assist the client to establish own partnership agreement with International Management Centres Association (includes all financial arrangements).	**1** | 2 | 3 | 4 | 5
(3) Roll out:		1 | 2 | **3** | 4 | 5
CORPORATE LEARNING:		
Annual memberships	Internalize procedures for managing annual memberships (graduates, faculty) of the CVU and the International Management Centres Association.	
(4) Candidacy:		1 | 2 | 3 | **4** | 5
Review and development	Internalize procedures for action research and review re: effectiveness of the learning infrastructure, course designs, coaching and mentor interface and action learning process.	
(4) Candidacy:		1 | 2 | 3 | **4** | 5
INVESTMENT:		
Initial investment	Link the benefits of Internet-resourced action learning and return on investment to recognition of the cost structure and training and development of client's own CVU team (supplied by lead partner).	
(1) Prototype:		**1** | 2 | 3 | 4 | 5
Long-term investment	CVU Dean initiated, ongoing action research to track the benefits of establishing a corporate virtual university (financial, company, learner) and quantify the outcomes.	
(4) Candidacy:		1 | 2 | 3 | **4** | 5
MARKETING:		
Market planning	Finalize orderly roll out plan and implement, with guidance from the IMCA Partner relations team and the lead partner.	
(3) Roll out: Market planning	Consider wider client networks (customers, suppliers, 'benchmark' firms) cost recovery/profit centre operation.	1 | 2 | **3** | 4 | 5
(5) Autonomous: Brands for learning	Agree on client branding for own corporate virtual university.	1 | 2 | 3 | **4** | 5
(1) Prototype:		**1** | 2 | 3 | 4 | 5

Components	Key tasks	Stage of activity
	Establish positioning and role of International Management Centres Association (as a professional association for career-long learning) and the accredited status of the University of Action Learning.	1 |2 |3 |4 |5 | M ▨ O n ▨

Components	Key tasks	Stage of activity
(1) Prototype PR and promotion	Create own CVU brochure for recruitment and PR.	| **1** | 2 | 3 | 4 | 5 |
(2) Development:	Use brochure and internal conferences and briefings to assist with roll out.	| 1 | **2** | 3 | 4 | 5 |
(3) Roll out:	Use CVU core team of Dean, sub-Deans and regional CVU staff to manage internal/international communications.	| 1 | 2 | **3** | 4 | 5 |
(3) Roll out:	Focus on success via the annual APC and Congregation Events and related festivities to build visibility and interest.	| 1 | 2 | **3** | 4 | 5 |
(3) Candidacy:		| 1 | 2 | 3 | **4** | 5 |

KNOWLEDGE MANAGEMENT:
Published learning Explain the value added of published learning

Components	Key tasks	Stage of activity
(1) Prototype: Learning harvest	Capture pilot programme learning outcomes in article format and establish client-only, password-protected electronic journal for knowledge management.	| **1** | 2 | 3 | 4 | 5 |
(3) Roll out: New products created	Use knowledge capture process to create customized learning pathways and new programmes for organizational development.	| 1 | 2 | **3** | 4 | 5 |
(5) Autonomous:		| 1 | 2 | 3 | 4 | **5** |

Exhibit 3
CVU
internalization
programme:
key project areas
for the Diploma in
Virtual Training &
Development/
Master of Science

Diploma in Virtual Training & Development

The Diploma in Virtual Training & Development (Dip. VTD) (mandatory for core team members) adopts a 'hands-on approach' and prepares this group to act as trainer/developers for the roles of Faculty Induction, Set Advising, Programme Management and Registry Management. (Duration: 10 months) (60 M Level credits)

Credits	Assignment elements	CVU core team activities
5 credits	(1) Participation in the Web Forum	(1) Mandatory
10 credits	(2) Career review analysis for Accreditation of Prior Learning & Experience in 3,500 words	(2) APEL training for accelerated learning
10 credits	(3) Own organization monograph/career development in 3,500 words	(3) For own learning template
10 credits	(4) Evaluative assessment of virtual learning (shared: up to 3 per sub-Set) in 4,000 words)	(4) Based on: (Options): • Specific Training & Development Project *or* • Faculty Induction, Set Adviser, Programme Management, Registry Management training sessions (T1–3 or T1–2; T4–5)
25 credits	(5) Project in 8,000 words	(5) Based on (Options): • Specific Training & Development Project *or* • CVU Blueprinting *or* • CVU Credit mapping
	(6) Oral presentation and defence	(6) Mandatory
60 credits	Total on completion	

Dip. VTD to Master of Science (MSc) additionally prepares the core team members to take on the CVU management roles of Dean/Sub-Dean and to manage the implementation of the CVU at the roll out stage and beyond. It also incorporates the 'blueprinting' work at the Prototype stage. (Duration: 14 months) (120 M Level credits).

Credits c\f 60 credits	Assignment elements	CVU core team activities
15 credits	(7) Written analysis on specialist topic with action plan in 4,000 words	(7) Based on: (Options): • Specific Training & Development Project *or* • CVU Credit mapping: implementation *or* • CVU specialist role/procedures/ systems development
90 credits	(8) Work-based action research implementation project (with literature) 20,000 words	(8) Based on (Options): • Specific Training & Development Project *or* • CVU specialist role/procedures/ systems implementation *or* • Implementation of Dip. VTD Project (e.g. blueprinting)
15 credits	(9) Evaluative assessment of learning and future action plans in 3,000 words	(9) Mandatory
	(10) Oral presentation and defence	(10) Mandatory
180 credits	Total on completion	

Project Development/Investment/Corporate Learning:

- How should our CVU embed its virtual training and learning goals? What are the 'business case' issues that need to be addressed and how do we demonstrate the added value of the CVU approach, in terms of a wholly integrated training and learning approach that yields tangible return on investment?
- How should our CVU integrate its training programmes with certified learning? What is the most effective model for this? How might it compare (and improve on) traditional university practices?
- What are the key competences of a virtual learning organization and its human resources? How might our CVU embrace these? What balances need to be struck between 'virtual' versus 'face-to-face'? Can our CVU adopt different models for very different circumstances (e.g. geographical, multi-cultural, multi-lingual operation)?
- How can our CVU establish effective organizational mentoring structures? How do

we recruit and develop mentors? How can we prepare managers to mentor and/or CVU Associates to mentor 'new' Associates?

Learning Infrastructure:

- What do we know about Internet-based research and resourcing? How can we leverage the capabilities of the Internet in support of our CVU and its focus on action learning?
- What are we learning about the best ways of re-purposing our training for Internet-based delivery? How does the approach fit with our CVU? How might the Internet enhance training delivery in the future?

Academic Management/Corporate Learning

- What role does the tutor play in supporting our CVU, how do we recruit, develop and retain them? How should they be contracted? How will this role differ from conventional academic tutoring roles?
- How do we 'internalize' the knowledge and 'cascade' this in terms of the Set Advising (SA) role? What are the key skills? How can we relate them to our CVU? How do we identify the ideal candidates for the SA role and then develop them on-the-job?
- What are the best ways of 'capturing' prior experience and learning (APEL) as a means of entry to accelerated processes for certified learning? How do we ensure comparability of approach? How should APEL portfolios be submitted and verified? How can we make this process as straightforward and effective as possible?

Quality Management/CVU Management

- How do we 'internalize' all the Programme Management functions? How do we identify 'ideal' candidates for Set-specific programme management roles and then 'cascade' experience to-date on-the-job? How should regional roles be organized and managed? (CVU registry, quality assurance co-ordination, external examiner support).

Account Management/Knowledge Management

- How might our CVU globally, embed and 'customize' action learning? What role might traditional university and other training and learning providers play in supporting our CVU? How do we achieve 'added value' by leveraging traditional learning partners behind our CVU without loss of focus and momentum re: own agenda for change?
- What are the practical requirements for our CVU faculty undertaking project supervision at all levels? How do we ensure that 'return on investment' is occurring (for the learner and for the company)? How do we develop and integrate our employees with 'external' CVU faculty so as to ensure a balanced mix of perspectives?
- How might our organization use the CVU framework for continuous improvement? What role should 'published learning' play in harnessing our intellectual capital? How do we get our CVU electronic *Journal of Knowledge Management* going?

Part 2
Practical Examples

Chapter 6

e.volution.com

Anticipatory learning in publishing

SARAH POWELL

Looking forward, looking back: MCB University Press – publisher and enterprise school of management

Gary Hammel has observed that 'If senior executives don't have reasonably detailed answers to the "future" set of questions, and if the answers aren't substantially different from the "today" answers, there is little chance their companies will remain market leaders!'

The 'future' set of questions facing MCB University Press over the period when the studies in this book were written could not have been more challenging. The publishing industry was facing a virtual revolution as new technology impacted on traditional ways of working and thinking. MCB University Press was quick to spot the potential contribution of electronic publishing and it invested heavily in a programme of rapid product development. Meanwhile much thought was given as to how the company itself should develop at this crucial time.

While many other publishers restricted themselves to what were little more than 'knee-jerk' reactions to change, MCB, both as a publisher and an enterprise school of management, was involved in an exercise of intense intellectual analysis which encouraged a higher level of debate and great originality in ideas. Crucially, this intellectual effort led the company not only to survive the upheavals resulting from change, but to respond innovatively to the paradigm shift in the industry, strengthening its leadership position.

Success did not come easily, however. For MCB, rapid market developments were coupled, internally, with differing values and visions which at times created barriers to change. It is these uniquely challenging circumstances, as MCB struggled to come to terms with the new electronic media, that make this book a fascinating and revealing case study both in publishing 'history' and in business transition and development. It also offers an excellent insight into an example of the role of action learning in reviewing and revising corporate goals and strategy.

The five authors of a forthcoming book entitled *e.volution.com* met in the autumn of 1999 to discuss developments over the period during which they wrote their MBA dissertations and in the months following the final study. Here we present some of their thoughts.

Anticipatory learning across a paradigm shift

Action learning in the shape of anticipatory learning across a paradigm shift under-pinned the studies in this book. Volatile operating conditions ideally lend themselves to this form of learning because they effectively build on existing knowledge, situations and challenges, in order to respond to the organizational imperatives of the moment. So how did this form of learning contribute to MCB's development? To what degree did it enable the company to survive, innovate and thrive during a period of quite frenetic and continuous change?

It was in 1992 that MCB University Press launched into electronic publishing; that same year Timmie Duncan commenced work on her MBA dissertation. This, and the other studies in this book, opened up a wide-ranging debate into the future of MBA's publishing operations and the potential impact of new technology on traditional publishing formats, distribution channels, and marketing methods. The debate also focused on the future shape of the company and issues of organizational renewal.

Timmie's focus was on the company's relationship with distributors whose sales, at the time, accounted for the lion's share of the company's revenue. Having explored the impact of global data networks on the traditional distribution channel and examined the critical issues facing subscription agents, Timmie concluded that strategic partnering with agents, to exploit the requirement for access to rather than ownership of journals through a new combination of product delivery, could increase both parties' revenue streams.

Bev Bruce saw strategic alliances with distribution or technology partners, i.e. allies with complementary skills, as a means to develop MCB's long-term electronic publishing strategy. Bev's study recommended hiving off the EP business into a company subsidiary, the idea being to seek a joint venture to enable building of required competences and consequent expansion of the electronic side of the business.

Mat Wills concerned himself with issues of organizational renewal, emphasizing the need for change in the way MCB University Press was led and managed, a need exacerbated by the technological revolution of periodical publishing. He stressed the importance of succession planning and highlighted some critical corporate skill and organizational shortcomings.

The changing nature of scholarly communication was investigated by Mike Cross for his study, which aimed to identify the areas of traditional publishing which would continue to provide competitive advantage for

MCB University Press in future years. Mike emphasized that brand value (i.e. MCB's individual journal titles), the key source of competitive advantage, was threatened by new technology and that the company needed to strengthen relationships with suppliers and academics to ensure that the company developed the products that scholars required.

The final link in the study chain was Clive Hoey's study which explored the potential of computer-mediated communication as a marketing tool both to promote acceptance of MCB's innovative products and to encourage key groups into the electronic arena.

So what has happened since?

A significant capacity for innovation

Surveying MCB University Press today, the company's continuing success points to a very significant capacity for innovation. The company forged ahead at a time when others hesitated. It proved capable of adapting to change, of responding to new market imperatives, of changing strategies when necessary and, throughout, of strongly promoting innovation; indeed the company was some way ahead of the customer in terms of recognition of the need for product development and realization of the potential of the new technology. The state of flux of the industry at the time, resulting from the rapid development of new technology, meant customers were frequently unsure of their own requirements. Stepping into the breach, MCB, as a learning organization, became a virtual 'trend-setter'.

The authors would be the first to recognize that the ideas outlined and strategies recommended in their individual studies were not adopted *per se* as MCB University Press moved forward from its traditional publishing role to embrace the opportunities of new technology. However, they have seen that their studies' focus on future options crucially widened horizons, encouraging extensive new thinking. Hence the whole process of action learning significantly contributed, and is still contributing, to the development of future strategy.

As said, the authors' studies were written at a time of continuous change and uncertainty in the field of information management. The publishing industry was faced with the need for change, yet was deeply uncertain of future developments, market potential, trends, and requirements. All these questions were set against a background of intensifying competition and growing price pressures. Meeting these challenges head-on, MCB has not only been notably successful but has frequently been a model for others in the industry, not all of whom were able to mimic its success.

One of MCB's strengths turned out to be its relatively small size which enabled it to move quickly and effectively. Consider, for example, the company's early investment in new technology – this led to substantial enhancement of products such as Anbar, the company's article abstracting service. The introduction of an electronic database greatly eased access to information and added value to subscriptions, bringing users an easily searchable archive at the touch of a computer keyboard – an invaluable asset to researchers or those simply wishing to keep up-to-date with latest thinking in their field.

Prior to the introduction of databases such as Anbar, sources of information were restricted to items stocked by libraries or works recommended by academics. Electronic databases have substantially widened access to information. Taking a Utopian viewpoint, a fully democratized model would make available all published material to academics and students. However, this overlooks the reality of constraints such as budgeting, among others.

Shifting the burden of cost onto academics and students is seen by some as a solution, but this would be likely to depress demand (by comparison, free access – as evidenced by free trials of MCB products – substantially boosts demand). Such issues underline the importance of finding a way of determining how much library content is worthwhile, i.e. actually used.

Clearly, establishing the requirements of information users is key, both for librarians and publishers. This realization has promoted an interesting shift in MCB University Press's strategic emphasis in recent years, which is reflected in discussions in this book.

The new customer/consumer focus
Up until the 1990s, MCB University Press's focus was very much on its products, and on pursuit of what was seen as the 'right' product strategy; there was very little emphasis on the customer. The studies presented in this book reflect this, being strongly focused on effective implementation of new technology. In contrast, the authors point out that today's publishing agenda is strongly driven by customers, i.e. those who pay for the subscriptions, and users, i.e. 'consumers', their roles in the business equation and their precise requirements.

This change in focus has meant that, most recently, service issues have become more and more prominent, e.g. helpdesks, online help, library workshops – all of which help 'sell' the benefits of MCB University Press's products and services. These concepts are seen to be not so much about selling *per se,* but more about forging 'partnerships' with customers to ensure electronic subscriptions are used to best effect. This signals a move from traditional to new values within the organization. In the past MCB merely supplied journals to libraries. With the advent of electronic databases, MCB University Press has itself become a library, with the consequent onus upon it to promote effective use of its products to encourage repeat purchases. In effect, consumer behaviour is increasingly central to sales and marketing patterns.

The marketing focus has, however, switched to some extent from users, for whom products and services are primarily designed, to customers who, in MCB's case, are mostly academic libraries. This has occurred as a result of a shift of power from academic publishers to librarians and library purchasing consortia resulting from library budgeting constraints. The problem in this for publishers is that libraries and library consortia effectively constitute a barrier between publishers and product users, which makes it increasingly difficult for the former to reach users with a view to assessing their prime requirements.

While librarians, as 'gatekeepers' to information, understand the value added of electronic publishing, their priorities are very different from those of users. Although users provide some feedback to publishers via librarians – and indeed it is users who have requested from MCB recent innovations such as reference linking – the latter, who control the purse strings, remain the primary decision-makers; but they are actively seeking manageable, institutionalized products, i.e. pragmatic rather than evolving product goals.

This said, electronic access simultaneously challenges the role of the librarian because it brings a far greater choice of articles to users, a choice which greatly exceeds the scope of the journals that the librarian would have chosen in the past, and this in itself creates demand. The challenge for MCB in its goal of continuous improvement in product design thus becomes to reach, and ensure communication with, the end user, to ascertain user needs and priorities, and to ascertain what impact usage has on the next buying decision.

Market considerations

Beyond academia, there would seem to be substantial corporate market potential for MCB products and services, and the company has recently been concentrating spending on marketing efforts. However, there is a question mark over whether either products or distribution are at an optimum stage of development for market expansion, while it remains unclear what the new publishing models for the future will be. Will MCB be able to sell cost-effectively to new markets? Might products such as Anbar even be 'over-engineered' because of their consumer orientation; is the company perhaps even moving too far ahead of customers? Conversely, is there perhaps a risk of under-estimating product development and of moving into the 'slow lane'? Finally, might the company be concentrating too much on the paradigm shift between paper and electronic publishing as opposed to wider market developments? And what, anyway, is the residual role for paper?

Leaving these questions aside, the primary question must be: how can the company take advantage of its lead in the marketplace and ensure maintenance of 'shelf space'?

Ultimately, say the authors, there are three issues here: the need to establish electronic publishing as a core activity in an established traditional marketplace – access to full text articles being the driver; the need to investigate issues of product and market, i.e. to exploit market potential and resolve issues of inappropriate material (which could involve investigating the potential for précis-type articles for the corporate market – see below); assessment of market direction in terms of technology, and the need to keep and stay ahead of the game, investing both in technology and content, while avoiding moving too far ahead of the customer.

While the potential of the corporate market has long been recognized, and the scope of electronic publishing for sales of individual articles would seem to increase this potential, MCB products themselves pose problems for the marketing effort. Much of MCB journal content is far too in-depth and academic for corporate consumption. It is known that the search for information within a corporate organization often occurs at crucial 'moments of truth', for example when managers are uncertain of their own futures or are facing an unfamiliar situation when they feel the need to demonstrate that they are abreast of latest thinking. So what sort of product would be suitable for this market at such times? Might précis of original articles be the answer, to act as a 'vehicle' to lead the reader back to original articles which at first sight might appear dauntingly 'heavy'?

To reach this wider corporate market, one suggestion is that MCB might consider extending access to its databases via a range of management portals, i.e. partnering as many organizations as possible to give leverage to the distribution system while bringing in outside resourcing and expertise. The downside would be that MCB would not be in full charge of such portals; however, it is accepted that MCB is a relatively small player and cannot alone target all markets; and is not a 10 per cent share of a large and growing market more enticing than 100 per cent of a small, limited market? This argument, and that of offering different levels of subscription to target different markets, makes issues of product identity and differentiation paramount, and raises those of varying subscription content and licensing terms.

The studies – looking back, and forward

Going back to the five studies, what conclusions can be drawn? What prevented adoption of the options proposed by the five authors? What were the barriers to implementation, and were they essentially external or internal? Should past managers such as our authors have fought their corners more aggressively? Finally, what has actually developed since initial publication of these studies?

Drawing closer to agents

The first study was written in 1993/4, when MCB was making its first forays into electronic publishing through the introduction of CD-ROMs. Author Timmie Duncan focused on the desirability of strengthening partnerships with leading subscription agents which were not only MCB's best distribution channels, but were seen to provide an invaluable 'window on the world' for a publisher that, at the time, was still comparatively 'inward-looking'. Agents were required to add value to distribution, and this they did by passing on information about customers worldwide. However, Timmie's wider-ranging proposals were largely thwarted, both by the agents themselves who were reticent about drawing closer to publishers, and by MCB which was slow to pick up on the ideas suggested.

At the time, there was much discussion about the future of the various participants in the triangle of publishers, agents and librarians. The much-hyped 'death' of the publishers failed to materialize. Librarians too survived the upheavals created by the advent of electronic media. Agents, who traditionally worked closely with librarians to ensure a seamless subscription system, have been affected the most by the changed environment.

Since Timmie's dissertation was completed, libraries have remained the consolidation point, playing agents off against one another; they are now increasingly using buying groups in order to benefit from discounts; meanwhile publishers too can bypass agents by aggregating journals and selling collections such as Emerald directly to libraries. It is the agents who seem to have failed to find a new niche for themselves. They proved slow to move towards closer relationships with publishers, and their aim to be a 'one-stop-shop' was never realized.

The newer purchasing groups such as CHEST are faring far better as they can offer benefits to librarians that agents cannot. Hence market concentration among agents is taking its toll while the roles of surviving agents have had to evolve. At the time of writing, at least one agent is targeting consortia – this would have been unthinkable a short time ago. While new players are now emerging in developing countries, where they are setting up infrastructures to bring publishers and librarians together, in general subscription agents would seem to be presiding over a declining business.

So what of Timmie's proposals? Her attempts to work more closely with agents for mutual benefit were, she reports, an uphill battle and she found that continuous efforts were needed to maintain relationships. Another problem was that agents did not always have the means to support publishers adequately. In one instance, an initiative agreed with MCB involving provision by an agent of product demonstrations, reimbursed through commission on new sales, failed because the agent was insufficiently geared up to carry this through.

MCB, too, was slow on the uptake. An agent's suggestion of brainstorming sessions involving MCB, librarians and outside organizations with a view to promoting alliances, has only recently been implemented.

Exploiting electronic publishing

Fearing that others would 'cannibalize' its customer base if MCB failed to move decisively, Bev Bruce's study proposed taking a partnership approach to development of a core electronic publishing subsidiary through the formation of strategic alliances. The idea was to ensure a more saleable commodity, whether the intention was ultimately to buy or sell. Bev suggested partnering with organizations in such a way that there would be shared responsibility and shared risk. This proposal involved identifying complementary skills, co-operative cultures and compatible goals. MCB's strength was recognized as being procurement of journal content. What was required was a wider electronic distribution network.

At the time, MCB's relatively small size, while sometimes an advantage, had led to its operating efforts being 'spread thinly', making it difficult for the company to perform well in all areas. In addition, production of three distinct product categories, the MCB University Press hard copy journals, the Emerald electronic database, and the Anbar abstract journals and database, meant there was a tendency for staff to champion different products, leading to conflicting visions of corporate priorities. In addition, many in the company were slow to come to terms with the new media.

It was against this background that the proposal was made to spin out MCB University Press's electronic publishing division (EPD). However, because within MCB traditional operating models were considered still to be working, this proposal was not followed through. Bev and the other authors of this book cite the influence of politics and divergent viewpoints and visions within the company as limiting factors.

In contrast to the study's proposals, the EPD was developed within the company. This, Bev considers, was a disadvantage. Had the division been hived off as recommended, it would have had to work harder, in isolation, to make a profit, while it would not have been held back by traditional print 'rules'. Meanwhile, as feared, the marketing of electronic products was left to current resources and simply subsumed in the commercial activities for traditional products, which meant electronic products did not get the dedicated resourcing they required.

The major question then in the option recommended, which is still considered valid today, is: who would be an appropriate partner to exploit the potential of electronic publishing? At the time of writing, several possibilities are being actively explored.

Renewing the organization

Mat's study, written in 1996, focused on MCB in terms of its structure. He applied to it the theory of corporate life cycles, i.e. how organizations grow, evolve and develop over time and the requirement for organizational renewal to ensure flexibility and adaptability to change. Mat's study reports that, while MCB had been founded by a co-operative group of some 50 academics, by 1996 it had just four owner-managers. Since then three of these have left the company, leaving it in the hands of a single owner.

Mat points out that entrepreneurs typically find it difficult to transfer control to others and he suggests that this is one explanation for the failure of the vast majority of family companies to survive the process of transfer of control. An environment of rapid change, he notes, makes a transfer even more difficult. In MCB University Press's case, the challenges posed by electronic media and the new set of competences emerging among younger managers suggest the need for a new, technologically-oriented generation to take over.

The failure to address succession planning has damaging implications as it both hinders change and breeds frustration. MCB University Press's policy towards employee development, for example, in itself highly desirable and valuable for individual members of staff, was also designed to enable the baton to be passed on to a younger generation. Yet this has not happened. Consequently some senior managers have come to question whether company directors really believe in them. An unsuccessful management buyout seems to bear out this concern, and senior managers' motivation has been eroded by a situation in which they see themselves as working hard and being innovative solely for the profits of others. Results-based remuneration would go some way towards resolving this situation; but ultimately the company risks losing well-qualified and experienced people.

For the wider business and its development, Mat points to a problem posed by the absence of academics from the board. When the company was started, the partners, academics themselves, had their fingers on the pulse of the business environment, of what was being written about it, and of the quality required of submissions. This link and the related networking potential are now lost and the company has become increasingly dependent on journal editors to determine quality of content. The Literati Club and Peer Net were designed to go some way to redress the balance, but there remains an absence of inside knowledge.

Maintaining competitive advantage

Prompted by upheaval in the industry and fears that publishers would see their role eroded by self-publishing authors, Mike Cross's study, written in 1996/7, investigated how MCB University Press could maintain its place in the information chain and ensure continued demand for its publications in an increasingly competitive market. Mike emphasizes that brand value – vested, in MCB's case, in individual journal titles – is the key source of competitive advantage.

To maintain this the company must attract top quality articles from the best authors. Provision of appropriate systems and support are seen as crucial to this process of ensuring maintenance of the quality of branded journals which will be attractive to top-ranking authors. The idea of Peer Net, whereby authors review the work of other authors, was developed to ensure this quality focus, and in recognition of the fact that traditional peer review (involving review by editors who are sometimes considered too much of an 'old boy's network'), was too restrictive. The Internet-based Peer Net was seen as a more meritocratic process. Meanwhile MCB would be able both to generate more journal content and to exert greater control over the quality of articles published, justifying premium prices for MCB publications.

However, while Peer Net has been operating for some time now, negative reaction to it from editors has thwarted its full adoption and development. Managing editors have, on the whole, also failed to champion the concept as their prime concern is the timely flow of material rather than its quality. The organizational structures in place within MCB meanwhile have prevented the proponents of Peer Net from lobbying editors directly. Hence, to date, very few journal editors have approved and adopted the system. A strategy of pinpointing and working with a few known enthusiasts has, however, proven successful.

To recap, while 'selling' Peer Net to editorial management staff has proved problematical, the concept itself is considered both viable and valuable. The problem is that editors at times constitute a barrier between MCB and its authors.

So the question is – how can Peer Net be effectively exploited, bypassing editors and managing editors for whom it poses a problem? Should it perhaps be marketed directly to authors via MCB's Literati Club which boasts a database of some 10,000 authors? Or might MCB consider either hiving off the concept into an independent company, or going into partnership with another organization, to create some sort of an authors' 'agency'? The Peer Net concept, it is suggested, would be likely to prove more acceptable to both authors and editors, and hence be successful, if it were not seen to be exclusively an MCB product. In addition, it could become a more widely marketable concept.

The communication conundrum

The last and most recent study explored what electronic communication meant to MCB University Press both in terms of the electronic products' sales process and the overall communication process. Clive Hoey, the study's author, set out to investigate how the communication process was changing, how librarians and academics were using electronic media, and how MCB was adapting to this. His goal was to demonstrate the role, scope and importance of electronic marketing communication with a view to creating a database environment to enhance marketing potential.

The study discusses such questions as how to attract visits to websites, and how to promote involvement, for example in discussion groups and virtual conferencing. How too does a publisher like MCB University Press assess who is visiting a site? How does it 'capture' information? How does it generate awareness of its products, and communicate with potential customers and product users? Finally, how does it encourage sales and appropriate product use to ensure customers use its products to best effect, maximizing the value of subscriptions and consequently encouraging repeat purchasing?

Clive points out that the creation of customer databases based on take-up of free trials, website visits, Internet conferencing and meeting-place participation can now bring the publisher direct access both to journal readers and authors. A system of grading these has been set up and the ongoing challenge is to ensure MCB communicates the right message to the right people and has something to sell to as many of these as possible.

Target markets are students, librarians, academics and senior decision-makers. To develop the database as a marketing tool, there is a need both to generate traffic and then to 'whittle' this down, analysing site visitors to enable close targeting of potential customers. Work in this direction is in its early stages. One major development is that, while until now Internet marketing has been kept separate from the traditional marketing effort, it has recently been incorporated into the mainstream marketing effort. This has been reorganized according to type of market, i.e. academic, corporate, and institutional, rather than marketing media. Hence, in terms of Clive's study and recommendations, not only is the Internet marketing infrastructure he envisaged in place and working, but database marketing will now also be able to influence what is happening in the mainstream, i.e. it is no longer working out on a limb.

So, whither MCB University Press?

Ever more questions emerge when looking forward. While consolidation is seen as key to future strategy, MCB is continuously evolving.

What new developments will there be in the field of technology? For MCB, might future changes focus on the way the company markets and services its products rather than on the shift from paper to electronic media? More generally, what will be the roles of librarians, publishers and agents as the electronic era intensifies?

The answers to these questions will doubtless emerge over time. Meanwhile, other questions, posed both implicitly and explicitly in our authors' studies, still remain to be addressed.

Internally, one major question to be posed is to what degree MCB's ownership structure has been an inhibiting factor in its development.

Continuing the discussion into today's situation, what is the overall impact of a family business culture? The authors see part of the problem as being that the shareholding and financial decision-making structure in place today still tends to view investment as a potential encumbrance; hence leeway in essential decision-making is hampered by short-termism. Yet investment to compete in a fast-changing market is seen by our authors as crucially important.

The main barriers to change then are seen as having been longstanding shareholders with fixed ideas. In recent years there has been both a failed sell-out to the *Financial Times*, and a failed management buyout. The latter is particularly regretted as it might have addressed strategic weaknesses while it would have transformed the youthfulness of the top management team. So, the corporate succession question remains.

It is the authors' contention that MCB needs clear resolution of this corporate succession question. The company also needs a more forward-looking leadership to address the strategic issues facing it. Another major weakness in MCB, being a private company, is the lack of independence of the financial director. In addition, the impartial advice of a strategic financial adviser to co-ordinate management and financial input would be of value. There is also an urgent need of an injection of specialist, outside talent into other areas, and particularly those of sales and marketing.

The prevailing corporate culture has proved a major hindrance, say the authors. Because of the company's academic foundations, this culture has traditionally focused on supporting, educating and promoting employees – 'downsizing' or cutting salaries, even when necessary, go against the grain. The academic bias, it is argued, while part of the strength of the company, has at times also led to a tendency to philosophize rather than act decisively. Finally, a policy of promoting from within has hindered injection of new blood into the company. This is considered to have impacted particularly adversely on divisions such as sales and marketing where there is a strong argument for outside expertise. Such recruitment, it is suggested, has been actively blocked by the directors' refusal to countenance paying market rates.

As noted, the corporate culture and structure is also responsible for frustration at senior management level where traditional decision-making structures mean managers find themselves unable to put their visions into effect; the lack of an adequate reward structure further erodes job satisfaction with the consequent risk of loss of some of the company's best people.

MCB's strategic priorities, e.g. regularly increasing prices which became unacceptable, have themselves been a limiting factor in the company's overall development. Meanwhile, the company's many-stranded operations have led to a marked absence of a shared vision, while entrenched structures and habits have created actual barriers to change.

In general, the company must develop and promote a clear vision for the future while maintaining the dynamic for improvement which will enable it to continue into a second cycle of development. Ultimately MCB University Press has shown its ability to adopt and successfully exploit new technology. Where it fails, the authors believe, is in issues relating to people. Investment, for example, has always been available to upgrade equipment, i.e. the tools of the trade, but it is notably absent to enhance structures, streamline procedures or reward the company's people.

The consensus of opinion is that the way forward for MCB University Press involves focus on fewer objectives, improvement of efforts and performance towards these, relationship building with consortia to promote sales, and use of other organizations' portals to extend distribution. The most significant challenge then remaining will be that of differentiating the company's products and segmenting the market.

In the meantime, the authors warn that MCB University Press must 'keep tabs' on its competitors, and notably online newcomers such as Ingenta which have no historical 'baggage' regarding how material is put into print, and are unhampered by hard copy journal publication costs. Ingenta, like other, newer players, has built up a business geared specifically to an electronic working environment, and so is tailor-made to respond to today's changing market demands.

This said, the profitability to publishers of supplying librarians in the future is not expected ever to return to past levels. However, the authors have no doubt that there remains a substantial volume market to be tapped. Hence a major question that remains to be addressed is how MCB University Press, now also a creator of databases boasting exceptional search engines, should market its products in the future.

A final word
This book endeavours to show how organizational learning has contributed to MCB University Press's self-awareness and decision-making at a time of rapid transition. The action learning underpinning the authors' conclusions has effectively questioned the *status quo*, explored new avenues and, where necessary, encouraged MCB to think the hitherto unthinkable. The authors' questioning has thus generated a wide-ranging debate, suggesting options which otherwise might never have been imagined. This process was, and is, crucial to the pursuit of change. As our authors only too clearly recognize, in today's fast-moving world, leaving the future to providence is not an option.

Chapter 7

International Management Centres as a learning organization

GORDON PRESTOUNGRANGE AND CAROL OLIVER

The tradition of story telling as the effective way to pass on learning from generation to generation is well founded and of course preceded the written word. In this chapter we seek to bring them together, as many organizational sociologists have.

1964 saw the completion in Buckinghamshire, at Slough Technical College, of the first cadre of practising managers from a night school Diploma in Management Studies in the UK. They resolved, as most such socially reinforced groups do, that they should continue to meet together to keep learning together. They (and the group included the author) had enjoyed working together, yarning in the canteen at supper time and discovering new knowledge with and from one another and from tutors. It seemed normal enough and the tutors, including Ruskin College-educated Geoff Pitt, a newly minted MBA (Chicago) graduate who had masterminded the whole experience over three years, encouraged this initiative.

First stop was the British Institute of Management (BIM), the national professional body that had forsaken its own professional qualifications in 1961 and passed responsibility for the Diploma to a national committee. From the late 1930s until that time the BIM and a more intellectual grouping known as the Institute of Industrial Administration had offered their own professional programmes lasting, in the BIM's case, for seven years part-time. The first question was: would they like to sponsor a Chapter for the new wave of Postgraduate Diplomatists emerging from the Technical Colleges under the new scheme? And the answer to that was no: don't be elitist.

The second question was: would they like to launch a new postgraduate-level journal on the model of the world-famous *Harvard Business Review*, alongside their own professional journal called *The Manager*? And once again the answer was no, there would not be a big enough market for it.

The notion of the journal had arisen because most of the group were already professional and were accustomed to using such information media. During the course of the programme all had been aware how good British material was being little used by tutors; it was mainly American, and that trend was reinforced by Geoff Pitt's Chicago MBA.

There was no way the group's learning had taught them to take no for an answer: so they immediately set to work to accomplish their goals independently. The Institute of Scientific Business was established in late 1964 and, with the collaboration of an outside resource, published a journal – also called *Scientific Business.*

That Institute has been known since 1982 as the International Management Centres Association (IMCA). The journal has gone from strength to strength and has been known as *Management Decision* since the late 1960s.

IMCA was in its turn the world's first fully Internet-based provider of professional qualification programmes from 1994. By 1995 *Management Decision* was the cornerstone journal for a suite of 150 journals from MCB University Press which became one of the most significant e-publishing houses on the Internet from 1994 onwards, and in 1999 saw 10 million hits on its renowned virtual library known as Emerald.

This chapter looks at the IMCA as a learning organization over the years 1964 to 1999.

Phase One: learning to sustain association
It was straightforward enough at the beginning. Everyone knew one another in depth after three years of shared adversity: new jobs, promotions, problems to discuss and a determination to read around the subject in which intellectual as opposed to simply practical or skills interests and curiosity had been aroused. There were seminars and congresses and decisions. It sounded like an alumni association that would wither away after a few years. But it was soon determined that membership of the Institute should extend well beyond the original graduates to as wide a grouping of like-minded people as could be found. This was to make the meetings more interesting and varied and the seminars economically viable. Associate and Fellow grades of membership were introduced, the former being those who were still learning at a college and the latter for those who had achieved the output of an award. Buckinghamshire Fellows very soon invited graduates from Portsmouth and Northampton College and Regent Street Polytechnic in London to join, and they did. (Today these institutions are known as Thames Valley, Portsmouth, City and Westminster Universities.)

Economics of organization of meetings could be managed from internal resources – but not the publishing activity. The working capital and the launch investment of the journal was beyond the risk-taking preferences or perceived competences of the members (and thereby hangs a tale for later). The external ownership certainly managed to build the circulation of a serious intellectual management journal to be the UK leader with some 3,000 subscribers. But by 1970 they had lost interest and were determined to discontinue publication. Nothing daunted, three of the founders of the IMCA agreed to spend 6s 8d pre-decimalization each, making £1 in total to buy the title and publish it themselves from Bradford where two of them had become business school tutors at the University. And as they say, the rest is history.

By the inspired use of management theories of new business-start venture groups, the enterprise grew into MCB University Press with some 50 equity holders from among members in discrete subject fields. The boom in management education found no dedicated professional and academic intellectual journals in almost all emerging fields, from logistics to marketing and human resources, operations management, quality management and so forth. MCB moved again and again to launch, with enterprising clusters of investors working through a service company support framework. And the whole momentum was funded by an initial risk capital rapidly supported by incoming subscriptions in advance.

Whilst the phenomenon of the IMCA-sponsored and resourced publishing enterprise was occurring, the meetings and associating of IMCA members was highly focused in the venture groups. But the very success of publishing activity nationally facilitated the most worrying of developments for the practising managers who were the Councillors of the IMCA. The whole process of developing adult managers in mid-career into an intellectual understanding and contemplation of their roles was being replaced by an overwhelming academicization. Managerial concerns *per se* were no longer the issue of the curriculum; a body of knowledge admirably captured in the journals was to be tutored.

Those who were joining IMCA as Fellows were increasingly concerned with the academic rating of their awards, which by now had escalated in the UK from postgraduate Diplomas in Technical Colleges from the national committee to University MSc and MBA degrees. As a professional association in 1982, IMCA was approaching the same destination as the BIM had reached by 1961. The structure and substance of professional development was being 'taken over' by the main institutions of undergraduate education and the curriculum was being defined away from the practitioner and the place of work; and our own members had become party to the determinism of that process.

Tough decisions had to be made, and in 1982 they were in the room at the White Hart Hotel in Lincoln where the original plans for the First World War tank were first unveiled. The leading members of the IMCA, who were mainly teachers of management in the universities but could clearly remember why they came into such a field, resolved to raise the banner for a movement that insisted management development must return to the mid-career manager's needs and wants. It must eschew the academic curriculum.

Endless debate had surrounded the ultimate decision to strike out with the IMCA's 'own' qualifications. The grade of Associate was henceforth to describe managers who were following a route to an IMCA grade of Graduate membership. The Fellows were the tutorial team. The confidence with which IMCA proceeded was all down to one man whom they scarcely knew, Dr Reg Revans. He had been Professor of Industrial Administration at Manchester University in the 1960s but had left to work in Belgium as he saw the process of academicization taking hold. He was an individual of great distinction who since 1944 had proposed a well-articulated alternative learning process known as action learning. It was that process that IMCA from that time exclusively espoused and Reg Revans became IMCA's President.

The strategy was simple and bold. The IMCA introduced grades of membership for its Graduates that were at Bachelor, Master and Doctoral levels, all levels at which the leading members were well experienced in their university roles. But they were only achievable by action learning. Ironically, the funding then for the new qualifications strategy came from the outstanding success of the academic journal publishing that IMCA had fostered in MCB University Press. IMCA had learnt that the sources of profit in any endeavour would not always be from the mainstream activity. But for the bold decision at the outset that the journal should go forth and find its own funding, and the entrepreneurial spirit in 1971 to take it on at Bradford, there would have been little scope for the launch of IMCA's own action learning qualifications programmes.

The launch cost was in the region of £2 million from 1982 to 1987 when it finally broke even and a Fellow buy-out team took over the financial underwriting just as a small group had earlier taken over the publishing enterprise in 1971. The success had been achieved by the outstanding support of major corporations in the UK and Europe such as NatWest Bank whose global CEO today was the IMCA client, Dow Corning in Brussels and IDV. There had also been exceptional success in Malaysia, South Africa, Hong Kong, Singapore and Australia as the action learning qualification programmes captured the practising managers' imagination. But in 1988, for reasons 'not intended to impact on IMCA' according to the UK government, the Association was supremely challenged. Its work was made technically illegal. Worse than that, it was informed by government ministers that its continuation must be based on gaining the approval of the very institutions it had been established to contradict – the universities.

This was the moment when the IMCA realized more powerfully than ever before that its strength lay with its membership and that action learning for the Association itself was required. IMCA refused to accept subordination to the academicization processes. It provoked anger and sustained opposition from the university sector for its continued determination to assert its own professional awards as degrees of IMCA membership. And it found that the way to accomplish this was by accepting that IMCA had already become an international institution and that that could avoid the legal restrictions forthcoming from the UK government. From 1988 IMCA ceased to be a Buckingham-driven professional association and became multinational. It incorporated in Australia and Vanuatu and New Zealand immediately and has since gone on to incorporate in a further eight countries – the USA, Papua New Guinea, Singapore, Canada, Finland, The Netherlands, Curacao and South Africa. The major face-to-face meetings for Graduation Congregation and Annual Professional Congress began to rotate around the globe. IMCA made an advantage of its adversity, and whilst its critics now rue the day it was driven offshore by the 1988 legislation, IMCA looks back with something resembling gratitude for the push it provided to reflect on what it had really become.

The financial break-even accomplished in 1987 enabled the publishing enterprise to spin out the IMCA activities to a new shareholding group from among Fellows. It made an auspicious start and soon realized it needed major additional funding for expansion globally, most particularly in the light of the 1988 legal constraints in the UK. This was readily found with a major listed public company, Doctus, with some £150m annual turnover. The Fellows recouped their personal investments plus a substantial gain in three years. But their luck did not hold out. In the financial and economic crisis in the UK in the early 1990s Doctus collapsed, leaving the profession with extensive debts. Once again the publishing enterprise obliged with the recovery which was vigorously led from the Far East and The Netherlands. IMCA's multinationalism was once more its very great strength, even though the UK was its ancestral home. Fellows and Graduates around the world formed action learning 'recovery' Sets and the IMCA was back in its stride in two years. It had learnt that when it resolved to work with outside investors there was limited empathy and few of the 'beliefs and values' in lifelong action learning that characterized the global profession. Action learning was consciously used to reposition IMCA's physical centre in Buckingham as a self-financing support resource, and the global registry was transformed by the emerging electronic data interchange systems.

And thus was the IMCA positioned when the capabilities of the Internet arrived for its global activities, and when MCB University Press resolved to become a leader in the field of e-publishing in 1994.

Phase 3: virtual global associating is born

In 1994 IMCA had already been a multinational association for a decade as the Internet effectively arrived. The determination to be included from the very earliest days in 1964 to broaden the learning experience of all members had been inexorably reinforced when the IMCA espoused action learning in the workplace in 1982, which rapidly spread across the world. The UK's legislative programme in 1988 gave a further inexorable push. And the recovery in the aftermath of the Doctus financial collapse in 1991/1992 took the face-to-face meetings onto a rotating global pattern.

No organization could have been more clearly expectant of the burgeoning communications revolution which the Internet has provided than the IMCA. The multinational association had been in a state of aestivation for ten years when in 1992 the members from Australia and The Netherlands proposed that Bulletin Board Systems (BBS), and swiftly thereafter the Internet with its http facilities, should be adopted. An Internet Research & Development Centre (IRDC) was formed immediately and, working with the Electronic Publishing Division of MCB University Press most especially for the virtual library services, created the world's first online professional association by 1994/1995. And more was accomplished by the creation of continuously updated courseware resources with automatic literature access against key words, clustered into specialist areas and regional forums.

In one step via the Internet, one of the telling challenges of distributed learning – access to the literature at out-of-the-way locations – was not only overcome, but the service provided exceeded that of most fixed locations. In addition, distributed learners could, via Web meeting places, not only stay in better touch on a regular basis than with face-to-face activities, but could correspond with other members and Associates around the globe. Global virtual conferences that vastly outdistanced the mainstream face-to-face conferences and seminars of the IMCA of old were convened on the Internet under the aegis of MCB University Press journals and integrated by IRDC.

It was during this transformational period in the latter half of the 1990s that the IMCA also explored whether it could approach the world's universities to joint venture together in the new medium for workplace action learning. As described elsewhere, however, the universities were not ready; they were not empathetic to the paradigm of learning for the learner with quality defined as fitness for that professional purpose. Accordingly the stage was set for the second half of the Internet revolution to be played out for the IMCA as the new millennium dawned.

Phase 4: twenty-first-century association portals and resources for career development

The Internet has done more than transform IMCA's abilities to be an effective and efficient multinational professional association: it has brought in its wake a broader definition of its outreach, of its ability to be inclusive. The Internet can reach to all corners of the globe in any language that may be desired. It can deliver cost-effectively the smallest item of knowledge or understanding. To take but one example, it is economic to deliver an action learning doctoral qualification for individual Associates in New Zealand, Hong Kong, Barbados, Toronto, Singapore, Alberta and Texas, without the need for them to come face to face with one another or with their tutors. The Internet for IMCA aggregates individuals into virtual groups that flourish where the economics would formerly have prevented any activity at all. The Internet takes IMCA's finest facilities and resources and support to corners of the earth where they have never been before, such as Vanuatu in the South Pacific or to African townships or up-country Yukon in Canada.

Whilst all the productivity gains have been gladly accepted at IMCA, there has been the growing realization that the medium is indeed the message. Three vectors have emerged for technological development that reflect IMCA's enduring purpose – but in quite different manifestations.

The first of these is the creation of an online Action Learning Institute (ALI) which offers open access and modest pre- and post-qualification-level participation in the activities of the IMCA.

The second is the realization of a global mega-portal in association with major lifestyle and career development partners, with the objective to be a contextual participant in the big framework. Here the IMCA is taking the lead. And this is of course in addition to participation in myriad other portals on an alliance and tenancy basis.

Third, the twenty-first-century definition of e-publishing includes for the IMCA what we call action learning rather than a simplistic knowledge base. Our twenty-first-century initiative to parallel the twentieth-century creation of MCB University Press is arising from IMCA's Site 2000 project. It is building, just as MCB University Press did, one of the finest resources for individual and corporate use which will be available both through the IMCA and independently.

Whilst the first vector is funded in-house, the second and third build on the corporate learning gained over the period 1987 to 1999 and introduce external capital allied to capital generated from Fellows and Graduates. The net outcomes of these three vectors of the global activities will be greatly increased contact levels measured in millions of hits at the website per month, and the provision of professional services and support in more digestible units. And the language of the Internet and the Web meeting places all make their distinctive new medium message contributions.

In this framework, the conduct of IMCA's qualification degree of membership programmes is open for modular/incremental participation. Their co-ordination and intellectual leadership has now been placed under the aegis of the Association's professional/corporate university located in cyberspace, IMCA's own University of Action Learning. The IMCA is also, through its 'Internet inclusive' outreach, offering credit mapping for prior experiential and structured action learning to corporates and training and development providers at large which can accumulate towards the IMCA's professional qualifications.

How do we learn what we learn?

This chapter must surely conclude with an analysis of the learning mechanisms IMCA put in place in 1964 for individual learning and to ponder whether they have been sufficiently robust to stand the test of time.

1964 saw IMCA established in the interest of its members' lifelong careers and managerial development by them helping one another. The processes of institutionalization seem not to have overwhelmed that, because no centralized structure was ever created. The learning and activity was always seen as being from the place of work and with the members. When its senior members became deeply involved in the universities' academicization, IMCA's ethos was strong enough to provide them with a way forward by adopting action learning, and this was immeasurably reinforced by embracing the Internet. Both presented themselves as 'beliefs-appropriate media' for the extension of the fundamental purposes, and the IMCA was able to go with them. Resistance to such evolutionary change was virtually non-existent.

It could be argued that any incipient institutionalization by 1991/1992 was effectively destroyed and the IMCA was required to regenerate itself by the demise of Doctus at that time, and that to regenerate, the Association went back to its members and reinforced its beliefs. But however the story is told, IMCA has demonstrated truly amazing resilience to adverse legal, financial and educational adversities. The conclusion has to be that its ethos and espoused learning approaches are up to the task. They are sufficiently open and the situational leadership sufficiently robust to be able to permit the IMCA to learn faster than the forces of entropy.

The strength of Reg Revans' message that action learning will take place whenever people who 'know, care and have the power to do something about it' are gathered together has been vindicated many times over. It is the self-confidence of knowing that the IMCA itself uses its own philosophies to manage its own affairs that gives it the credibility to offer them to millions more who are not yet members but can see the way it can help them too. Protective institutionalization has been the Achilles heel of much professional development provision from time immemorial. Placing members' articulated needs permanently at the centre of the IMCA by the action learning process has proved its worth.

Chapter 8

Strategizing at work

*Practitioner perspectives on
doctoral Set working*

JENNIFER BOWERMAN

The value of experience

'Just because you have read *Oliver Twist*, doesn't mean to say that you know what it is to be an orphan .' These words, from the character played by Robin Williams in the popular 1998 film *Good Will Hunting*, will strike a chord with many of us. They speak to the fact that knowing something cognitively and rationally doesn't have the same impact as experiencing something using all of our senses.

These words are particularly haunting for those of us who work in organizations that are experiencing change at an unprecedented rate. Continuous change has taken away our sense of organizational stability, our ability to predict what will happen. Changing conditions mean that there are no longer any right answers, only those appearing to be the best at the time. We see a need for fluid processes that will help individual employees cope with change, and at the same time bring the organization to where it needs to be in order to cope with the ongoing pressures of global competition, privatization and increased technological innovation. These fluid processes are new, and emergent. They are worthy of study, and we read lots about them. I believe, however, that they are best studied by participating in them directly.

My experience with these issues in part arises because of my own personal journey. I relate the following story because it speaks to so many of the themes of self-direction, action learning and the virtual business school, which have become increasingly important to me as a doctoral practitioner in the workplace.

The journey

In 1997, after 22 years in a government job, I decided to return to university – to fulfil my dream of obtaining a PhD. In many respects this decision was my way of rescuing myself and making sense of a public sector world that had drastically changed over a very short space of time. In my own department, more than 50 per cent of the workplace had been 'displaced' or laid off over a period of three years. Middle managers had been demoted, including myself. Many of the services we had previously offered as a government department had now been outsourced or privatized. If I was to survive, with mind and passion intact, it was going to be necessary to take seriously the idea that organizations were changing, and to consider my own role in the change.

Taking the notion of organizational change seriously, it occurred to me that one way of confronting my own disappointment at being demoted was to study change rather than just be a victim of it. After the managerial demotion, a new role as an internal training consultant gave me the opportunity to see change as an opportunity to experiment and work with people through learning. As the organization developed competences, implemented broad banding, and built teams, I began to believe that what we were doing was important. This was more than just work. We were strategizing, building and creating new systems and knowledge about the workplace that were worthy of sharing with others. I started to write essays about organizational change and its impact for the university classes that I was taking on a part-time basis. I was even successful in having an article published in a new book on the learning organization with the then deputy minister. Three years later, the changes that I had helped to create came to a crossroads with the appointment of a new deputy minister who had a quite different and more traditional philosophy for the public service. Because I was committed to the changes we had implemented, I felt as though my career was also at a crossroads. I decided to leave, and with the desire to learn more about the implications of learning in the workplace, saw a doctorate at the local university as an appropriate choice.

Returning to university full time after 25 years in the workplace was a shock. Because I had changed, I was expecting the university to have changed; to acknowledge that I was now an adult with full earning power and a lot of experience in organizational transformation. The university, however, seemed to have changed little from the days when I had completed my Master's Degree in my twenties. Even though I had developed wonderful relationships with some individual professors as a result of my organizational change work with my former government department, the university administration was bigger than all of us. The Faculty of Graduate Studies still had me jumping through bureaucratic hoops. The road to the PhD was littered with hurdles that were not about me and my abilities or interests: they were all about what others had pre-determined to be important, without any input from me.

Within this system, I could only ever be a student, lucky to be worthy of a scholarship, or a measly stipend through a teaching assistantship. Such a situation would have been fine in my twenties, when I had no work experience or expertise to fall back on. But now, after 30 years in the workplace,

I was at a different phase in my life – a phase where I expected to have more control over what was happening to me. The university was still catering to me as though I was twenty. I had moved on: they had not. It was clear that my journey to a doctoral degree within this institution would be very difficult.

After two months, I realized that I was going to have to reassess my dream, or at least the means I had chosen to realize it. What I was beginning to see about myself was that my personal dreams of learning through a doctoral programme were tied to my passion for working in an organization, strategizing, implementing, and learning in an ongoing way. I was at a stage in life where I wanted to be able to see the impact of my work and my learning directly where I was working. An opportunity to work with Reg Revans through an international seminar at Salford made me aware that this method of study was called action learning. I realized that studying other people's work was not so interesting as the study of my own developing and emerging practice.

Over the years, I realized that my living experience of working in a change environment had moved me from being a passive recipient of knowledge to seeing myself as a co-creator of new knowledge through my own actions and strategy in practice; in other words, I saw myself as empowered. I decided to quit the university, and returned to the workplace as an organizational learning specialist in a quasi-governmental organization needing to become more entrepreneurial. Putting my doctoral dream on hold, I threw myself into organizing, developing and implementing action learning programmes intended to create culture change and realize new business results.

My doctoral dreams were finally realized when I came across the International Management Centre (IMC) in partnership with Oxford Brookes University (OBU) in Great Britain offering a distance, thesis-based, action learning programme. Using IMC as the medium, this virtual business school gave me the opportunity to draw all the themes of my life together, my desire for self-directedness and self-management, and my interest in action learning as a method of bringing about personal and organizational transformation.

As a result of my own personal experience, I have come to believe that:

- action learning as a strategy for learning at work, and for creating new knowledge best fits those adult learners who are self-directed; and
- the virtual university through IMC and OBU with its open system complements the desire to be self-directed with the opportunity to create new knowledge through action learning.

The rest of this article develops these themes in more detail.

On being self-directed

A major assumption of action learning is that subjects learn only when they wish to do so, and not at the will of others. If such an assumption is at the heart of action learning, it is also perhaps the essence of what it means to be self-directed. When Malcolm Knowles (1970, 1981) first coined the term 'androgogy' to explain the difference between adult and childhood learning, his thesis was that adults are internally motivated to learn because of their life experience, and the desires that arise from this experience. Other writers such as Bernard Lievegoed in his book *Phases* (1993), identifies the critical inner stages that adults go through as they live their lives. He suggests that the inner qualities and challenges arising at each stage of life, from adolescence through to our thirties, forties, fifties and beyond must be recognized and acknowledged. There is nothing new about the idea that as we go through our lives we go through key developmental phases. Much of what we know about the human psyche comes from the work of Carl Jung, whose theory of human maturity is based on the notion of individuation – a gradual process of maturation as our inner and outer selves interplay and evolve toward wholeness (Quenk, 1993). This is somewhat similar to Maslow's concept of self-actualization (1954).

Neither of these propositions, that adults bring their life experience to the learning process, and that they go through key developmental phases as they progress through life, are particularly earth-shattering. Indeed many of us who are in the business of developing learning programmes in the workplace advocate a practice based on principles that correspond to them. What is surprising however is our difficulty in implementing the practical application of these principles. In the workplace for example, much of what we believe about Knowles' work has been translated into humanistic principles that we advocate for use in the classroom by trained adult instructors. Despite our adherence to concepts such as the learning organization, with its inherent principles of adult autonomy, we are quick to ignore the fact that many of our workplace classroom learners are present to learn at the will of the instructor, or the will of the manager, rather than at their own will.

Take the case of the design and implementation of new performance development or performance management systems. The two organizations in which I have been involved over the past seven years have designed new performance management systems. These systems require employees to be self-directed, empowered, team players, and at the same time encourage personal goals to be aligned with team goals, and corporate goals. How have we implemented these systems? The answer is that we have used human resource trainers such as myself to provide compulsory classroom training for employees throughout the organization. The new systems were devised outside of the line, by a centralized human resource function, with little or no reference to the adult employees for whom the system is intended; and they were not successful.

It can be argued that factors responsible for the lack of implementation and buy-in on the part of employees likely include a sense of *déjà vu* on the part of the employees being 'trained'. Often this is translated as a groan of 'Oh no! Here we go again' by our captive audience. It is also difficult for these initiatives to impact the 'culture' of an organization that has become ingrained over time into the ongoing practices and daily activities of the line operations.

In today's organizational world, classroom training of the sort described above confronts a real dilemma. Downsizing and fear of layoffs have created a workforce that is sceptical of new performance management systems, and many of the other initiatives perceived as coming from the top. What we see is a workplace filled with the same paradox as my university experience described above. On the one hand, employees are sophisticated enough to manage their own finances, buy houses, raise children, plan vacations, and a dozen other myriad of things indicating that they are mature adults. On the other hand, we drag them into the classroom to improve their communication skills, or develop their leadership, or set goals so that they can do what we believe is right for them to build our business. On the one hand we want their loyalty and their skills, but on the other, we lay them off when the corporate circumstances dictate it. For employees this is like walking through a minefield. Sometimes, it doesn't matter what they do, or what they learn in the classroom, it may not be right for the business. It is as though the changes are outstripping the very initiatives that are designed to implement them. Under these difficulties, our best ideas are bound to be challenged about how to integrate learning into organizations so that it is effective.

So how do we recognize that often employees, as adults, know what is best for them? It is simply not enough to pay lip service to adult learning styles or humanistic classroom design methods. What about demographic factors, lifestyle choices, and the stages of life that we all go through? How do we tap into the passions that energize people so that these same passions can unleash their creativity and innovation and contribute to resolving the workplace problems that we all face? How do we allow employees to have a voice in the decisions that affect their lives, and advance their own growth? How do we make the workplace learner-centred around the problems that employees face in the course of real work so that they can impact ongoing practice and culture, and not us-centred around our problems that we perceive them to face?

On action learning

One possible answer to these rhetorical questions is to take an action learning approach. The assumptions behind action learning are that learning does not simply happen as a result of listening to a lecture, or receiving a piece of information from another individual, or a book. Learning happens when we take that information, and actually apply it in our behaviour. It is believed that we do this best when we are confronted with a problem that involves us personally. By taking action, and then reflecting on that action through good questions, in the company of others working on similar problems, we learn. When we learn, we will have gained new knowledge, including more about ourselves, our blind spots and barriers, as well as those of others. In short, action learning is a method of expediting the process of learning from experience. It refers not only to cognitive understanding, but also to the development of self-awareness and the ability to behave differently (Revans, 1998). As we work to resolve our problems through action and reflection, we take with us our passions, our phases in life, our psyches; and as our problems develop and become workable projects, so too do we grow in parallel fashion.

Action learning works best when individuals work on particular projects that address real problems in an organization. By working with others to define the problem, and then applying a proposed solution, action learning provides a structured environment for individuals to receive feedback as a result of their own actions. Thus the purpose of action learning is not only to complete a particular project, but also to provide for individual self-development and growth through an awareness of the emotional and cognitive factors implicit in the way one sees the world. This is why action learning is about self-direction. To the extent that a person can work with others and is open to being intellectually and emotionally stretched, then action learning is a vehicle where personal and professional interest and passion can coincide.

This does not mean that action learning is necessarily a substitute for training: it isn't. Training may be a very appropriate strategy when dealing with particular skills or knowledge that people need to have. But the point is that we often conduct training in the belief that we are following principles related to self-direction when we are not. Our processes when dealing with adult learners in the workplace should be transparent so that they can work out for themselves through dialogue with us what it means to be self-directed. Self-direction in its purest sense is about allowing people to find their own way, to find their own solutions and answers, and knowing full well that these may well be different from yours.

At the same time it is important to recognize that this happens unevenly. People have varying degrees of maturity. We are all at different phases in our lives. Transparency is one way of dealing with this unevenness. If we can de-expertise ourselves as facilitators, or people in the front of the classroom, concentrate on process, and at the same time 'expertise' the learners so that they are able to share their practices and knowledge with others, then we help to build maturity. This in turn builds accountability, leadership and empowerment, all qualities that are believed to be important in today's changing workplace.

On the virtual university

As a doctoral researcher in the workplace, not only are issues such as self-direction and action learning important to study, they are also of major importance from a personal dimension. Because I am working on particular projects, and studying them at the same time in terms of process and outcomes, then I am necessarily involved in the creation of what I am studying. I make decisions about what is important, and the kinds of partnerships and relationships that are necessary for implementation. As the projects grow and develop, then through the process of reflection, I too will grow and develop. The virtual university, based on client needs such as these, is an open system that allows me the opportunity and freedom to define my own learning outcomes, develop relationships and build my own competences around the objects of research. In contrast however, a traditional university programme with strict residency requirements, demands that the role as student take precedence. Under these circumstances, personal learning outcomes are taken for granted, and the university provides the context for research.

In addition, most universities are themselves models of traditional organizations. They are known to be bureaucratic, and functionally and disciplinary siloed. This can be limiting when the object of study, and the methodology in use, transcends many disciplines. As Michael Marquardt so eloquently points out, action learning has many theoretical roots, including education, psychology, sociology, management, anthropology, political science, systems thinking, and ethics (Marquardt, 1999). Undoubtedly universities are changing, but are they changing fast enough? For myself, the organizational structure of the university made such an interdisciplinary approach of the sort suggested by Marquardt difficult to implement. Yet such an interdisciplinary approach is necessary when one is studying personal and organizational development within a context of global and technological change.

The virtual university built around an action learning approach has permitted me the freedom to work with others in an ongoing global Set through the use of sophisticated electronic technology. This provides a dedicated infrastructure so that I can communicate with other doctoral candidates around the world, in a variety of organizational positions, with different research interests. While the relationships may lack the spontaneity and sociability that are possible in face-to-face encounters, the advantage is that we each have action learning as a common frame for understanding the purpose of the group, and within which we can share our learning. Such a global Set may well be different from those initially envisioned by Revans which were based on his work in physics at the Cavendish laboratory, but few environments are as rigorously defined as that one was (Marquardt, 1999). For me personally, the difficulties of building relationships over the Net really do mean that we become colleagues in adversity as we respond to one another's circumstances and situations from a common action/reflection learning perspective.

Just as the doctoral Set provides a global world of colleagues, so it also provides the opportunity for knowledge to be actively created and shared in an ongoing way. As ideas and experiences are shared with others, and reflected upon within the Set, so new configurations of knowledge can be built. This in turn leads to more opportunities for publishing, described by Gordon Wills as 'conceiving, creating, capturing, transforming, disseminating, archiving, searching, and retrieving academic knowledge and information' (Wills, 1996). The partnership between International Management Centres and Anbar Electronic Intelligence means that I have at my fingertips a virtual library which is constantly being updated, as well as access to online conferences in subjects of relevance to my interests.

Action learning and the virtual university in practice
The experience of being a working practitioner undertaking a doctoral degree on the work being practised has led me to a number of exciting places. In particular, I have been able to actually experience action learning programmes in the workplace, both from the perspective of participating in them, and also administering them. In keeping with Wills' contention that managers 'learn best at work', my strategy in the workplace has been to implement learning programmes built around the organization (Wills, 1993). In this way, not only am I learning, but so also are the participants, who, through pursuing goals and objectives related to the business, help the organization achieve its business outcomes. Two programmes are worthy of mention in this regard. They are:

- *Leadership In Action.* This is an action learning programme designed to build leadership and learning capability for supervisors and managers. In this programme, supervisors and managers brought real, live issues and projects to be worked on over a time-frame of six months, based on their business needs. Some of the individuals in this programme have gone on to develop evaluative assessment papers of their own learning, for which they have received certification. The papers are a reflective component of the actions that the participants took, and serve in themselves to contribute to the ongoing knowledge of adult learning theory. Also, they are a permanent record of the real results achieved by the participants.

- *The Coaching Network.* This programme is designed for individual and organizational development. It provides a framework for individuals paired as coaches and performers to coach each other based on just-in-time learning principles within a twenty-week time period. The role of the coach is to use good questions and coaching ability to help build the capacity for action on the part of the performer. As the performer's horizon of possibilities for action is expanded, problems are dissolved, and goals can be achieved.

The programmes have several things in common. Specifically, they both:

- are based on action learning principles in that they are learner-led, and require participant self-management;
- can be evaluated in terms of achieving specific business results; and
- have the capacity to transform both participant individuals, and the organization.

Working on these programmes towards doctoral research has enabled me to explore many emergent issues in the world of organizational change. Both programmes have been written up in recent publications (Bowerman and Peters, 1999; Bowerman and Collins, 1999). Both provide a vehicle through which to examine the nature of personal and organizational transformation, and the real nature of organizational resistance as individuals walk the tightrope between espoused theories for change, and those that they use in practice (Argyris and Schon, 1978). They also provide insight into my own ability to market and sell such programmes internally within an organization. Just because I believe they are effective programmes and will lead to organizationally beneficial results, does not mean that they will necessarily be bought and implemented by the powers-that-be. A traditional view of research means that the student studies other people's work. In my case, it is necessary to design, implement, evaluate, and sell the programmes I believe in, within the organization through the ongoing creation and building of effective relationships. Studying and judging other people's organizational and political savvy in the implementation of effective change programmes is one thing: building and developing my own as I work to implement such programmes is something else. Such a process demands intensive strategizing, and retroactive sense-making (Weick, 1995), and is best studied in an open and transparent environment that encourages ongoing reflection and dialogue with fellow practitioners.

Summary and conclusions
In Karl Weick's seminal book entitled *Sensemaking in Organizations*, he mentions the need to 'use one's own life as data, and a search for those out-

croppings and ideas that fascinate' (Weick, 1995, p. 191). In this chapter I have used certain events in my own life as data to develop themes that are increasingly common in literature such as adult learning, self-direction, and the difficulty organizations face in dealing with the rapid changes that are befalling them.

The fact is that to experience change, reflect on it, and grow from it is different from reading about, imagining it, or having others try to teach you about it. Unfortunately today in many of our organizations, we view the teaching part as the most important. We downplay the importance of experience and fail to use it as a focal point from which we can take action and learn. At the same time our organizations lack the flexibility and open processes to incorporate the learning that does occur. Despite a humanistic rhetoric about the need to accommodate differences, and the need to learn from experience, most organizations fail on these counts.

One way of dealing with these apparent contradictions is to use the process of action learning. It is no coincidence that one of Revan's favourite quotations from the Belgium executives after his work with the steel industry was 'What is an honest person and what must I do to become one?' The quotation points to the ongoing need to open up one's 'theories in use' to the scrutiny of others.

Finally, the virtual university, whose operating principles are based on Revan's theory of action learning, becomes the place to put it all together. Its flexible structure, and open learning process, enables the reality of the learner's experience to be recorded as it happens, so that it can be incorporated into ongoing research and knowledge. In this way, it is learner centred, permitting personal experience and theory to effectively mesh together.

References

Argyris, C. and Schon, D. (1978) *Organizational Learning: A Theory of Action Perspective*, Reading, MA, Addison Wesley.

Bowerman, J. and Collins, G. (1999) 'The coaching network: A program for individual and organizational development', paper presented at the Learning Company Conference, Warwick, UK.

Bowerman, J. and Ford, R. (1996) 'A new vision for government: Learning in the public service', in K. Watkins and V. Marsick (eds) *In Action: Creating the Learning Organization*, American Society for Training and Development, pp. 211–19.

Bowerman, J. and Peters, J. (1999) 'Design and evaluation of an action learning program – a bilateral view', *Journal of Workplace Learning*, Vol. 11 No. 4, pp. 131–9.

Knowles, M. S. (1970) *The Modern Practice of Adult Education*, New York, Associated Press.

Knowles, M. S. (1981) *The Adult Learner: A Neglected Species*, 2nd ed., Houston, Texas, Gulf.

Lievegoed, B. (1993) *Phases: The Spiritual Rhythms of Adult Life*, Bristol, Rudolf Steiner Press.

Marquardt, Michael, J. (1999) *Action Learning in Action: Transforming Problems and People for World-Class Organizational learning*, Palo Alto, Davies-Black.

Maslow, A. H. (1954) *Motivation and Personality*, New York, Harper.

Quenk, N. L. (1993) *Beside Ourselves: Our Hidden Personality in Every Day Life*, Palo Alto, Davies-Black.

Revans, R. W. (1978, 1983, 1998) *ABC of Action Learning*, London, Lemos and Crane.

Weick, K. (1995) *Sensemaking in Organizations*, Thousand Oaks, Sage Publications.

Wills, G. (1993), *Your Enterprise School of Management*, Bradford, MCB University Press.

Wills, G. (1996) 'Embracing electronic publishing', *Internet Research: Electronic Network Applications and Policy*, Vol. 6 No. 4, pp. 77–90.

Chapter 9
Cyber tutoring and learning
How to facilitate action learning online

ERIC SANDELANDS

Introduction

'Cyber tutoring and learning' – a phenomenon of recent years, and a timeless one. The sub-heading I have chosen is much more specific: 'How to facilitate action learning online'. The word 'facilitate' is one that has been chosen with care – it is a process that underpins the function of a 'tutor' in the action learning process. In our introduction to *The Virtual University: An Action Paradigm and Process for Workplace Learning* (Teare *et al.*, 1998) we state:

> A virtual university must be a real university offering learning opportunities otherwise denied. It must be, above all, a network for lifelong learning which meets the new learning needs of a new century.

Our central point was, and is, a challenge to classroom-based paradigms. Our belief, backed by evidence, is that the process of workplace, action learning is central to new learning architecture for postgraduate and post-experience learners. The benefits of action learning have been outlined by Marquardt (1999) as:

- Shared learning throughout various levels of the organization.
- Greater self-awareness and self-confidence due to new insights and feedback.
- Ability to ask more questions and be more reflective.
- Improved communications and teamwork.

He goes on to outline six distinct interactive components of action learning:

- A problem.
- The group.
- The questioning and reflection process.

- The commitment to taking action.
- The commitment to learning.
- The facilitator.

International Management Centres (IMC) has been facilitating action learning programmes in companies, and for individuals, since 1982. It currently operates in 44 countries. These benefits have been sought and experienced by many managers undertaking IMC's action learning programmes. In 1993, the Enterprise School of Management (Wills, 1993) was developed as a process and architecture for embracing action learning within organizations, through a corporate business school mechanism. This has been prototyped with MCB University Press at its Bradford headquarters. In becoming an Enterprise School of Management, organizations embark upon a journey designed to enable them to generate and systemize new knowledge as an organization, while developing individuals' abilities to learn and grow – and keep on learning.

Increased understanding of the Internet as a mechanism to facilitate action learning through discussion, access to course materials, online libraries, global forums and so on (Teare, 1998) has enabled global organizations to become Enterprise Schools of Management. The international hotel company, Marriott, became the first global ESM in 1998. According to Vice President Jim O'Hern:

> ... the new action learning experience at Marriott is designed to help participants become more effective in their jobs. It is driven by outcomes, not content. All assignments reflect real workplace challenges – there are no formal exams. Our approach is to test the application (not recall). Participants undergo 'exams' at the end of the course to draw out what they have achieved, both personally and for the company. (Marquardt, 1999)

This chapter proposes a method for facilitating action learning online that is currently being delivered by my colleagues within the Canadian School of Management (CSM), an academic partner of IMC. In drafting and testing this procedure, the detailed feedback from an action learning set learning online while designing their own corporate business school is compared with feedback from the general population of action learners within IMC globally. The insights provided are rich, and were often expressed in emotionally charged terms.

The corporate business school Set is from an organization that began in the USA in the early part of this century. Today it employs well in excess of 100,000 people globally. A motivating factor is to continue to be regarded by its staff as an excellent place to work. The objective of this university is to offer supervisors and managers the chance to grow and be more effective, while enjoying benefits like flexible scheduling, shorter course completion time and the opportunity to earn advanced university degrees for work-related education.

Overview of experiences from IMC learners worldwide
Each year, prior to graduation, IMC runs evaluative workshops with candidates (the 'graduands'), backed up by a questionnaire examining the nature of the learning experience. The feedback reveals something of the learning journey in moving from:

> We gained confidence to talk to people at all levels in the enterprise. (Wills and Oliver, 1996)

through to:

> My employer invested $2 million to fully implement the project. We gained a threefold return in the first 12 months.

If, overwhelmingly, the results from the Wills and Oliver survey are positive, then there are areas of weakness too:

- Faculty members unable to meet the expectations of demanding, action- and context-based managers.
- Problems in the place of work where top managers and colleagues are less supportive than is hoped.
- IMC's own organizing skills for action learning sets around the globe.
- Managers' own inability to effectively manage time.

Bringing the story more up-to-date, analysis of the questionnaire results for the period 1996 to 1998 revealed (Prestoungrange, 1999):

- Just under half the graduands had been promoted during the programme.
- The Set as a learning support group retained first place in the rankings of 'most helpful', but IMC faculty and the set adviser made a better showing than previously.
- Boss/mentor support at work was reported as bi-modal – either it was good or bad. The balance was more towards good than previously.
- Not surprisingly, the most positive highlights once again were the Set and the discovery of action learning as a way to learn; the most frustrating were variable faculty support, lack of sufficient time and problems with fellow Set members.

- The most valuable benefit of the assignments was reported as 'helping to solve real problems'.
- Graduands emphasized how they had gained more self-confidence as a manager and how their objectivity had improved. They had broadened their horizons as they put academic theory into practice. They believed they had come to put greater emphasis on people and come to a better understanding of how to change cultures at work.
- They were once again overwhelmingly assured and confident about implementing the recommendations they had made as a result of the programme. Some 30 per cent reported they were authorized to do it themselves and a further 50 per cent had their employer at large seeing them through. The balance was made up of 'minimal' (12 per cent) and 'some' (8 per cent) implementation.
- 25 per cent of graduands were implementing recommendations with soft/non-financially quantifiable outcomes whilst the others were looking at modest to spectacular ROI, e.g. £18 million and £3 million overhead reductions, EBIT increase of some 100 per cent, sales increases of £2.5 million per annum and of 10 per cent per annum, etc. One graduand reported it had meant the organization actually managed to stay in business. The most frequently mentioned figure was £500,000 improvement.

While problems remain – in particular the gap between expectations and reality relating to the role of faculty and interaction within the Set – the action learning experience viewed by those graduating is perceived as very positive. Since the early 1990s, learners with IMC have utilized the Internet in support of their learning programmes – face-to-face meetings every six weeks or so have been resourced by access to online course materials, library, discussion forums and more.

For the client's trainers, the emphasis is squarely upon action learning in the Internet age. The face-to-face sessions are six months apart. How will the learners' experience compare? What can be learned about action learning online? Will the group be able to recognize the cost/benefits of various communications media?

Clearly the client group is not a typical group: it is a group of senior training professionals coming to terms with defining and delivering an Enterprise School of Management within their own organization. Yet the rich experiences and new learning generated by the client's team is truly at the forefront of action research into this area. The hard-won lessons the team have learned seem certain to influence all who follow – within the organization and beyond – into research into organizational learning.

Aligning learning with business imperatives

The breakthrough being made by the client's team is in developing a corporate university capable of delivering action learning experiences on a global basis. This is recognized by all participants and supported by them. The role of the Client Virtual University (CVU) is one of realizing those business imperatives where learning is the key. In doing so, the CVU was realizing a vision of learning that had already been articulated and shared, envisioning learner-centred learning, delivered just in time and harnessing communications technology.

The group therefore saw one of its prime focuses as one of alignment – relating group learning to business imperatives, relating individual projects undertaken within the virtual university to business measures, aligning outputs with business needs. In achieving this, senior management commitment was recognized as essential, both from senior managers within the design team (i.e. having the right design team in the first place) and from the senior management cadre within the client's global business.

The group were intensely aware of the internal circumstances within their organization, including the need to consider budgetary cycles and budgetary responsibilities, and sell the message of the benefits of action learning, while being able to deal effectively with issues of timing and where and by whom funds are allocated. Clearly the benefits messages need to be understood and bought into by appropriate senior managers and budget holders. Involvement in the process personally is a priority.

Characterizing a supportive learning environment

Within the trainer group there has been great excitement about being at the 'cutting edge' of the corporate university movement. However, a wide range of emotions has been logged by the participants reflecting upon their experiences of action learning when visioning and developing a new future. There have been feelings of 'abandonment', of feeling 'set up', of not being included in the decision to launch the Client Virtual University, merely in its realization.

Personal learning issues quickly emerged from the group – issues of time management, fear of failure, of being left behind by the group. A requirement for even greater emphasis on team building was a strong theme, including understanding the interdependence between the sub-Sets (groups working on specific themes) and the main action learning Set. Not enough group support was cited as being a major disappointment. The learning styles analysis approach (Mumford, 1995) was found to be useful in enabling learners to discuss their learning characteristics with the team, and it was recommended that it should be maintained.

The group saw a key role of the action learning Set and its facilitators as setting a positive climate for learning, recognizing that the organizational context is also important. It is clear that some of the experiences are a necessary part of coming to terms with the action learning process. However, the group feedback provides some very useful pointers regarding future action learning programmes, with even earlier inclusion of the group in defining its function, even greater emphasis on the action learning process and on team building.

The timeless lesson of the need for action learners to be willing volunteers is clearly underlined by the feedback from these managers. Also of significance is the crucial role of the facilitator in communicating, clarifying, questioning and summarizing.

Ambiguity within the action learning process

Harnessing ambiguity is a lesson within itself. It's a high-level skill that most of us aspire to. For the design team the strategy was, and is, emergent and the future unclear. It was a substantial leap of faith to realize that this is how it should be. This whole area of strategy is emergent and the design team, as an action learning Set, are inventing the future.

Much of the angst within the group has been about coming to terms with these issues. Those without a formal university education have felt disadvantaged, without realizing that the entire group was similarly afflicted – giving voice to these fears should have been part of the group bonding process had this issue been recognized in time. This uncomfortable feeling, where no clear roadmap has been provided, caused motivation levels to fluctuate with some learners, depending upon how comfortable they felt regarding the emerging future plan.

Practical recommendations within this process of developing emergent strategy generated by the group included:

- the development of a very simple demonstration of what action learning means and can achieve; and
- the development within the process of a common language between the 'academics' (facilitators and supervisors) and the 'practitioners' (the trainers and subsequently Marriott managers).

Discovering appropriate media for conversational learning

Before moving on to consider the benefits and shortcomings of various media used for conversational learning, let us first sketch in something of the nature of the group. The senior training team meets around twice per year. In their working lives, the trainers host and lead training sessions. Much of the skill-set within the group has been developed around interaction with people in a group, face-to-face context. Not surprisingly, engaging with action learning where the Internet is the prime method of content delivery, and with conversational learning, has proved to be quite a challenge for many. The group knew that these issues must be wrestled with in order to deliver action learning programmes, utilizing the Internet. However, the group quickly came to consider the various modes of communications available and reach conclusions as to the appropriateness of each medium.

The discussions of the training team members can be characterized as:

- Efficient versus effective communications – recognizing that posting a message in a newsgroup is different from communicating with its need for messages to be understood, debated and internalized.
- Synchronous versus asynchronous communications – a big issue for a global team. Face-to-face sessions were seen as providing rich experiences, but expensive in terms of time and money. Newsgroups and e-mail were viewed as highly convenient, but lacking in nuances, quick-fire exchange of ideas, and so on.
- The media available – face-to-face, telephone conferencing, online newsgroups, e-mail – what is the right blend? What triggers usage of a particular medium?

One sub-set viewed limited face-to-face as being a distinct disadvantage. Another pointed to misunderstandings that can occur with the written word, particularly in a group where English is a second language for many. The group did not seriously address the cost benefits of each mode of communication in the submitted evaluations of their virtual learning experiences – something that will be tackled in the next phase. What, for example, can be sacrificed in order to make worthwhile financial savings, cost being a serious factor to consider at all times in the development of the CVU?

The experiences crystallized the variety of communications media there are within a 'virtual' university. It also reinforced the view that the conversational aspects of learning within a group are vital, in fact one of the central pillars of action learning. This is worth noting given current pressures to streamline and pare down the amount of messages, particularly e-mails, being posted.

Roles of tutors as facilitators
All who have fulfilled the facilitator role are likely to empathise with Nelson and McFadzean's (1998) observations that one needs:

> ... an ability to work with a group which may contain people of sharply contrasting interests and concerns, and the intellectual agility to guide a process in the direction that is most likely to prove beneficial to the participants.

Table 9.1 outlines facilitator competences.

Category	Specific competences
1. Understanding context	• Understanding of requisite theories, methodologies, processes and techniques • Understanding of business environments • Understanding of particular 'problem situation'
2. Technical competences	• Time management • Planning and preparation
3. Rational skills	• Objectivity • Judgement
4. Interpersonal skills	• Communication • Active listening • Clarifying • Questioning • Summarizing
5. Task process skills	• Development of a structured set • Problem-solving agenda
6. Human process skills	• Establishing trust

Table 9.1
Facilitator
competences

Adapted from
Nelson and
McFadzean, 1998

In considering the roles of those facilitating and supervising the action learning process within the team, truly deep feelings and emotions became evident. People were uncomfortable with taking ownership of their own learning process. They were used to seeing 'class rosters' indicating how they were doing relative to other individuals, and sought practical tips and strategies on how to cope with the uncertainty, and greater guiding subject matter expertise.

'Clarity' is a word that characterizes much of the feedback from the group. Where so much is uncertain, the group looked for greater clarity in those areas that were defined:

• Assistance in clarifying the scope of projects.
• Supportive yet challenging feedback.
• Better understanding of the facilitation roles.
• Establishing clearly the role of the external academy in relation to the organization.

The competence of the facilitators clearly emerged as being important to this set of learners, including an ability to motivate where learners were unable to self-motivate, and an ability to balance both emotional and intellectual components within the Set learning experience. Building the Set as an effective group, able to motivate each other and tackle ambiguity collectively would move this to another level. The CVU development project is complex, but the basic action learning principle of attention to Set dynamics holds true.

These experiences stress the need for good, solid facilitation. The requests of the group are fully consistent with the competences outlined in Table 9.1, while at the same time an explanation of the role was sought by the group, indicating a desire to understand the total process.

Online learning resources

The potential of the Internet to deliver rich learning resources has been observed by many (e.g. Rudenstine, 1997). Literally, the world's finest knowledge is being made available to workstations around the globe, transforming the learning experience. In IMC, through alliances with official publisher MCB University Press, including its Anbar electronic library division, ensuring access globally to the management body of knowledge was an early breakthrough, followed by the instant availability of full-text articles, reviewed books with hot-links to bookshops. The next phase saw the reinvention of the course materials as learnerware, providing structured access to vast management databases, with hard coded keywords linking the learner to the very latest literature in a given field (Sandelands, 1998).

Within a corporate university context, such resources must be present to be imported into the client organization. How to hold the data then becomes a vital technical question – currently Site 2000 is being developed as a solution to the mass customization of resourcing within corporate university partners of IMC. In doing so, Site 2000 will also be designed to import data for utilization within a corporate intranet environment. The issue server reliability of partner publishers' resources is being addressed, having become increasingly a concern as critical mass is built.

However, the debate has now moved forward to tackle two major issues:

1. What is the role of IMC in creating and disseminating new knowledge?
2. What is the role of the organization in capturing and systemizing bespoke knowledge?

Action learning as a process fosters the creation of new knowledge almost daily, but in particular as assignments and projects are implemented and as learners are invited to reflect and capture their reflections, either individually or as a group. IMC's unique contribution to knowledge comes from harvesting outputs from action learning and from capturing the new knowledge generated about the action learning process itself. Both areas are being targeted with specific publication requirements for faculty and Associates (learners with IMC), co-ordinated by the Director of Published Learning. The outputs, published as journal articles and within scholarly books, are then fed back into the resources available to learners.

For the organization, capturing bespoke knowledge and acting upon it becomes an early priority: it is a next-phase assignment for a member of the design team. Already within the team, the debate is one of how to share new knowledge effectively. The culture is one in which mistakes are welcomed as learning opportunities, but in which new mistakes are sought as knowledge is shared, rather than constantly learning from the same mistakes.

Within the group, the learning resources were broadly found to be useful. However, it was felt that more emphasis should have been placed on introducing the learning resources to the group. One lesson that can be gleaned is that appropriate approaches must be further developed to enable learners to access the knowledge they need to take smart action and learn. Some of this can be engineered into the resources by:

- creating explanatory 'start-up' materials;
- re-engineering courseware resources;
- enabling facilitators to collect and disseminate favourite papers and generic advice.

However, much of this must also come from the online facilitation process and the Set dynamics. It is at this point when the material being promoted is being customized to the needs of the learners by the facilitator (acting as tutor) and by the Set members themselves.

A further thread for this debate is to understand the cost/benefits of Internet-resourced and facilitated learning and face-to-face workshop and other events. There are manifold benefits available from the Internet, including libraries, globally distributed learners and more. However, it is clearly different from a face-to-face context. Learning designs in which the two are combined provide the potential to combine the benefits of each, leading to the question 'What is the requisite amount of face-to-face contact within an Internet delivered programme?' This is a question that must be addressed each time a learning design is created for a group of learners.

Experiences of using technology
Using the technology as a vehicle for learning proved to be challenging. The group accepted that the technology will get easier to use as technologies converge, and that their own expertise in using it would improve now they had a real need to come to terms with it. A golden rule proposed to the Set had been that we should not blame the technology when it failed, but work

out how to fix it or get around the problem. This proved to be difficult to accept by learners in countries where Internet connectivity is unreliable.

Some clear, key issues emerged, important to the success of future action learning programmes within the CVU:

1. That a clear technology briefing be given at each programme start-up.
2. That PC training issues not be underestimated, albeit learners will overcome challenges during the action learning process.
3. That, from a practical point of view, the client should commence its roll-out of programmes in countries where Internet connections are sound, and then review.

This particular aspect of the learning will change rapidly, almost from day to day. The much heralded convergence in technology is both real and gathering pace. The challenge for the learning provider is to understand which technologies are most appropriate to its learning designs. The challenge for the facilitator is to be able to adapt to new technologies and harness them to benefit learners while not losing sight of the fact that these are only tools.

Comparing the client experience with the IMC global community
Every action learner's experience is a unique one. In being the first group to envision and create a global action learning corporate university, there is the propensity to have generated many unique experiences and learning opportunities. However, there are similarities too with IMC's broader action learning community. Many of the uncertainties and ambiguities experienced are manifestations of a healthy action learning process. There is evidence too that, taken as a whole, the group is beginning to intuitively understand the action learning experience and empathize with the feelings of fellow action learners.

There is the same desire to focus on the emotional aspects of learning, particularly the Set dynamics, and the same need for excellent facilitation, albeit it may be that the client's team put greater emphasis on this aspect than the general population. Where everything is emergent, maybe there is a greater need to ensure the facilitation is first rate, including the feedback, attention to the needs of the Set, access to specific subject expertise, and so on. The CVU design team is different from IMC's graduands in seeking to understand action learning in order to facilitate it for others – either directly or indirectly. In this sense, this group behaves more like inducted IMC faculty – a comparative population, for whom, unfortunately, no feedback is currently available, but who would make an extremely interesting comparison.

Where the client's group stands out though is in living and reflecting upon action learning in an online learning environment. They are the first global corporate training team to go through such an experience. Their learning is truly new, and needs to be tested as to whether it can be generalized from – i.e. how much is a factor of the characteristics of this particular set, of the organizational culture, and so on. However, very powerful learning has taken place on a number of levels which, after bringing the story up-to-date, we will draw out.

Facilitating action learning courses

The Canadian School of Management is pioneering online facilitation within the IMC global professional association. CSM provides modular action learning experiences for in-work managers, primarily delivered by Internet, but with optional action learning workshops held twice per year.

The eight-phase model provided is for online facilitation, taking the theoretical concepts of action learning and building upon the experience of CSM tutors (with their correspondence school roots) and the IMC action learning community. The final output from the majority of modular courses is a 'Written Action Case (WAC)', a write-up of action and implementation showing reference to requisite theory and stressing personal learning and organizational results. Two interim assignments are built into most modules as building blocks.

Phase 1: Setting the scene
- On the first day of term post Part 1 of the introductory memo (Annex A, page 121). Three days later post Part 2.
- Require learners to post an introductory message – to include their name, job, organization, location, the current challenges facing them and the benefits they are seeking from this course.
- Summarize, synthesize and encourage a social discussion.
- Use the application questions throughout the course to encourage immersion in the key issues of the subject. How this is achieved is at the discretion of the facilitator. A useful tactic can be to give each group member a question to research and report back on for everyone's benefit, then invite comments.

Phase 2: Selecting the Written Action Case (WAC)
- What are you trying to do?
  - Require each learner to outline their proposed WAC.
  - Invite learners to look at the assignment outline and the marking scheme.
- What is stopping you from doing it?
  - Ask each learner why this problem hasn't been tackled before.
  - Summarize the answers and invite further comment from the group on what each has learned from this question.

- Invite learners to look up the marking scheme for the assignment giving Web address.
- Learners submit Assignment No. 1 – Project Proposal. Encourage learners to share insights from proposals and help improve each other's work. Provide feedback to each on whether the proposed WAC will also meet the academic requirements of the course.

Phase 3: Questions to clarify objectives and methods
- Require each learner to further contribute regarding their WAC:
  - What they might do about the problem.
  - Who knows about the problem?
  - Who cares about it?
  - Who can do something about it?
- Encourage learners to constructively comment on each other's challenges.

Phase 4: Discovery of data
- Ensure effective use of the online library:
  - Invite each learner to comment on the literature search strategy they have been following.
  - Invite each learner to highlight some particularly appropriate readings they have retrieved.
  - Advise on search strategies where appropriate.
- Research methodology:
  - Invite each learner to justify why their chosen method is appropriate to the task.
  - Trigger a group discussion on methods chosen and those deemed inappropriate.
  - Advise on appropriate approaches where needed.
- Learners submit Assignment No. 2 – Action Learning-based Case. Encourage learners to share insights from assignments. Provide feedback.

Phase 5: Feedback and analysis of data
- Ask group members for updates on data as it is gathered. Keep a sense of urgency.
- Ask group members to comment on analytical approaches they are using.
  - Advise where appropriate/refer to theory.
- Ask for comment on anything surprising emerging from the data.

Phase 6: Discussion and agreement on action
- Request that each group member highlight the options they have available for change, together with the option they are recommending as a

course of action. Why?
- Invite the group to comment on each other's work.
- Provide both group and individual feedback.

Phase 7: Action implementation
- Ask group members to consider who will influence their implementation plan.
  - Who will champion it for them? Why?
  - Who is likely to resist change? Why?
  - What strategies do they have to ensure effective implementation?
- Invite the group to comment on each other's work.
- Provide both group and individual feedback.

Phase 8: Assessment of change
- Ask group members to consider how successful change will be measured.
- Ask group members to highlight changes already taken place.
  - What did they learn from this change?
- Invite learners to consider their main learning points from the course.
- Invite learners to complete the online evaluation form (part of the courseware).
- Invite learners to make entries in their learning logs.
- Thank participants.
- Provide an overview of the collective achievements of the group, including their own learning points.
- Seek to motivate participants to continue their studies.
- Advise on when marks and comments can be anticipated.
- Learners submit Final Assignment (No. 3) – Written Action Case.

Summary
My recent experiences in facilitating online action learning programmes have led me to two not unsurprising conclusions.

1. That the ability of the facilitator to understand the role fully and interpret into effective action is, if anything, even more important than in face-to-face sessions.
2. That the learning architecture and resources need to be designed to support the facilitative style of learning 'delivery'.

This leads me to a third conclusion:

3. That the facilitator has a vital role in conducting the access of the learner to appropriate knowledge. The vast amount of content being published

does not detract from naïve enquiry – vital to the action learning process – but can be overwhelming without a sensitive guide.

References

Marquardt, M. J. (1999) *Action Learning in Action: Transforming Problems and People for World-class Organizational Learning*, Palo Alto, CA, Davies Black.

Mumford, A. (1995) *Effective Learning*, Institute of Personnel and Development.

Nelson, T. and McFadzean, E. (1998) 'Facilitating problem-solving groups: facilitator competences', *Leadership & Organization Development Journal*, Vol. 19 No. 2, pp. 72–82.

Prestoungrange, G. (1999) 'Congregation feedback from graduands 1996/98', IMC internal document available from http://www.imc.org.uk/imc/.

Rudenstine, N. L. (1997) 'The Internet and its uses in education: a close fit', *The Chronicle of Higher Education*, 21 February, pp. 28–9.

Sandelands, E. (1998) 'Creating an online library to support a virtual learning community', *Internet Research: Electronic Networking Applications and Policy*, Vol. 8 No. 1, pp. 75–80.

Teare, R. (1998) 'Developing a curriculum for organizational learning', *Journal of Workplace Learning*, Vol. 10 No. 2, pp. 95–121.

Teare, R., Davies, D. and Sandelands, E. (1998) *The Virtual University: an Action Paradigm and Process for Workplace Learning*, London, Cassell.

Wills, G. (1993) *Your Enterprise School of Management*, Bradford, MCB University Press.

Wills, G. and Oliver, C. (1996) 'Measuring the ROI from management action learning', *Management Development Review*, Vol. 9 No. 1, pp. 17–21.

Introductory Memo, Part 1

Annex A
Introductory
Memo from
Canadian School
of Management's
modular action
learning course

Paragraph 1 – The benefits to the learner of undertaking this course.

Paragraph 2 – Who you are/your experience.

Paragraph 3 – About action learning, but very practical, e.g.
- Tackles current real issues.
- Group-based learning.
- Learning about self.
- Study own organizations.
- Starts with questions, causing you to refer to theory.
- Involves planning and doing.
- Output result-based.
- Present and future-orientated.
- It is active.

Paragraph 4 – How you will approach the tutor role. What the learner needs to do, e.g.
- Log on once per week – share successes/failures, talk to the tutor and

fellow learners, debate both sides of a question.
- Comment helpfully on postings by fellow learners/don't be afraid of expressing views and opinions and sharing knowledge/making mistakes is fully acceptable – you will get constructive advice.
- Get to know your 'buddies' online (fellow learners)/don't be afraid to post humorous and social comments – they help the process, but keep to less than 10 per cent.
- Expect good feedback from the tutor and from each other.

Paragraph 5 – A motivational parting shot/sharing of an anecdote or insight.

Introductory Memo, Part 2

Paragraph 1 – Briefly outline the content of the course. Cause the learner to refer to course materials for more information.

Paragraph 2 – Flag up the assignment requirements and invite learners to read up on what will be required.

Paragraph 3 – Remind learners of the resources at their disposal, particularly the online library, but also subject forums and so forth where appropriate, together with your preferred links to specific Web material. You may wish to comment on textbooks at this stage.

Paragraph 4 – Remind learners that you are here to facilitate their learning and to ensure that Set members learn from each other.

Chapter 10

Internalizing action learning

A company perspective

KATHY BIERMANN, JACQUELINE CANNON, HADYN
INGRAM, JANE NEIL and CATHERINE WADDLE

Introduction

This article reflects on the experiences and lessons learned from the delivery of a pilot management development programme delivered from November 1998 during the following twelve months. The programme was groundbreaking in that it was developed through a partnership between Marriott Hotels and International Management Centres Association. Marriott identified the need to develop their junior managers with minimal disruption to their work on a Certificate of Management Studies (CMS) programme that could be applied to the Associate's work (Marriott describe their employees as 'Associates'). International Management Centres Association have a track record of delivering a range of management development courses around the world using the Internet and e-mail as the main communication resource. Whitbread (who operate Marriott Hotels in the UK) managed the pilot programme of fifteen Associates training staff so that this means of developing hospitality managers could be internalized and replicated in a number of situations throughout the world. Just as, in the cycle of action learning, reflection follows action, this paper represents the reflection following the experience of the authors, who managed this programme. In particular, the focus is upon conceptualizing those practical factors that are critical to the success of subsequent programmes with Marriott world-wide. These lessons, based on practical experience, may be applicable to any organization that seeks to internalize learning processes effectively.

Critical Success Factors (CSFs)

The term 'Critical Success Factors' surfaced in the management literature in the 1980s when there was concern about why some organizations seemed to be more successful than others, and research was carried out to investigate the components of success. Freund (1988) defines CSFs as 'those things that must be done if a company is to be successful': in other words, those factors that are critical to the success of a project or undertaking. CSFs must also be few in number, measurable and controllable. In any project the relative importance of these factors may differ with the stages of the project cycle, but it is essential to put the right people on the project team (Pinto and Slevin, 1989). The Marriott project team was composed of training professionals who were committed to the precepts of action learning and who were acting both as teachers and students, because their experiences on this programme were being formalized into a diploma of virtual training. As well as receiving an award for their efforts, this programme enabled the team to fully reflect on the pilot programme, and this chapter represents some of the fruits of their reflective efforts.

The practicalities of action learning

Newbold (1993) defines action learning in the following way:

> In action learning real managers (student-managers and manager-students) should share ideas and tackle real problems with their counterparts, which effects change in the real world by helping each other.

Bravette (1996) suggests that action learning in management education helps to develop self-knowledge and underpins critical thinking skills. The ability to think is a competence that is much sought after by employers, which can enable students to become effective managers. As such, action learning teaching and learning strategies tend to engage the student more fully and involve deeper learning than more traditional passive strategies. Accordingly, action learning can be resource- and time-consuming, and the implicit student-centredness has implications for flexibility of approach required of the programme team. The action learning approach adopted by International Management Centres Association uses a core of resources and a virtual library to enable students to address work-based problems that add value to their participation on the programme. Much work is done virtually, but students attend residential sessions that are led by members of the IMCA faculty who act as facilitators, rather than traditional teachers. The Marriott pilot project used academic and university lecturers to lead the workshops. In this programme, these tutors were chosen with care, but there is a danger that the facilitative and student-led approach of action learning might not be adopted by university lecturers who may be steeped in the traditional approaches that Ramsden (1992) describes as 'depressing'. The 'open' paradigm of action learning, described by Davies (1998) is a challenging approach that requires a management and facilitation team that is able to cope with its challenges.

This approach poses challenges for the action learner too, not least in recognizing that the open paradigm requires a greater level of participation and group co-operation, and it is important that the learning Set is fully briefed at the outset. In any learning Set that works closely together, group dynamics will have an effect on social interaction, thus careful consideration must be given to the configuration of the three or four action learners that will comprise the sub-Sets.

Establishing CSFs for the pilot programme

It is essential that any project be evaluated both while it is running (formative) and after it has been completed (summative). In the case of the Marriott programme, the lessons of the pilot programme had to be distilled because it needed to be replicated in many different geographical locations. The summative evaluation of the programme was drawn from the experiences of those concerned Associates, management team, company members, tutors and external examiners. The questions that were asked were:

- What had gone well/badly?
- What could go wrong?
- What needs to go right?

The answers to these questions and the lessons learned were encapsulated in four key areas as shown in Figure 10.1.

Figure 10.1
Key issues in
internalizing
action learning

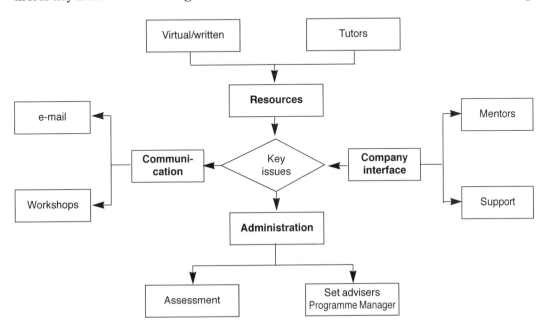

1. *Company interface:* the relationship between the sponsoring company (Marriott) and the course provider (IMCA). Both should be mutually supportive and have an open and flexible approach to learning. The role of an in-company mentor is an important one.
2. *Administration:* those backup services and personnel that manage key processes such as programme management and assessment. These include tasks such as arrangements for meetings, marking assignments and recording grades and marks.
3. *Communication:* this is an essential activity in any project, but distance learning courses require that the technology of e-mails and Internet infrastructure is effective and well supported.
4. *Resources:* represent the range of people, systems and technology that contribute to supporting the learners. In an approach that is learner-centred, it is vital that the action learner has a range of accessible and effective resources to enhance learning.

1. Company interface

In the business world, there has been a recent trend for organizations to form deeper relationships with key suppliers of goods and services in order to ensure that each party understands what the other needs, and to solve problems together, rather like an effective marriage. Nichols (1994) comments that: 'These days, there is a strong trend in strategic thinking away from products, markets and towards intent, competences and capabilities.'

Accordingly, in the Marriott programme, there was a period of intense consultation while the parties worked out a course structure that accorded with Marriott's strategic objectives, which were to:

- develop a suite of management development courses that could be 'rolled out' worldwide;
- foster a deeper culture of learning in the organization;
- ensure courses are relevant to work needs and do not affect the operational work of the hotel;
- enable junior managers to be more 'promotable' and have deeper strategic awareness;
- use the course to help to solve relevant work-based problems;
- provide cost-effective courses with internal control and external validation from a university;
- produce more effective managers who would work 'smarter' and develop a career progression path in the company.

It was felt that an established 'virtual university', as provided by IMCA, would fulfil these objectives and provide management development programmes that could be delivered anywhere with the support of Marriott staff and other external tutors. Marriott had had exploratory talks with a number of conventional universities, but the inflexibility of a normative, awards-based and rigid curriculum and delivery locus did not meet their needs.

The other partner in this UK pilot, Whitbread plc (who operate Marriott Hotels in the UK) also needed to accept this approach and support it from the outset. Both organizations have the reputation of being growth-oriented, customer/Associate-centred and recognize the importance of their human resources in delivering a quality service. In essence, there was a fit between the opportunities provided by the virtual university and the strategy of the two participating organizations.

The internalizing process worked rather in the same way as a strategic alliance, in that there was a resonance in the cultures of the stakeholder organizations, which ensured that there was understanding of the process of action learning. This compatibility manifested itself in the interest that was generated within Whitbread and the support that was given by top management in attending the residential sessions and giving strategic input where required. The experience of this programme suggests that it is important that, at an early stage, senior managers are made aware of the nature of such management development programmes and that this information is cascaded down the line to unit general managers. In this case, there were regular meetings to brief unit managers and explain the role of the programme in the overall training and development strategy for the company. At a practical level, Associates need to have the 'space' to be able to attend residential workshops and the time to complete work-based assignments.

MENTORING

> a protected relationship in which experimentation, exchange and learning can occur and skills, knowledge and insight can be developed. (Mumford, 1995)

An essential component in these virtual courses is that an in-company mentor supports the Associate's learning. MacFie (1998) comments that internal mentoring is a relatively commonplace occurrence in many organizations and that mentoring is a powerful means of transmitting learning, wisdom and experience. A mentor is usually a senior member of an organization, often one step removed from line management, who can assist a more junior person with problems and challenges and, in the context of this course, help with the work-based assignments. Mentors can provide an objective 'sounding board' for problems or can challenge the biases and preconceptions that even the most enlightened leader can have. The seniority of a mentor can help with the awareness of organizational politics or strategy, and can 'open doors' to finding the person who has valuable contacts or specialized information.

The characteristics of a good mentor include:

- Perceptive.
- High performer.
- Secure.
- Accessible.
- Patient.
- Humorous.
- Good listener.
- Genuinely interested.
- Good network of contacts.
- Style complementary to mentee.

The experience of the Marriott programme suggests that mentoring can be a powerful tool for effective learning and a source of satisfaction for both parties, provided the mentor/mentee relationship is a good one. As with group dynamics, there are some styles that complement one another and others that can clash. Using Honey and Mumford's (1992) learning styles as a framework, effective mentor/mentee pairings include:

- Activist/Theorist.
- Reflector/Pragmatist.
- Reflector/Theorist.
- Activist/Reflector.

In the Marriott programme, Associates were given advice as to the role of the mentor and were free to select the mentor of their choice. Mentors were briefed at a special meeting where they were informed as to the nature and demands of the programme, and their role in supporting the Associate's learning. In this prototype programme, the mentoring role was a central one between a range of stakeholders, as shown in Figure 10. 2.

2. Administration
The second factor that was critical to the success of the programme was the course administration and management. These were regarded as the 'hygiene' factors of the programme; in other words, those issues of logistics that needed to be in place if the Associates were to maximize the learning opportunity. Further, for busy practising managers, administrative failures can be frustrating and can give an impression of inefficiency.

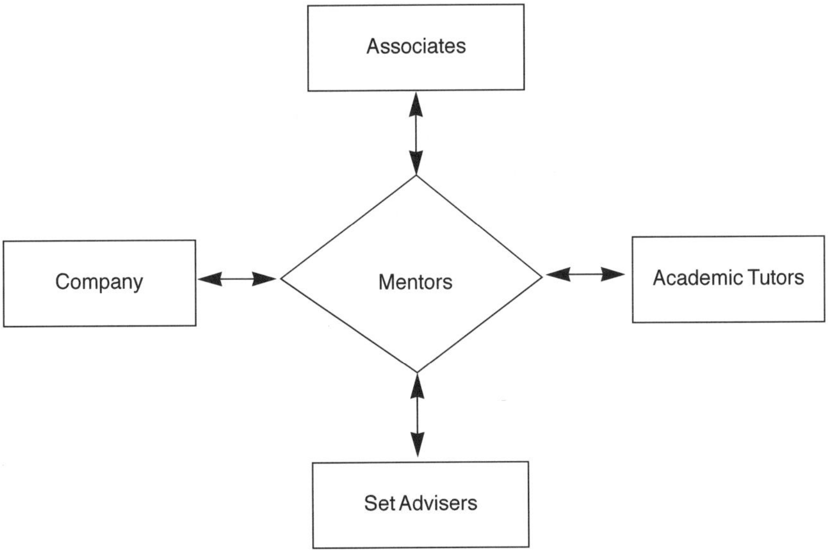

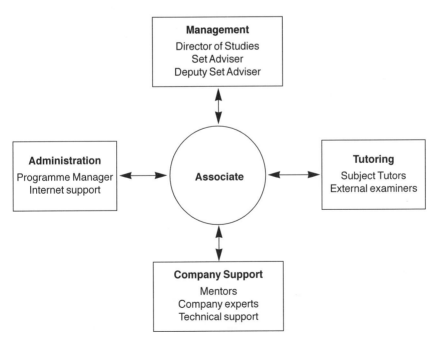

Figure 10.2
The central role of
mentors

The programme support infrastructure included a number of key roles, which can be categorized into management, tutoring, company support and administration, as shown in Figure 10.3.

Figure 10.3
Course infrastruc-
ture and key roles

MANAGEMENT ROLES

- *Director of studies:* Works with the set adviser to design the programme and address such issues as start dates, number and duration of residential sessions and subjects to be covered. Also responsible for identifying and appointing appropriate academic tutors and external examiners.
- *Set adviser:* Has a dual role as a facilitator for the Set, not the leader or chairperson. In the early stages the facilitator's role is a fairly active one, but once the group is comfortable with the concept of action learning, the need for facilitation diminishes. In addition, the set adviser liaises with the programme manager to administer the programme. This includes communication with the tutors to agree plans for residential workshops, and liaison with company mentors and experts. There may be one or more deputy set adviser(s).

TUTORING

- *Subject tutors:* The internalization of a virtual programme can permit emphasis on one or more of the core disciplines of business strategy, operations, marketing and human resource management programme. In the Marriott CMS programme, it was decided to concentrate upon operations and human resource management, as it was felt that these most affected the Associates' work. Accordingly, specialist tutors were recruited from the ranks of university lecturers who were responsible for leading the subject sessions and marking the assignments.
- *External examiners:* In order to ensure rigour, objectivity and the quality imperatives of ISO 9002, an external examiner is always appointed to oversee the process and conduct the *viva voce* examinations that form the final part of the assessment process. External examiners should be experienced in this role, perhaps in higher or further education, and have no direct link with the provider (IMCA).

COMPANY SUPPORT

- *Mentors:* The role of the mentor has been described above in supporting the Associate's learning and assignments. It is important that the Associate selects someone who they can approach readily and express their concerns in an open way. In return, the mentor supports the Associate's learning by providing ideas for further research and 'opening doors' to other resources.
- *Company experts:* In order to ensure that the organization's agenda drives the curriculum, it is important to involve senior personnel in virtual programmes. For example, in this CMS programme Marriott directors of human resources and operations each gave an input to the course.
- *Technical support:* As programmes of this type rely heavily on access to

Internet and e-mail, it is essential that Associates are supported in case of technical problems. One of the key lessons of the Marriott programme was that technological breakdown can be a cause of intense frustration. The programme should also include technological training for those who need it, although, in many cases, Associates learned quickly by 'doing'.

ADMINISTRATION
- *Programme manager:* The programme manager has responsibility for the operational delivery of the programme and its efficient administration. There are responsibilities for registry (applications, induction and correct retention of scripts and records), quality assurance (ISO 9002 demands) and co-ordinating assignments (deadlines, delivery of scripts and marking).
- *Internet support:* Represents the link between the programme management team and the technical support given by the provider in, for example, ensuring that the virtual resources are maintained and that the Set Web page is updated with Associates' contact details.

3. Communication
Effective communication is at the heart of all programmes of this type in order to enhance learning and ensure effective administration. The essence of action learning is the co-operation and communication between learners and facilitators, and this may be achieved in several ways:

- *Written:* Assignments need to be written, and this can present some learners with initial difficulties. It is important that Associates are made aware of the constituents of 'good' and 'bad' assignments and the criteria and weighting with which they will be assessed.
- *Virtual:* One important dimension of the Marriott programme is that virtual communication enabled the group, tutors and Set advisers to communicate with each other from anywhere in the world. Further, any company member could observe the virtual interplay and take part, if required.
- *Face-to-face:* Although the Associates on this prototype programme worked in different locations and could communicate virtually, it was felt necessary to incorporate some face-to-face meetings and workshops. These had the effect of enhancing group cohesion and helping the Associate to focus on the demands of the programme in an environment away from work. The initial induction meeting was aimed at ensuring that Associates understood the structure of the programme and the principles of action learning, as well as demonstrating how to access the online resources, Set website and meeting places. Subsequent workshops

focused on the disciplines and assignments that were based on functional integration and work-based projects.

One important effect of the programme was felt to be the improvement in communication skills of the Associates, not least because managerial effectiveness is linked to communication skills. These include the ability to listen (summarizing, restatement, reflecting feelings and clarifying), questioning (open and closed questions) and feedback (giving and receiving). The management team and Associates felt that communicating virtually is sometimes more difficult than communicating face to face because verbal clues such as intonation are missing and body language cannot assist understanding. As a consequence, there may be a mismatch between meaning and perception and the wrong impression may be given or misunderstood. The face-to-face meetings at least ensured that the understanding of Associates could be measured against 'the way that they said it', and that individual problems or concerns could be addressed. These concerns might be felt 'petty' by the Associates, but could grow to problems that might affect the quality of learning. Action learning is a learner-centred approach.

4. Resources
The final factor that is critical to the success of internalizing virtual management development programmes is that it should be well resourced. Resource support includes financial, human and technical support. Initially, it is important to cover the costs of the following elements:

- Salary and the cost of time for Associates, management team and other company members.
- Travel and accommodation for those attending workshops.
- Oral examination costs.
- Internet costs.
- IMCA charges for resources provided.

Human resources and support are also necessary in order to imbed the programme into the organization and its agenda for the future. Technical support includes providing the Associate with access to a personal computer that is loaded with Internet and e-mail software, ideally a notebook-type computer that can be used in a range of contexts (home, work or workshops).

VIRTUAL/WRITTEN
Another important factor is that Associates have access to a range of academic resources to support their understanding and enhance their written assignments. The IMCA virtual library includes a large range of

online resources on generic core subjects, as well as access to the search-able databases of Anbar Management Intelligence and the full-text retrieval facilities in the Emerald database. These virtual resources enable Associ-ates to track down specific articles on their area of study and to download journal articles to a file or a printer. This was felt to be a powerful resource which covers a broad range of management literature and ensures that time is not wasted in finding and filtering sources of reference. In addition, the virtual library was supplemented in this programme with several special-ized books, because of the information that it contained and because many of the Associates felt more comfortable with 'real' books.

TUTORS

It has been explained that the role of the subject tutors is to facilitate workshop sessions in areas of study identified by the company and to lead the workshops and assess the assignments. These assignments are based on the work-based problems of the Associates, and use the core resources to investigate and pose possible solutions. In this case, tutors were drawn from university lecturers who teach hospitality management courses, but this degree of specialization may not always be necessary. It is more impor-tant that subject tutors have a knowledge of the subject, not necessarily of the industry, and have a style of facilitation that accords with the 'open' paradigm of learning. Associates communicate with tutors via e-mail, and can be given a lot of individual attention with assignments, comment and assessment feedback.

Discussion

It is clear that each of these four Critical Success Factors is important to the success of virtual programmes, and combine to create the environment in which such courses can be replicated in a large organization. Another key area is the selection of people to manage, support and take part in the course. A lesson of the Marriott prototype was to determine the selection criteria for the course, which included:

- Current position and responsibilities.
- Managerial potential: 'promotability'.
- Skill levels and gaps.
- Loyalty and desire to stay with the company.
- Technological competence/computer skills.
- Previous experience and other courses undertaken.
- Openness to action learning.
- Motivation towards management development.

The management team have yet to finally evaluate the prototype, but the primary results suggest that the key factor in selecting candidates for the course is the desire to see it through to the end. While Associates who had undertaken university courses or had computer experience showed an initial lead over others, their expertise was shared in the Set through the medium of action learning. Some Associates whose native language was not English or who were not used to the formality of written reports did find difficulty with the early assignments.

An area that many Associates found difficulty with was time management. It is, of course, not easy to undertake an intensive programme of study in addition to working as a practising manager, and in the hospitality industry, long hours and an operational focus are common features. Associates felt that it was difficult to balance the needs of work with the desire to complete the assignments, and extra training was given on time management. In particular, Associates were advised to try to prioritize tasks and to delegate more effectively to subordinates in their departments.

It became clear in this pilot scheme that the process of action learning is a challenging one for those participating in and managing such programmes, but that it can also be an enjoyable experience. Because action learning is collaborative and interactive, it can work better if the atmosphere is informal, with workshops sensitively designed around the needs of those taking part and appropriate use made of humour.

Conclusion

It is essential that any project should be periodically monitored so that the team is aware of problems, and that solutions can be built into future programmes. In the case of the Marriott CMS programme, it was even more important that these lessons should be reflected upon and captured by those taking part in the prototype. This article has encapsulated these Critical Success Factors in the areas of company interface, administration, communication and resources. Each of these areas must work well if virtual management development programmes are to be internalized in a company.

These areas can also be categorized into 'hard' and 'soft' areas. 'Hard' areas include resources that are necessary to 'oil the wheels' of the process, such as computer hardware and software, an efficient administrative system and financial support for the programme. Without these essential 'hard' areas, there may be problems in initializing such programmes, or frustrations in keeping them going. The other, and more important, area can be described as 'soft' and includes issues of human relationships between parties, communication and goodwill. These represent the real key to success because such non-prescriptive courses require a flexibility and openness that not only helps to achieve course objectives, but may be an essential contribution to organizational learning in the future.

References

Bravette, G. (1996) 'Management education: valuing differences in the classroom', *Proceedings of the 5th Annual Hospitality Management Research Conference*, Nottingham Trent University, pp. 37–48.

Davies, D. (1998) 'Towards a learning society', in R. Teare, D. Davies and E. Sandelands (eds) *The Virtual University*, , Chapter 1, pp. 17–26, London, Cassell.

Freund, Y. P. (1988) 'Critical success factors', *Planning Review*, July/August, Vol. 16 No. 4, pp. 20–5.

Honey, P. and Mumford, A. (1992) *The Manual of Learning Styles*, Maidenhead, Honey.

MacFie, C. (1998) 'You don't want to do that . . .', *Independent on Sunday*, 26 July, p. 3.

Mumford A. (1995) 'Learning styles and mentoring', *Industrial and Commercial Training*, Vol. 27 No 8, pp. 4–9.

Newbold, D. V. (1993) Introduction, in R. Revans, *The Origin and Growth of Action Learning*, Bromley, Chartwell-Bratt.

Nichols, J. (1994) 'The strategic leadership star: a guiding light in delivering value to the customer', *Management Decision*, Vol. 32 No. 8, pp. 21–6.

Pinto, J. K. and Slevin, D. P. (1989) 'Critical factors in R & D projects', *Research Technology Management*, Vol. 21 No. 1, pp. 31–6.

Ramsden, P. (1992) *Learning to Teach in Higher Education*, London, Routledge.

Chapter 11

Challenges for service leaders

Setting the agenda for the virtual learning organization

RICHARD TEARE AND JIM O'HERN

The aim of this chapter is to use a literature-based review to frame the questions for tomorrow's learning organization. The review is contained in Section 2 of the book *The Virtual University: An Action Paradigm and Process for Workplace Learning* (Teare *et al.*, 1998b) and some of the applications are related to the pioneering work conducted by the global lodging organization, Marriott International, during 1998/1999, in partnership with International Management Centres Association. The contention is that the multi-faceted challenges of service leadership, competitiveness, profitability and return on investment, require a highly responsive and supportive learning community. This delivers on the challenges and derives benefits in the form of rapid access and reduced cost, by utilizing a 'virtual' network of university design. This chapter depicts a sequence of 'change factors', 'enablers' and 'impacts' that provide a reference point framework for learning and for focusing on business outcomes. If these are the key deliverables, what kind of learning process is needed to ensure that managerial and organizational activity is properly aligned? It is proposed that work-based 'action learning' is the only sustainable means of building the intellectual capital and competence of the organization to achieve its service leadership and business goals.

Change factors: how do you assess information needs and external change?

Teare and Bowen (1997) examine the managerial activity of learning about events and trends in the organization's environment by profiling the 'top 30' hospitality industry issues as reflected by UK-based and North American hospitality management journals.

Figure 11.1 portrays a thematic picture of the clusters of research-based articles that reflect patterns in management, service improvement and business performance issues. These themes sit at the centre of organizational purpose and form a logical starting position for framing a learning agenda.

In seminar discussions with a group of 25 experienced UK hotel general managers during 1997, the Worldwide Hospitality and Tourism Trends (WHATT online) research team sought to draw together the participants' own 'top 10' priority ranking. Industry's priorities reflected a very real sense of concern about both customer and employee retention and development, as well as the means of enabling these goals to be achieved. A summary of the key issues and priorities is included here.

Some key issues:

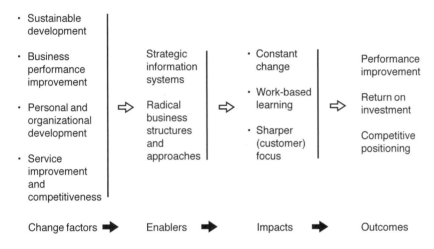

Figure 11.1
Patterns in
management,
service improve-
ment and business
performance

People
- The problem of retaining high calibre employees in the UK is related to the industry's inability to attract the right people (managers claimed that entrants have unrealistic expectations about hours of work and wages). The highest level of turnover occurs if expectations are not met during the first few weeks of employment.
- High turnover is also attributed to inadequate training and lack of ongoing development for employees – a need exists for initial management training and continuous, self-directed learning for all. The 'Investors in People' scheme is seen as a positive step (especially for managing front-line employees) but other areas were viewed as equally important, e.g. leadership training, 'adaptive manager' techniques, information management skills and responding effectively to challenging financial targets (among many others). Maximizing 'effectiveness' both individually and in team performance is seen as the prime means of delivering better results – financial, customers, employees and systems.

Business
- Participants were keen to see industry-wide improvements in strategic systems, especially relating to information and yield performance. In turn, it was thought that this would help industry to focus more attention on organizational indicators that are harder to monitor and measure but are potentially important measures of success (e.g. effectiveness of communications, morale, 'best practice breakthroughs').
- Branding and brand awareness coupled with operational consistency and perceptions of quality were seen as a key issue then and in the future, especially in relation to the UK trend towards the 'outsourcing' of hotel restaurants.

The top priorities
- Overall, the discussion groups felt that the most pressing priorities for the UK hotel sector were: (a) customer retention and being customer-focused; (b) motivating employees with a vision of the long term; and (c) personal development so that employees are equipped with the skills necessary to 'make things happen'. Other key benefits will include improved retention rates among the pool of 'good' managers and operatives, and this is linked to development initiatives to lead, motivate, inspire, recognize and reward the workforce.

Enablers: how are strategy, structure and performance related?
In reviewing the inter-relationships between the external environment, strategy, structure and performance, it is possible to draw out a number of challenges for business learning (Teare *et al.*, 1998a). In summary form, they are as follows.

Strategy and external analysis
- How might the organization assign environmental scanning tasks to detect and interpret the likely impact of external events?
- Who should be involved in 'inside out' environmental scanning? Who will identify information needs and sources and assign scanning tasks? How will information be stored, processed and disseminated so that it provides timely, well-focused and meaningful inputs to organizational learning and updating?

Strategy and structure
- How should the organization seek to develop and sustain forms of competitive advantage now and in the future?
- Should unit managers adopt an enhanced role in the ongoing task of maintaining alignment between the strategic variables of structure, strategy and environment? What additional contributions could they

make to organizational efforts to improve processes, embed a customer-focused culture and maintain 'open' internal communication networks?
- How might workplace learning programmes be used to optimize: flexibility (e.g. employee participation in idea generation and decision-making); adaptability (e.g. responding quickly to changing market conditions); empowerment (e.g. giving employees the scope to be creative and to experiment); innovation (e.g. allowing employees to 're-invent' processes and procedures); and team support (encouraging, sharing and providing mutual support).

Strategy and performance
- To what extent should financial, functional, asset and investment performance influence the organization's strategic direction?

While these challenges have the appearance of 'strategic' level complexity, they provide meaningful categories for organizational learning that can be subdivided and 'cascaded' as project assignments to an operational level.

Impacts: how can learning be linked to interpreting and responding to customer needs?

If managers have discerned the main business issues, how should they interpret and respond to their customers? How do you close the loop on managerial learning by relating industry issues and imperatives to customers and customer-led processes for delivering and assuring customer service? These challenges give rise to a number of questions for workplace learning initiatives related to customers (Teare, 1998):

Understanding customers
- Which services might be standardized and which should be customized (or personalized)? What are the design and delivery implications of these approaches for hospitality services?
- In what circumstances are customers likely to attribute more credibility to internal information than external information sources (and *vice versa*)?
- How does prior experience and familiarity with the product affect the customer's 'preference structure' and the formation of expectations, assessment criteria and 'reference point experiences' as key performance indicators?
- To what extent does role specialization in family purchase situations influence choice? What are the implications for the marketing of hospitality services?
- When are customers likely to use a 'decision rule'? How does this approach help to confirm the appropriateness of the decision?

- How does a customer's 'personal rating system' operate and vary between different customer groups and across different hospitality settings?
- In what circumstances might customers be willing to 'compensate' for a feeling of dissatisfaction with hospitality services? How might a feeling of dissatisfaction affect the approach to a re-buy situation?
- What practical steps might the organization take to minimize the potential impact of dissonance?
- How might the experiences of customers and employees be used to monitor and improve customer satisfaction levels?

Designing and delivering services
- How should the organization integrate or at least co-ordinate its customer service, quality assurance and marketing effort throughout the 'value chain'?
- How might the organization re-focus its internal service culture so that it is customer-led? What practical steps does this involve and how should they be reinforced?
- To what extent could the organization benefit from service branding?
- How might the organization inter-relate its efforts to maintain customer loyalty and product consistency?
- How might the organization 'localize' its operations to adapt and respond to culturally and geographically different customer needs and expectations?

Assuring total quality services
- How might customer-perceived quality measures be used to identify and rectify 'quality gaps' in the organization?
- What practical steps does the organization need to take to design and implement its own programme for service quality benchmarking? To what extent might this activity drive organizational learning both internally and in partnership with other service providers?
- How might the organization ensure that its quality and performance improvement efforts are customer-focused?

The answers to what seem to be technical questions can, in the main, be addressed by attaining and sustaining a service leadership position. Whatever else this might mean, the over-riding task is to learn from mistakes and to find ways of embedding an 'active learning' habit. To underline this, it is helpful to note one of the main findings of an Anglo–US benchmark comparison of service practice and performance report on the competitiveness of UK service. The report observes that 'training alone is insufficient – a concerted effort is needed to retain employees and develop their potential to its fullest extent' (London Business School, 1996).

If those who deliver service are themselves 'capturing' the best ways of improving it (given that those in the front line are truly the 'eyes and ears' of service leadership) then work-based learning might well be the key that unlocks the full potential for learning from customers.

From impacts to outcomes: the virtual university – tomorrow's learning organization?

While a great deal was written during the 1990s about the 'learning organization' there is no magic formula for embedding better ways of working and, in turn, learning from work. At its simplest level, individuals have a capacity to learn and to share their experiences with others. If team or shared learning can be nurtured, with imagination and courageous leadership it can, it seems, be cross-pollinated. But what are the consequences? If the organization is too rigid or hierarchical, then the 'good ideas' will live with the enthusiasts and perish with the die-hards that refuse to renew their learning regularly. How do you embed a culture of learning and, most significantly, how do you enable it to 'catch fire' so that it becomes infectious and quickens the pace and the competence of the people who make an organization what it is?

Step 1: How do you support managerial learning in the workplace?
A thematic review of the following areas – managerial learning and work; coaching, mentoring and team development; competences, managerial learning and the curriculum and work-based action learning (Teare, 1997a) – reveals a number of key questions for embedding managerial learning:

- How are the participants' roles defined (scope, tasks, responsibilities, relationships), how do they currently enact their roles (gather information, take decisions and action, contribute to key activities such as planning, organizing, staffing, leading and controlling) and what improvements would participants like to achieve for themselves, their work group and the wider organization?
- What are the external variables affecting managerial work (e.g. related to sources of discontinuity, uncertainty, ambiguity, complexity) and how might the programme enable parallel, ongoing learning to occur so that managerial skills and knowledge keep pace?
- How can the programme encourage participants to enhance their capacity to learn from work by using a variety of ways of analysing experiences (e.g. intuitive, incidental, retrospective, prospective approaches) so that learning becomes self-sustaining?
- What forms of learner support should be used (e.g. coaching, mentoring, team development) to help people to learn, widen and strengthen

organizational participation and embed a culture of learning?
- Who will coach and mentor, and what are the resource and development implications?
- What are the core and specialist levels of competency, how will these be built in to the programme and measured for attainment? How will these considerations affect the form(s) of learning and the methods of delivery?
- How will the efforts of participants be recognized – formally (e.g. accredited learning and the completion of an academic award), informally (e.g. support, encouragement, study time) and professionally (e.g. enhanced career prospects)?
- How will programme outcomes 'add value' for participants and the organization as a whole? How can the programme encourage others to take responsibility for recognizing and responding to their own development needs?
- How can the benefits of workplace learning be readily identified and 'sold' to participants, their superiors and subordinates? How can the reactions of sceptics and opponents be anticipated and effectively dealt with?
- How might 'return on investment' (time, resources, individual and organizational effort) be measured and monitored?

Step 2: What is needed to enable organizational learning?
A thematic review of the literature relating to organizational vision, leadership and motivation, organizational change and performance (Teare, 1997b), reveals that for both formal, programmed learning and informal self-reflection, it is helpful to consider the following:

- How can the organization equip itself to detect and respond appropriately to market trends? What processes and procedures are needed to isolate any given pattern of external events, devise suitable responses and ensure that the implications for re-aligning resources and competences are addressed? How should the organization assimilate the 'new' knowledge that it acquires from this continuous cycle of adjustment and re-alignment?
- Should the organization make a deliberate attempt to inter-relate complex internal and external environments to planned organizational cultures for learning and creativity? If so, how might the concept of an 'evolutionary organization' (EVO) be launched? What are the organization's ideals or vision for an EVO? How can organizational members be encouraged to think and act responsively and without unnecessary constraint so that natural curiosity drives workplace learning?
- What kind of organizational structure is appropriate now and in the

future? To what extent could and should the organization move towards facilitated self-organized learning networks so that budgets, resources, targets and goals for learning are 'released' to groups of employees each 'managing' enterprise activities? How will the differing roles of 'knowledge workers' and generalists be reconciled if this approach is adopted?

- How should the organization adjust its information flows so as to take advantage of real-time communications (virtual office, global networking via Internet and intranet) for transacting its business? How could communications technologies be used to create a searchable knowledge network within the organizations to support the learning effort?

- What action is needed to ensure that learning from experience is 'captured' and that opportunities for organizational learning from self-reflection (individual and shared learning) and from studying other organizations are acted upon?

- How might learning partnerships with external catalysts be used to organize joint discovery and research projects, workshop and benchmarking activities, in-company tailored partnership programmes and organizational network activity assessments?

- What performance measures does the organization currently use most often, and why?

- Should 'soft' employee-related performance measures (e.g. commitment, employee satisfaction, self-development, morale) be given more emphasis? How might the full range of organizational performance measures be related to improvements arising from the organizational learning effort?

Step 3: How do you put managerial and organizational learning together?

So as to 'ground' some of the key 'learning organization' concepts, several themes were explored concurrently during an Internet conference with managers from airport owner and operator BAA plc (Teare and Dealtry, 1998). The aim was to identify ways of creating a supportive learning environment and to relate this to an agenda for organizational learning and renewal. A summary of the main recommendations arising from the discussion is given in Table 11.1.

Having created the information and communications infrastructure, what should be the syllabus if we are to support learning organization environments? Peters (1996) proposes a syllabus-driven approach for the aspiring learning organization, inter-linking six areas that can be addressed by designing interventions for individuals, groups and organizational systems. The syllabus areas are:

1. Learning about the participant's own job in the organization and how to do it better.
2. Learning how to create alignment between culture and strategy in the organization so that initiatives 'fit' the context from inception to implementation.
3. Learning about the future by exploring the value of techniques for scenario planning and anticipating the likely implications for personal and organizational competency development.

Themes	Recommendations
Modelling the learning process in organizations	• Use internal communications to explain and encourage personal learning and to promote its application to ongoing business improvement. 'Sell the benefits' as often and in as many different ways as possible, throughout the organization. • Aim to recruit and retain people with different cognitive styles and skills to avoid 'organizational cloning'. • Aim to use taught and discovery methods and, where appropriate, a combination of both. • Encourage creative thinking and its application to 'opportunities for learning'.
Organizational readiness	• Seek to enact change through individuals rather than 'overlaying' an agenda for organizational change on the workforce as a whole. Use workplace learning founded on core values of trust, honesty and integrity to encourage personal development. • Establish one or more independent action research Sets to examine future scenarios and implications. Draw the Set membership from people with different learning styles, skills and from a variety of organizational functions.
Teamworking and learning	• Communicate the benefits of teamworking as widely as possible and link individual inputs to team outputs via the appraisal process. Use a learning log to enable team members to reflect on the effectiveness of their own inputs. Establish targets for team participation (ongoing and different teams) and encourage shared learning.
Networked learning	• Seek to embed a culture of learning by devoting time and resources to developing a wider and deeper understanding of the concept of empowerment. Link this to on-the-job training and development, explain and communicate the benefits at all levels of the organization and emphasize the benefits to individuals as well as the organization.

Table 11.1
The learning organization: some recommendations

4. Learning about the operating environment and the supply chain – essentially Peter Senge's 'fifth discipline' of systems thinking.
5. Learning how to challenge existing schools of thinking and avoid myopia so that personal and organizational mindsets are open to change and to new ideas.
6. Developing an organizational memory for the purpose of capturing, storing and retrieving knowledge and expertise.

The syllabus is for the organization as a whole and its members, who should participate according to their personal learning agenda and the organizational imperative. However, the sequence of its implementation is of some significance. Peters suggests that the learner's own job should be the starting point, as improvements here will yield organizational benefits from the outset. After this, the longer-term debates should be established about the future competences and how to network learning throughout the organization's supply chain. The framework also provides a basis for monitoring the kind of organizational adjustments needed to maintain creativity and productivity and for routinizing improvements by creating and drawing upon a knowledge base that constitutes the organization's 'bank' of knowledge capital.

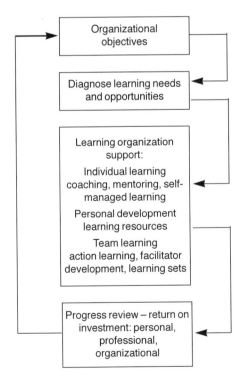

Figure 11.2
Systemized
organizational
learning

Adapted from
Buckler,
1996, p. 37

The issues raised in steps 1 to 3 can be described as the ingredients of a learning organization and they are depicted in Figure 11.2. But how do you make this happen and integrate learning and work?

Step 4: How will workplace learning evolve in the information age?
Work-based, career-long learning is increasingly seen as the route to personal effectiveness, and the new communications technologies *are* revolutionizing the delivery of learning experiences. Access to global domains of knowledge is now a reality and the Internet brings the generators, brokers and users of knowledge closer together than ever before. The Internet provides the means of interacting with 'communities of interest' wherever they exist and of accessing, searching and using learning resources linked to databases of articles, current awareness and archive material. This capability offers the means of enabling a new form of online business learning and providing 'real time' links between the knowledge stakeholders – authors, editors, publishers, readers, learners, tutors, industry sponsors and educationalists.

The virtual university represents the most advanced form, so far, of this emergent network of learning. Its design and implementation should necessarily reflect the challenges of 'working smarter' and team-based learning. The final section profiles the pioneering design work undertaken during 1998/99 by Marriott International, working with the multinational Association of International Management Centres.

**The Marriott Virtual University (MVU):
a global design for localized, accredited learning**
The Marriott organization has an unrivalled reputation as a service leader and for the breadth and depth of its training and development activity around the world. Yet, in seeking transformational change in training and learning, Marriott International concluded that it would need to embrace the Internet and the processes of action learning, a combination that has been pioneered by the International Management Centres Association (IMCA), the world's first global business school dedicated to work-based, action learning. The obstacles to building an integrated framework for just-in-time learning seem complicated enough without overlaying 'best fit' resource configurations for both micro and macro variables, some of which are cited below as challenges for the MVU design team. But these are the operational realities that present a daunting challenge. Our aim was to design a robust, low-cost learning network for 'high flyers' at every organizational level, regardless of their prior academic background, that is capable of supporting an organization of nearly 200,000 people working in every world region.

Micro level	Macro level	Best configurations?
Owner involvement	Six-continent scope	Communications
Legal variance	Multiple languages	Multiple brands
Cross-cultural differences	Business in 52 currencies	Systems integration
Franchise integration	Political impacts to balance	Technical expertise
Casino operations	High-risk environments	Policy adaptation

Challenges for
service leaders

Table 11.2
International challenges for MVU

Marriott International had set itself the task of constructing a framework for accelerated, 'active learning' so that it could build the competence levels of its managers as quickly and cost effectively as possible.

Human resource challenges
- Generate and retain competence.
- Leverage technology.
- Develop future leadership performance capabilities.
- Create rapid development routes for managers.
- Accelerate paths for competency.

Put simply, the goals are to work smarter and add value to the business by helping employees (called Associates) to learn at work.

Human resource goals
- Maintain a high performance work environment.
- Demonstrate added value services.
- See that continuous learning is the key to being a world-class organization.
- Continually raise the 'performance bar' and accelerate development.
- Build expertise in the knowledge of the business.

In order to do this, it is necessary to speculate on the challenges that tomorrow's service leadership organization will need to embrace.

Working with IMCA, which is able to create industry 'themed' learning Forums, Marriott International set out the design criteria for its MVU Internet resourced learning environment, the priorities being:

- Learning at work, with minimal 'time out', using Internet-resourcing to deliver 'learnerware' to the work environment and engaging high potential employees on the projects that frame the organization's own learning agenda.

- True partnerships between industry and education, with 'localized' university support around the world – based on the client organization's 'dynamic' learning agenda rather than a 'static', more traditional learning agenda.
- A 'seamless' connection between accredited training and learning for career-long, 'just-in-time' development in the workplace. This should recognize the importance of learning outcomes (and the evidence of achievement) as the means of aligning training and other forms of accredited workplace learning via a 'credit mapping' process.
- Parity of status for non-traditional forms of learning achievement, using practitioner-oriented mechanisms for accrediting prior experiential learning so that no Associate is discouraged or impeded from learning at work and gaining formal recognition for the outcomes of their study.
- Accelerated learning that is no longer bounded by traditional academic structures, yet is recognized as equivalent to conventional degree award frameworks – at all levels.

If this was to work, it would need to be a well-resourced, highly supportive learning process with opportunities for Associates to 'customize' their own learning and to share their learning with the 'Learning Sets' and 'sub-Sets', both face to face and via the Internet.

In 'selling' this radical agenda for learning at work to busy, successful Associates, it is essential to set out the benefits and opportunities for

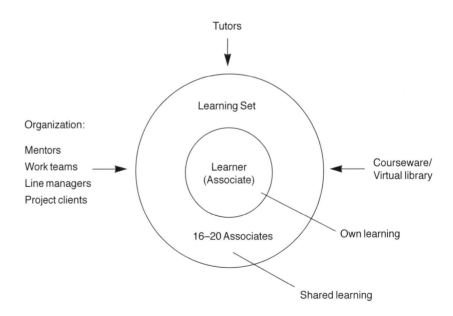

Figure 11.3
The process of
action learning

personal development and for the company as a whole. In practical terms, this means stating 'how' and by 'whom' the learning process is directed:

How is the learning process organized?
- It uses computers and the Internet to deliver a total learning infrastructure at low cost, nationally and internationally.
- A single Internet access point in any given work location provides complete access to all learning resources. A 'hands-on' induction to Internet-resourced learning is provided so that those with no prior experience of computers or the Internet are not disadvantaged. Our Internet resourcing is easy to access, navigate and print at the point of use – with no time wasted and minimum fuss. The resources are constantly updated and used internationally to ensure they are relevant to industry's needs.
- Associates can access their 'learnerware' at work so that they can relate it to the world of work – with minimal travel costs or time out for formal, 'classroom' study.
- MVU courses integrate with all existing in-company training courses – they do not replace them.

By whom is the learning process directed?
- The learning process is transformational and is built to the organization's specification.
- The learning process is professionally accredited and university validated: a consortium of universities around the world supports the process – not control it. MVU's business objectives and the needs of learner-associates come first and drive the curriculum.
- The learning process is designed for busy managers – its purpose is to help them to function more effectively in their current job and to prepare them for their next job and/or promotion – not to create 'academically oriented' managers for the sake of it.
- The learning process delivers return on investment as Associates work on the company's key issues and, in this sense, the 'value added' is trackable and quantifiable.
- Evidence shows that action learning actually increases commitment (and employee retention). Associates can see the relevance and value of what they are doing by working on the projects that really matter to them and to the company.

How do you make it happen?
The international scale and scope of MVU required the maximum possible engagement of Marriott's senior training team in the phased design, 'internalization', implementation and evaluation of the 'first wave' of action

learning Sets. In order to embed the Internet-based quality assurance protocols and procedures used for managing all aspects of the courses offered at Certificate, Diploma, Bachelor and Master's degree levels, a prototyping process was established. The essence of this meant that all trainer team members who engaged in the architecture/design process undertook projects aligned with Marriott's training and learning strategy. The total 'project map' sought to explore, test, review and refine all aspects of the MVU model prior to its launch. This included:

- Internet resourcing (such as forum design, courseware design, Internet communications and learning, use of online publishing resources, learning Sets and learning dynamics for workplace learning – nationally and/or globally).
- Accreditation of prior experiential learning (APEL). This would enable the senior training team to mentor and undertake or supervise the learning portfolio assessments of its Associates. The purpose is to recognize workplace learning achievement as a basis for entering MVU courses as a 'proxy' for possessing conventional qualifications.
- Aspects of credit mapping. This enables the senior training team to 'credit rate' the organization's existing training resources by mapping the learning outcomes against IMCA's accredited and validated courses. Where outcomes are equivalent, academic credit can be given and the length and content of MVU courses can be customized to reflect this. In effect, this provides an integrated approach to training and accredited learning, by creating a career-long framework for 'just-in-time' personal and professional development. It also means that the MVU team learns how to 'build-in' learning outcomes to achieve the maximum possible quantum of academic credit, when designing future training materials and courses.
- A fully customized and prototyped course for front-line, operational staff, using the full extent of IMCA's courseware with own organization contextualization.
- The transfer of expertise in tutoring; inducting tutors (who are members of both MVU and IMCA's global faculty); running Internet Forums as meeting places for virtual learning; managing all aspects of dynamic quality assurance (ISO 9002 certified) and equipping the team to run their own evaluative research programmes for training and learning.
- The transfer of expertise in 'harvesting' the learning outcomes of projects and formalizing this as internal systems, procedures and routines so as to build on and fully utilize the intellectual capital of the organization as a whole.

In essence these components are reflected in four strands of concurrent activity over a two- to three-year period of design, prototyping, implementation, evaluation and incremental improvement.

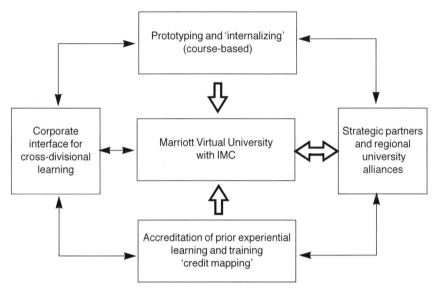

Figure 11.4
Designing the Marriott Virtual University

Beyond the initial design phase, the MVU trainer team is organized so that it might make rapid progress in three main areas of course-related activity:

Pilot course delivery teams
An MVU trainer team responsible for organizing the support functions for the pilot courses (each with sixteen course members or Associates per learning Set) in every MVU world location. Additionally, each Associate has his or her own mentor and a 'client' for the main dissertation project and/or other assignments as appropriate. The main challenge here is to 'cascade' the early successes of the initial UK prototype course and to build MVU's 'mentor' network so that every single learner has a 'helper' close at hand.

The key 'hands-on' experiences for these teams are:

- The course start-up process (when individual and team learning mechanisms are established).
- Taking action to ensure the 'organizational fit' of the course, linked to the Associates' own work.
- Project assignment specification and marking (all based on 'real' work-place challenges).
- Maintaining momentum in course Set and sub-Set working (face-to-face

and Internet sub-Set interactions) as well as organizing and facilitating both academic and company-specific inputs.

- Operating the programme management functions, including registry and quality assurance.

Partnership

The main role of the partnership trainer team is to internalize the IMCA partnership framework so that MVU might run its own accredited and validated courses. This should necessarily be built around Marriott ways of working and so the team must interpret the MVU design framework from their own experiences and knowledge of 'how things are done'. The team reports on all aspects of organizing and customizing MVU Internet-resourced workplace learning. The infrastructure includes:

- All courseware, and ISO 9002 accredited quality assurance with full 'hands-on' guides relating to all aspects of course design and delivery.
- All aspects of accreditation (Distance Education Training Council, US and the British Accreditation Council UK) and university partner support around the world for joint awards with IMCA and MVU.
- All aspects of 'virtual tutoring' and 'Internet-resourced learning' including the 'virtual library' (access to some 1,500 journals online) and other resources designed to provide learner support at work.
- Mechanisms used to 'capture' knowledge and track 'return on investment' in workplace learning – these are key deliverables for MVU implementation and for Associate retention and development.

Credit mapping

This team is learning how to 'map' the outcomes of internal training courses against IMCA's practitioner/academic awards so that a 'seamless' pathway between training and learning can be created. The 'hands-on work' includes:

- Prototype 'mapping' of existing Marriott training courses (if the 'academic value' is known then Associates can progress directly from internal training courses to Certificate or Bachelor's level awards and obtain a 'fast track' qualification at work).
- Accreditation of Prior Experiential Learning (APEL) portfolio building. The credit mapping team is also learning how to coach and counsel potential Associates with non-standard or no qualifications, the aim being to help applicants to complete the APEL workbook so that it might be successfully verified and enable them to gain entry to MVU awards at the appropriate level.

The development of the 'corporate university' concept was a feature of the 1990s, and this phenomenon quite probably reflects a sense of frustration with the perceived 'narrowness' of conventional management education in a business world that is obliged to work at a much faster pace. The Marriott Virtual University represents a significant step forward in that it quite deliberately leverages the best that the world of education has to offer so that it might be applied to learning at work. In effect, it is both a corporate university and a 'real' university with some ten university alliance partners supporting MVU's agenda in their respective world regions and languages. In this, the role played by IMCA is key – it provides all the resourcing, quality assurance and accreditation mechanisms and experience to enable learning to flourish in a sophisticated business context and on an international and multicultural basis. IMCA also acts as a 'broker' with MVU of university relationships for joint awards and seeks to ensure that academic inputs are both meaningful and relevant. This is a challenging and difficult task, but the goal is worthwhile as it 'aligns' university support with Marriott's global enterprise. In this way, the global network, orchestrated by MVU and IMCA, adds value to a global firm's enterprise rather than seeking to 'control' the learning process and the curriculum as in the past. At last it is possible to say that we have applied a commercial mindset to business learning that achieves global scope in resourcing terms and local attention to the issues and challenges that matter to individual learners, their business units and in virtual university terms to the Marriott International business as a whole.

In summary, MVU reflects a radical industry-based response to the issues and challenges of retaining service leadership. It has 'blazed the trail' by:

- promoting the workplace as a valid site of learning and giving prominence to continuous, lifelong learning with a truly open system of access and entry;
- designing an organization-wide framework of action learning with industry themed resourcing and accredited awards, supported by an Internet-rich learning environment with a single access point for all Associates anywhere in the world;
- aligning an array of university alliance partners with IMCA and MVU so that they deliver a meaningful support service with a curriculum that is rigorous, vibrant and dynamic, within a framework designed to Marriott's specifications;
- enabling MVU's own trainer teams to run the courses with external tutors and examiners to 'triangulate' a multi-dimensional view of quality assurance, characterized by 'fitness for purpose' and evidenced by the

attainment of learning outcomes that are derived from implementable
solutions to 'real work' projects with tangible benefits for the learner, his
or her work teams and for Marriott International – a world leader in
service.

References

Buckler, B. (1996) 'A learning process model to achieve continuous improvement and
innovation', *The Learning Organization*, Vol. 3 No. 3, pp. 31–9.

International Management Centres Association: http://www.imc.org.uk/imc/

London Business School (1996) 'Competitiveness of UK service: an Anglo-US benchmark comparison of service practice and performance'. Occasional Paper, Centre for
Operations Management, November.

Peters, J. (1996) 'A learning organization's syllabus', *The Learning Organization*, Vol. 3
No. 1, pp. 4–10.

Teare, R. (1997a) 'Supporting managerial learning in the workplace', *International
Journal of Contemporary Hospitality Management*, Vol. 9 No. 7, pp. 304–14.

Teare, R. (1997b) 'Enabling organizational learning', *International Journal of Contemporary Hospitality Management*, Vol. 9 No. 7, pp, 315–24.

Teare, R. (1998) 'Interpreting and responding to customer needs', *The Journal of Workplace Learning*, Vol. 10 No. 2, pp. 76–94.

Teare, R. and Bowen, J. T. (1997) 'Assessing information needs and external change',
International Journal of Contemporary Hospitality Management, Vol. 9 No. 7, pp.
274–84.

Teare, R., Costa, J. and Eccles, J. (1998) 'Relating strategy, structure and performance',
The Journal of Workplace Learning, Vol. 10 No. 2, pp. 58–75.

Teare, R., Davies, D. and Sandelands, E. (1998) *The Virtual University: An Action
Paradigm and Process for Workplace Learning*, p. 315, London and New York, Cassell.

Teare, R. and Dealtry, R. (1998) 'Building and sustaining a learning organization', *The
Learning Organization Journal*, Vol. 5 No. 1, pp .47–60.

Worldwide Hospitality and Tourism Trends Forum: http://www.mcb.co.uk/htgf/
whatt/.

Part 3
Outputs and Impacts

Chapter 12

Designing quality into action learning process

GORDON PRESTOUNGRANGE AND MOLLY AINSLIE

This chapter analyses the evolution of an Internet-driven dynamic quality assurance system for action learning programmes across the world. Its success was imperative for a global business school to comprehend how Sets were proceeding while avoiding 'controlling' processes that would contradict the action learning paradigm. This was further reinforced by several joint ventures between the authors' own institutions, the global Association of International Management Centres (IMCA), and tertiary educational institutions in Australia, Asia, Portugal and the UK. Each party was required to meet quality assurance monitoring requirements of disparate agencies globally. The outcomes are shown in Part 1 below.

When the protocols gained ISO 9002-accredited status, there was an immediate upsurge in the ever-present determination to continuously improve further patterns of faculty induction, continuous training and development for their facilitation skills through action learning scholarships and delivery effectiveness workshops. The approach is now operative in both fields for North America, Africa, Asia Pacific, Australasia and Europe, with gratifying outcomes. One of those outcomes was the search for the 'quality metrics' of the action learning process over and beyond the competence of the faculty who led or facilitated it. These particular outcomes are shown in Part 2.

Our organizational learning context
The effective delivery of action learning requires the deconstruction of the normative curriculum to allow the customer to drive its re-creation from challenges that are meaningful and actionable in the learner's own context. This gives rise to concerns among providers (who fear where customers might lead them) and among customers (who fear the responsibility they must assume for their own learning). And in the particular context of International Management Centres where we are involved with learning at and from the workplace, there is a further concern among the intermediaries/

brokers/funders of the process, who fear lest their backing of action learning is seen as a less worthy or credible process for the individual manager's career prospects than one driven by a normative curriculum.

Where such concerns are present – and they are not infrequent – one significant way to allay them is by means of visible, credible patterns of quality assurance. Providers, customers and intermediaries must all be reassured. This chapter is a case analysis of International Management Centres' journey of continuous improvement in this respect since 1982 when it metamorphosed itself from a professional association of business school graduates (established in 1964 from what are today the Universities of Portsmouth, Westminster and Thames Valley) into a qualifying workplace action learning business school awarding MBA, DBA and Practitioner Bachelor degrees wholly in its own right (Mumford, 1997).

The originating paradox

The 1982 metamorphosis was catalysed by research in the late 1970s specifically at Cranfield School of Management but more widely in industry and the management professions. It showed that, while student managers recognized the marketplace credibility of MBAs in their own career development, they criticized much of the tutorial as too theoretical. Employers for their part regarded it as deficient in skills to make use of the theoretical knowledge acquired. The paradox was that, despite such disappointments, MBAs were in great demand. Providers, finding themselves in such a seller's market, did little to respond to the concerns expressed.

IMCA, because it was an association of graduates, felt sure something both could and should be done, and after an extensive search determined that the action learning approach pioneered by Reg Revans (1971, 1982), advanced in UK coal-mines and health care and then latterly in Belgium, was ideally suited.

A foundation consortium of industrial concerns and business school faculties initiated the first programmes in 1982. Support came from IDV/Grand Metropolitan and NatWest Bank in the UK, Dow Corning in Brussels, and from academics at Cranfield, Hull, Bradford and Queensland Universities. It was a dangerous enterprise academically, if not for the customer or the broker. The deconstructed syllabus was not welcomed at a time when business schools had just set their chosen normative curriculum in concrete. However, success was assured by holding fast to the espoused customer focus and deploying those elements of the normative curriculum which were requisite for the re-created curriculum. Finally, at the conclusion of each degree programme the traditional pattern of external examination was conducted. Quality in these early days (Peters, 1988) was seemingly assured by our dedication to customers' needs and by the determination within each programme (known as a Set) by all concerned to expect 'quality' on a fitness-for-purpose criterion. Great effort was made to find tutors with the facilitation skills necessary in adult learning and to empower the Set first to counsel, then if necessary to remove, poor performers. Great attention was paid to the design and conduct of all assessed assignments to ensure that they reinforced the goals of actionable learning – that they benefited the career of the individual manager concerned and that they gave a measurable return on investment (ROI) for the sponsoring organization (Ball, 1991; Wills and Oliver, 1996).

Nothing succeeds like success. A glittering array of corporate names joined with the originating enterprises – Cummins Engines, Jones Lang Wootton, Shell, ICI, Midland Bank, Malaysia Airlines, Ernst & Young, and more. And they were seeking programmes across the world – in Australia, South Africa, Hong Kong, Singapore, Malaysia, Indonesia, Papua New Guinea, Finland, Holland, Vanuatu and elsewhere. Our lines of communication became rapidly extended and processes of quality assurance became a very high priority indeed (Kozubska and Wills, 1992). Our awareness of this need had been well highlighted in our successful submissions for accreditation by the British Accreditation Council and by the Washington-based Distance Education and Training Commission in 1985 and 1986.

Action learning's Achilles heel
The marketplace success of a customer-focused workplace curriculum did not surprise us. We had anticipated it, but our potential competitors, being in a seller's market, had neither the incentive nor the will to follow us until more than a decade had passed – rather they characterized us as oxymoronic and accordingly less worthy. Yet the founders of IMCA's action learning initiative were all products of the normative curriculum and were well aware of its particular benefits – benefits that action learning clearly did not offer. By the latter's determined focus on actionable customer-focused issues for the re-creation of the curriculum, a helicopter view of the totality of the body of learnt knowledge was not imparted and could not be obtained. Issue-driven learning left gaps, often quite substantial, that no thoroughness in attention to scholarship in the issue areas could avoid: and this was even after the fullest involvement with fellow action learners in Set discussions of one another's actionable issues, which of itself extended coverage greatly beyond the individual's own focus areas (Sutton, 1990).

We accordingly resolved from the outset to address this in two ways: the first was the inclusion in the programmes of 'courseware' covering the all-significant areas of the normative curriculum, for requisite use with total exposure only by deliberate browsing. Second, however, we resolved to place great emphasis on ensuring that all action learners were aware of, and became advocates of, 'understanding how we learn' and how to improve our learning styles (Mumford and Honey, 1986). This determination was institutionalized in myriad ways – through faculty training and induction, learning styles testing and action planning, evaluative assessments of learning, both at workshops to talk over learning log entries and as credit-earning outputs (Thomas, 1993). This attention was further continued after graduation through one- and five-year continuing renewal assignments leading to Companion Membership (Mumford, 1996).

In this manner we ensured a platform of learning and independent action for graduate managers to build on, as issues arose outside their specific issue-driven action learning. Areas not specifically addressed on any given programme were accessible by deliberately understood processes.

The 1988 UK Educational Reform Act was a supreme test of our faith in the action learning process and our customers' right to join with us in re-creating the curriculum. The academic establishment, encouraged by government, which deliberately reinforced the cartelization of higher education in the Act to eliminate magnified malpractices, sought to return our curriculum, via validation processes and legal sanctions, to its normative view. But we had seen sufficient of action learning's 'fitness for purpose quality' and the enthusiastic acceptance of our educational approach by customers to be willing to suffer the consequent slings and arrows of such outrageous fortune.

IMCA was especially sustained by its corporate clients, but most particularly by adherents in the Asia Pacific, Holland and South Africa, where traditionalist cartels were then less firmly entrenched. And so from our outrageous fortune a re-engineered global professional association was sensibly forged. This provision of action learning programmes in myriad countries then gave us an excellent basis for comparative benchmarking of quality achieved. Best Graduates at Bachelor/Master/Doctor, Best Academic Partner, Best Companion Member, Best Learning Organization awards were competed for globally and honours shared around the world. And twice each year, at Graduation workshops and Annual Professional Congress many met together at a single location – Helsinki, Amsterdam, Johannesburg, Curaçao, Hong Kong, Brisbane, Kuala Lumpur, London, Cape Town – to share and compare. At one of these, Australian and Dutch colleagues were most determined that we should come to terms with the advancing electronic communications systems for straightforward issues like the Multinational Registry and for interactive communications. The initial proposals were for electronic data interchange (EDI) and bulletin board systems (BBS), both of which went live in 1994. This was closely followed by the Internet in 1995.

Evaluative Research Fellowships were also set in place each year, one of which (Peters, 1995) quite specifically explored whether, and if so how, IMCA could usefully employ ISO 9000 approaches in its customer-focused action learning vision. The over-riding message from Peters, who headed

MBA in Quality Management in association with the British Standards Institution (BSI), was readily anticipated. The challenge was how to engender the enormous energy required to develop and implement an ISO 9002 approach globally. As often occurs when commencing such an endeavour, many of the component elements are present, but they do not have the coherence that a total quality management orientation affords (Peters and Wills, 1996) (see Figures 12.1 and 12.2).

Part 1: Evolving ISO 9002 protocols

Accessing requisite knowledge
We were determined to be true to our action learning, customer-focused vision as we advanced. A normative construction could not be acceptable and many doubting Thomases proffered the view that ISO 9000 processes often collapsed under the weight of their own bureaucracy. We resolved to evaluate the voluminous literature on ISO 9000 and in particular the experience of educationists – a process we have since continued on a dynamic basis. Here we shall focus in particular on the latter which was, and still remains, relatively scant. (Needless to say, there was an abundance of knowledge about ISO 9002 and quality management generally across the faculty and the body of members of the Association.)

Idrus (1996) most helpfully offered a comprehensive global review of TQM in the educational sector. While New Zealand (where he was Director of Otago Polytechnic) disappointed him, he found considerable evidence of successful applications in the USA and Europe. Yet he was critical of professional institutions and especially business schools that advocate TQM without taking their own medicine. His overall conclusion was that, unlike the inner drive within those coming from action learning, the majority of cases of implementation that he identified arose from outside pressures. This is exemplified in Asser and Haines (1995) at Oxfordshire County Council; Cave *et al.* (1995) at Brunel University; Doherty (1995) at the University of Wolverhampton; Hill (1995) at Queen's University, Belfast; Rippin *et al.* (1994) at Bolton Institute; and Sommerville (1996) at Swanley College. In almost all these circumstances it was the pressure of external competitiveness either for government resources or for customers that drove the initiative forward. Most contributions allude to a governmental desire to measure the performance of education whether via performance efficiency indicators or via input/output measures. The influence in the UK from the now defunct Council for National Academic Awards (CNAA) was profound. Throughout their 25-year history as the accrediting body for new higher education institutions they had built up and implemented a disciplined regime towards what they perceived as quality (CNAA, 1992a). In their last years they also began to embrace the customer-derived contribution to the quality debate (CNAA, 1992b) which has since gathered force globally, but they did not survive long enough to be true champions.

Marsh (1991) captured the dilemma as elegantly as any author when he observed: 'educational institutions should neither embrace the discourse and practices of the commercial quality culture wholeheartedly nor should they embrace them uncritically'. The creation of a total quality management environment that monitors nonconformities and calls for action demands the involvement of individuals in all internal processes that have the clear purpose of improving the academic quality of teaching, learning and the student experience. The challenge is how to bring this about in the typical higher educational structures without relying (exclusively) on external pressures. Vision from the top is readily offered as an effective way to achieve most organizational and cultural changes and the educational sector proves to be no exception (Schoengrund, 1996; Sommerville, 1996).

It would be unfair, however, to suggest that a considerable volume of activity and reported research was not taking place at the time on a pro-gramme-by-programme basis – oblivious to external pressures or top-down vision. There seem to be three strands. The first is either ISO 9002-driven (McRobert, 1995) or builds on the traditions of quality circles and teams (Asser and Haines, 1995; Boaden and Dale, 1993; Collins *et al.,* 1991; Goulden, 1996; Green, 1996). The second, expressed by Morgan and Piercy (1992) and O'Neal and LaFief (1992), urges marketing to enforce the customer-driven focus of the quality movement. But this strand goes further in studies that take a consumerist view, looking at the learner's own perspec-tives (Muller and Tonnell, 1993), focusing on the individual student as the true and direct driver for quality (Showalter and Mulholland, 1992) and even more interestingly via a simulation exercise (Bacon *et al.*, 1996). This latter example is a powerful way of helping students to learn how to learn and is worthy of considerable development. Schoengrund (1996) also explored the multilevel customer/consumer patterns in education which have strong rel-evance for workplace learning, as already indicated.

The third strand has been labelled quality function deployment (QFD). Pitman *et al.* (1996) applied it to MBA programme design in North America and assert that it 'helps ensure the voice of the customer is clearly heard and followed in the development of a product or service'. Originating in Japan, it works with cross-functional development teams to explore the 'Whats' and the 'Hows' and uses graphical displays to guide the process. Learning processes and curriculum compatibility are readily susceptible to such approaches (Lo and Sculli, 1996). Alitalia (Ghobadian and Terry, 1995) have made extensive use of it for customer service educational programmes, as have real estate agents (Campbell, 1996).

Finally, our review of the published body of knowledge at the time highlighted a number of other seemingly discrete fields of research and evaluation that contributed to our own thinking. Hosie (1995) described quality assurance processes in his analysis of human resource information systems that figured greatly during the development of our faculty and graduate databases for online searching against meaningful criteria. This database approach in particular highlighted the need for faculty development with appraisal feedback and mentoring, and ultimately gave rise to our own continuing renewal process as Companion Member, which is similar to Farrugia's model (1996), and addressed fully in Part 2 of this chapter.

Himmett and Knight (1996) most gratifyingly explored the determinism of the assignments set for any learning experience and agreed strongly that they must reflect the learners' needs, not those of the normative hierarchy. Cleary (1996) reinforces the point again, linking it with how students learn, using recognizable learning cycles but also working from disparate learning styles.

Focusing on ISO 9002

The dynamics of our learning approach, the exhortations of the Head of our Quality Management School, and the globally located delivery sites for our programmes readily came together to justify and give us the resolution to proceed with ISO 9002. We recruited one of our BSI collaborators as our consultant, and Registry and Bursar colleagues led by Molly Ainslie came to terms with what was going to be required. Like so many before us, we quickly came to understand that we had to delineate and communicate the managerial processes of our professional association's Business School that much more effectively, so that all involved with us – upwards of 300 faculty, 4,000 graduates and 400 current students (known as Associates) – could discern what they were entitled to expect. And then we had to measure our non-conformances and take deliberate actions either to emend the elements of quality or to deliver them more effectively. It took nine months for the Quality Team to complete the Internet site and associated documentation to win approval for the process in action – at their first attempt. Charters were crafted for Associates, faculty, graduates and partners that, by making use of Internet hyperlinks to our extensive site, were a major advance on the old paper systems and BBS (Ainslie, 1996).

Perhaps most significantly, the search engines created and their criteria meant that information that only a few previously knew to exist could be speedily traced. Almost as important, however, was our ability to keep all the desired information up to date. This included course materials, which were formerly, on average, two and a half years old, now being never less than six months since last revision.

The distribution of paperwork from the Multinational Registry and

Common Multinational Professional & Academic Board was replaced by website/e-mail proactive notification and user downloading. This ranged from full programme resources at one extreme to the Minutes of Statutory Meetings, Annual Congress outputs and outcomes and research findings. Paper was not eliminated but printing was done on demand at the point of use, eliminating global postal expense and delays, as well as increasing awareness. The sophisticated Web Forum/Virtual Academy framework evolved allowed not only for discourse among programme participants but globally for the Senior Tutor, Chairmen of MBA, Doctoral and Bachelor programmes, for the Annual Congress and all major meetings. These latter run as 'virtual' discussions of agenda items for six/nine weeks prior to the face-to-face event and enable those unable to attend physically because of geographical distance to participate actively.

A fillip for the process
The analysis of non-conformances for ISO 9002 readily showed that much of the infrastructure required for IMCA's effective management was dependent on others around the globe to supply data and to populate the sites concerned. We had previously re-engineered our Registry, in pre-ISO 9002 days, to use electronic data interchange from distributed sub-Registries in Australia, Malaysia, South Africa and Holland to great effect, as opposed to awaiting their transmission of paper-based records of application data, grades and fee settlements. We resolved to stay with the EDI strategy after ISO 9002 accreditation to create a wholly dedicated resource at the multinational monitoring point which would proact strongly with the sub-Registries, and *vice versa*.

Furthermore, the Internet resourcing of our programmes involved the creation and ongoing maintenance of virtual professions-cum-academies (Teare, 1996) in partnership with client enterprises, e.g. BAA, Fina and later Marriott Hotels International, as well as regionally, e.g. Asia Pacific Management Forum with its sub-Forums for Japan and Australasia. The creation process eventually evolved a series of modular templates, many of which could be routinized, but the challenge of ongoing maintenance and dynamic activities is, and will forever be, much more problematic. It calls not just for monitoring but also for self-starting motivation. Here, as with the learning process itself among Associates, the emphasis had to be placed on induction, training and group processes to achieve the requisite inspiration and desired fitness for purpose (Figure 12.1).

From fillip to imperative
IMCA's single-minded dedication to action learning in the workplace since 1982, together with its leadership position as an Internet-driven professional association, represent very considerable strengths in the

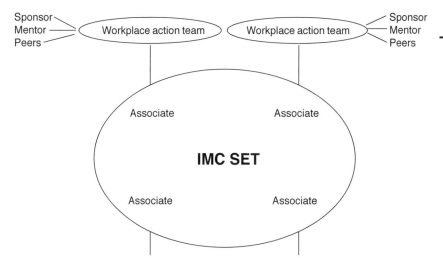

Figure 12.1
Partnerships with
client enterprises

contemporary, turbulent educational world. The external pressures, well rehearsed in the literature reviewed and referenced, are encouraging tertiary educational institutions at large to look ever more closely at the opportunities available in either or both of these areas – and globally, where once again we have unique strengths some fifteen years up the learning curve, with many challenges addressed and overcome to show for it.

Accordingly the joint venture which emerged in September 1996 between the University of Surrey and IMCA was not, on reflection, surprising. There were very considerable mutual advantages to be gained by both parties if they could agree on how to build on what had clearly been learned to be effective in global workplace learning, and what was being learned on the Internet – without damaging the vital reputation for 'quality' enjoyed by the University within the government-funded sector of higher education.

IMCA's non-traditional patterns of evaluative research and its strong emphasis on learning to learn constituted a good starting point. But problems were obviously present in terms of concern for sponsored in-post managers and traditional entry criteria. Some of the most innovative designs for our professional qualification awards, e.g. Practitioner Bachelors and Doctorates, Master's awards for Faculty Development and Post Qualifying evaluative awards called A+ and Companion, did not harmonize with the existing university framework. Validation panels for concurrent award schemes were unable to comprehend and evaluate the leadership role IMCA had gained on the Internet. University faculty, schooled in scholarship as an appropriate end in itself and an *ad hominem* approach to teaching, were not always accepting of the workplace realities of focused learning and team reliance.

While IMCA, which includes many current and former university academics in its faculty, would not presume to suggest how the University should operationalize its scholarly enquiry, the purpose of the joint venture was for IMCA to show the way for the University to be yet more actively engaged in the workplace and with Internet resourcing. As can well be imagined, the discourse on quality in terms of fitness for purpose speedily focused on 'Whose purpose?' and, as that matter clarified, gradually the requirements for quality action learning from the joint venture took on their own shape.

There was ready agreement that the EDI modelling for global sub-registries should be adopted from IMCA. It was also concluded that, once assurance was gained for the core curriculum resourcing of programmes (the courseware, as it is known), the design and implementation strategies offsite with corporate or regional theming were areas where IMCA's learning was well advanced. And the same resolution was also quickly reached in relation to faculty skills as action learning facilitators.

Indeed, the reliance on IMCA to show the way, which in retrospect should not have been particularly surprising, began to have the potential to make the joint venture heavily one-sided. The *raison d'être* for the University entering into the joint venture was not to have IMCA as a stand-alone unit but to forge links, share understanding across the University, and enable many others to evolve and develop in these areas. Failure to achieve this could be expected to undermine the joint venture's support, which from the outset was at the highest level, indeed unanimous at Senate. Accordingly, it was resolved:

1. to make dynamic quality assurance of the action learning processes our prime focus; and
2. to involve as many other University Faculty as possible in the processes beyond the immediate identification with management learning (see Figure 12.2).

Dynamic quality assurance
The quality assurance focus taken is conducted on the Internet. It is accessible at all times at the University or throughout IMCA globally by authorized individuals. It encompasses what are deemed to be the major elements of a quality action learning process and identifies the specific Registry elements involved. The dynamic or continuous improvement of the system lies in the requirement that, via EDI/online editing rights, the sub-Registries globally must update all elements monthly. Non-conformances are monitored and corrective action is taken.

While none will underestimate the challenge of keeping the information up to date, without the ISO 9002 disciplines and framework we would have been quite unable to respond as we have. But its elegant, visible success paradoxi-

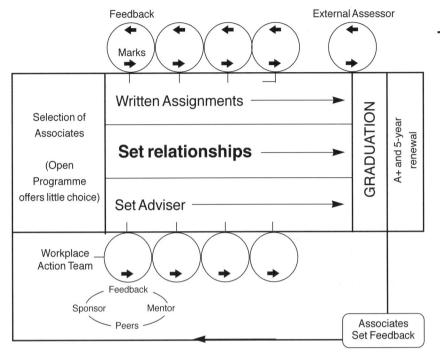

Figure 12.2
Learning Set
interactions

cally created much hubbub among faculty members. After many years of constructive and less than constructive criticism of the management of these procedures, the arrival of a state-of-the-art system caused concern too. Surely too much attention had been given to the administration, at the expense of the true seat of learning, namely within the Set with the Associates.

This was, of course, a happy message for IMCA's Senior Tutor who, with the Deans globally in support, is charged to ensure that all faculty who wish to tutor on programmes are professionally competent and refreshed in the processes used. The opportunity was rapidly taken to demand a higher level than hitherto of professional skills from all faculty and this happened concurrently and sequentially, as described in Part 2 below.

For all who were acknowledged action learning practitioners, two things were henceforth required:

1. Immediate refreshment and Internet induction.
2. Unless already qualified as an educationist, enrolment on IMCA's own Postgraduate Advanced Diploma/MPhil/DPhil programme with the benefit of a Faculty Development Scholarship forthwith. (At the time of writing (1999) several cohorts have completed at all these levels, with the specific focus for instance evolving to embrace online faculty skills, corporate virtual university resourcing and doctoral research advising.)

For those who were not yet action learning practitioners (and this included many from the University wishing to tutor on the action learning programmes), the refreshment phase at (1) above was replaced with a two-day induction/novice tutor period, with (2) still required.

Finally (and this is a matter of most considerable importance), IMCA faculty are seeking to build closer relationships with the University faculty in their discrete subject areas so as to be at the forefront of academic thinking/expertise as well as in the deployment of knowledge in the workplace. Whilst the Internet's access to almost all new developments via literature searching online has already made a major difference, the university's strength as a centre of academic excellence was obviously greatly to be welcomed.

In the spirit of continuous improvement

By bringing the two polarities in the educational quality assurance debate in the joint venture into one focused context – workplace learning – the potential for considerable continuous improvement and a forum for evaluative research emerged. Not that one can or should triumph over the other. Universities must always remain the guardians and catalysts for scholarship *per se*. But if as institutions they also wish to espouse market/customer-driven learning, and lifelong learning, they must also come to terms with and respect the workplace context and leverage it via appropriate media, including the Internet, in the cause of more effective higher education.

To be criticized as oxymoronic is, under such assumptions, to miss the point. The higher adult education challenge is to do both well, attaining the highest achievable quality levels of fitness for the twin purposes. Research must be clear as to which polarity is appropriate and outcomes measured accordingly.

IMCA's monotechnic approach for the past fifteen years has enabled it to hone many powerful workplace learning approaches, but it has lacked the especial strength that can be derived from a joint venture with a scholarly university institution. Equally, ambivalence about the legitimacy of workplace learning and its perceived threat to scholarly endeavour have meant that universities have often failed to serve a very large client group that greatly admires but frequently despairs of them.

To quote Marsh (1991) again: 'these differences of perspective can easily become caricatures and the resultant stand-off between the two partners ultimately does nobody any good'. The IMCA professional association's joint venture is no ideological stand-off. It hurts and it creates heat and lively debate and is consequently genuinely important as we try to keep what works and discard what does not. Fitness for respective purposes can be expected to prevail, but both parties can learn from one another.

Designing quality into learning processes

Part 2 is truly a sequel to the arrival of ISO 9002 quality assurance protocols globally. There was an immediate demand that a quality improvement approach be evolved for the action learning approach itself. There was little point, ran the argument, in ensuring the effective conduct of 'unimproved' processes. Righteous indignation that so much effort should have gone into ISO 9002 in the first place was considerable. It was a case of the tail wagging the dog. In terms of organizational *real politik* however, it proved highly effective. Designing quality into the process of action learning itself was actively on the professional agenda . The 'quality metrics' of the process were elicited and subjected to careful scrutiny to ensure continuous improvement.

Assignments and programme structures

Clearly, the structures of the programmes offered (e.g. frequency of meeting/style of Set behaviours/role plays by tutors as prescribed in the original design of, say, an MBA or DBA programme), have a critical impact on the learning processes. They demand certain activities that can then be managed for better or for worse. The sheer volume of words required to be penned for assignments, and the number and focus of assignments again greatly condition what can be accomplished. These requirements can, if not carefully managed, dominate the Set interactions, not just as a finale as assignments go in and as feedback is provided, but as a fascination or dread throughout the exploration of any topic.

As we examined the structures and assignments which had held constant for over a decade on MBA and DBA programmes, it became apparent that the originators' understanding and rationale for their introduction was lost on most contemporary faculty and most Associates. The sharing of these elements with every new cadre of Associates seemed to be a valuable way of increasing learning in particular through an understanding of the allocation of marks within assignments and the way in which Associates are perceived to have performed well or less well on each one. Indeed, the evaluation at this stage has already triggered a study of comparative marking around the world and the reallocation of marks to reflect, in particular, the implementation of action plans. We rediscovered the decision made a decade earlier that, because the implementation of projects within the time-scale of the programme of studies was seldom feasible, Associates were discussing how they might, rather than how they did, implement. Little or no learning was being captured and generalized about the challenges or the *real politik* of implementation of change, although considerable research had been accomplished on the cost benefit of the changes that did make their way through the enterprises concerned (Wills and Oliver, 1996). Attempts to capture 'what happened next' using a device known as A+, where graduates were asked one year after completion to share the outcomes, were valuable but not widely accomplished. It proved difficult to motivate a representative sample to create such evaluations spontaneously. The obvious way forward in this respect seemed to be to introduce action plans based on research earlier in the programmes so that implementation could take place and be evaluated prior to the completion of the programme. This was vigorously adopted in new programme designs for MBA and Master of Management.

Learning processes per se

The concern with learning about and from implementation outside the formal structure, and how the design of the programme could be used to bring it within, were surprising aspects of the search for useful metrics of the processes we used. The more predictable had been clearly articulated in the late 1980s as the composition of the Set and its consequent interactions; the workplace context from which the managers came and how it responded to them as they went about their workplace learning assignments; and the way faculty members and library resources complemented and empowered Associates. As reported in Chapter 15, the questionnaires administered for nearly twenty years at the Graduation Congregations have consistently reported that Associates meeting together from around the world, who have followed the imposed common structures and assignments, are literally amazed at how much of a common language and a common perspective they have gained on the processes of management. But more than that, they have all united behind the view that the interaction with fellow Set Associates was the most powerful learning trigger – both encouraging and sharing experiences in broadly similarly challenged workplaces.

A very considerable majority expressed relative disappointment with their workplace colleagues as supporters of their learning. Whether their expectations (because of how their fellow Set members who were similarly challenged had responded), were frankly unrealistic, we do not yet know. But we have come to the realization that a measure of how well the workplace does support an Associate is an urgent need. Once we can identify the elements of perceived supportiveness we can empower the Associates to manage them more effectively. Strategies have already begun to emerge on an *ad hoc*, but not on a well-researched basis.

Faculty members and library resources were seemingly taken for granted by Associates within the Sets. Provided they did not seek to dominate with traditional teaching models, expectations and demands were not high. They were treated more as equals in the process, and weaknesses were tolerated and compensated for rather than derided. Whilst this clearly gives faculty members an enjoyable and relaxed learning situation in the Set, it implied that metrics needed to be identified to bring out superior performances. And these are, of course, not meant to be about end-of-programme popularity assessments, but ongoing feedback which gives a fillip to superior contributions.

Interactions amongst the learning Set
It goes without saying, and notwithstanding the opportunities for Web-based discussion forums which we use, that attendance at Set meetings is a prerequisite for much desirable interaction. Yet we have eschewed atten-dance registers and been understanding and tolerant, as have the fellow Set members, of absences on business or because of family exigencies. And again, because we are seldom overwhelmed with applicants for any given Set, we have infrequently been in a position to attempt to select and catalyse a Set based on any prior model of how they can be expected to interact most powerfully. We have and do attempt this for sub-Sets within a programme, getting the Set themselves to understand how and why, as a critical element of learning for their own workplace. To achieve this we use teamworking preferences (Margerison and McCann, 1985) and most specifically shared learning styles (Honey and Mumford, 1986; Mumford, 1996) as developed by faculty members.

The role of the faculty member in knowing how to facilitate good interac-tions within the Set, and to share with the managers themselves how he or she is achieving that goal, should and frequently does outstrip the 'natural' interactions that the make-up of the Set will engender. And we believe that is as it should be. Management in the workplace is seldom about selecting and working with a perfect team; it is most frequently about making the most of the resources to hand. So too is it within a learning Set.

To assist the Associates come to a fuller understanding of how they learn from and with one another in a Set context, enriched and facilitated by process skills, is accordingly a valuable managerial learning outcome. It is one of the fields where not inconsiderable *ad hoc* research has been con-ducted (Thomas, 1993) and where assignments and Set meetings have been engineered to highlight the issues. The assignments gain significant credit points towards the qualifications awarded. Following Thomas' thesis however, that it must be a continuous process or there is a danger a shortfall will only be fully revealed at the end of the programme, the structured course materials and faculty guidelines called routinely for self-evaluation by the Set of how it is functioning. What was still missing was any serious attempt to measure, then capture and compare, the outcomes of that self-evaluation so that generalizations could be offered.

Cyril Atkinson (1998), IMCA's Chair of the Global School of Quality

Management, then proposed and implemented a quantified pattern of measures of Session Effectiveness (derived from Schein's work on Process Consulting) and of Set Health Checks (after Taylor's work at Hoechst Marion Roussell on Facilitation of Self Supervised Work Teams). The latter specifically enables the Set to create and evaluate its own Morale Chart over its life together, to understand what is falling short and to resolve to act to improve and measure again later. It is too early to say how powerful such an approach will eventually be, but it has gained immediate acceptance among faculty as both valid and valuable, and constitutes a real breakthrough.

We began this section by commenting on how valuable face-to-face interaction is. The arrival of Internet discussion forums within IMCA since 1994 has, however, led to heated debate about the relative cost benefits of face-to-face and virtual discourse. Not surprisingly the emergent solution is a mixture of the two, but our perception of what can be accomplished via Internet discussion forums is still growing daily – even though it is still frequently obscured by Associate and faculty difficulties with the technologies. Working with Marriotts International Hotel Group and early CyberSets we have established so-called Golden Rules for effective/quality action learning within the CyberSets. We have also crafted assignments, such as the Evaluative Assessment of Virtual Learning, which require all Associates consciously to assess how the new medium is working and its relativity with face-to-face workshop sessions.

At the completion of the first tranche of CyberSet programmes, Sandelands (1998) has distilled outcomes for the future balanced use of such virtual relationships in CyberSets and face-to-face high cost meetings.

Learning support from the workplace
We have identified already that the reactions and support of workplace colleagues to the action learning and action research work Associates were undertaking has been consistently disappointing in their eyes. Research showed that that was seldom the perception of the superiors or colleagues concerned, however. They saw what had happened, and what the Associate had achieved as well worth while and normally meritorious. As such, we have long concluded that there could never be enough support from colleagues at work for an Associate undertaking the programmes, which were always done in post rather than full time to ensure that connectivities with real work are not lost.

We resolved recently with British Airports Authority (BAA plc) in the UK, which placed 50 Associates on three joint IMCA/University of Surrey postgraduate programmes simultaneously, that we should take a different perspective on workplace support. We had exhaustively briefed colleagues and involved them via Steering Groups including project selection, and as Counterpart Tutors to the IMCA Faculty, to no apparent incremental improved effect. The different perspective was to take the outputs that were created by Associates, officially distil their crucial/best elements, and use the faculty team as advocates and disseminators of such distilled outcomes around the enterprise.

The endeavour is called Project Harvest, and a Director (Published Learning) as she is called, has been appointed full time to ensure that it is well carried forward. Its current manifestation gives high prominence to the Associates' outcomes and assertively requires attention from workplace colleagues. The outcomes are also 'published', so considerable pride can be taken in them. This does not of course replace the solo efforts of individual Associates to publicize and win support for their own propositions, but it adds status to them.

It must be said that it did not begin thus. Initially Project Harvest was conceived simply as a database of all the assignments produced, which was key-worded and searchable. But in successive debates at IMCA's bi-annual face-to-face global meetings it was enhanced into a proactive use of the outcomes. The database is still there, but the emphasis is on the creation of distilled crucial/best issues for determined communication. Faculty working with in-company Sets are required not simply to mark assignments but to draft the initial distillation, present it to the whole Set on the Internet as part of the feedback, and thereby invite all Set members to polish it prior to its 'publication' around the enterprise.

The Director (Published Learning)'s role is to monitor all this activity and to ensure that 'publication' does, whenever possible, also reach open dissemination in refereed journals. IMCA also maintains a suite of three of its own house e-journals, under the imprint of Internet Free Press, that carries all the outputs including literature reviews as first-instance publications for other members of IMCA globally, with the refereeing process seen as the responsibility of the faculty members concerned.

This lateral thinking looks well placed to trigger measures of effective enterprise dissemination and of refereed quality determination for the generalized body of knowledge. In this way, we believe ongoing workplace supportiveness will be enhanced because the dissemination is continuous throughout the programme.

To conclude on this element of quality in the learning process, it is important not to underestimate just how much support has always and continues to come from colleagues at work, even though it seems many Associates' appetites can never be sated. Since each assignment must necessarily be about the workplace, and since the assignments necessarily take the Associate into other realms of activity with which he or she does not normally engage, they cannot be accomplished without collaboration. Optimizing that quite clearly requires good interpersonal skills as well as the insight to play a non-zero sum game strategy. Quantitative measures such as those introduced by Atkinson on Set Health Checks are clearly worthy of early extension to this external collaborative activity and are now being incorporated into the assignment guidelines, with marks allocated for the way in which workplace colleagues have been motivated to contribute and assist.

Finally, it should be noted that the major impact of the above comments has been for in-company Sets rather than open Sets. Associates on the latter do also express disappointment at the lack of contribution by their own workplace colleagues, but seem to be more understanding thereof. As with in-company Associates, their response in line with Rosenthal's findings on teams (1997) is to strengthen the within-Set solidarity and perceived supportiveness.

Faculty and library resources
We have considered the significance of faculty members in facilitating self-learning Sets already. Here we shall look at the way in which faculty are looked upon as repositories of subject area wisdom, and the same applies to the 'library' function broadly defined as books/articles/grey literature/coursewares and guidance notes. But initially it will be useful also to comment on the authority role of the Faculty member in adult education.

In action learning, where the Associate is deliberately encouraged to define the curriculum to be studied, the faculty member clearly exercises a reduced but ultimately quasi-absolute pattern of authority. Each Associate will submit assignments to be marked, and the faculty member is responsible for allocating the marks. Among adult learners this, we have discerned, can only be achieved effectively if the Associate accepts the judgements implied and that the quality of feedback given is timely and actionable to improve subsequent performance. To ensure this, CyberSets are now inviting Doctoral Associates (one of the most adult and educationally experienced groups one could expect to work with outside 'own' staff development groups), who have received feedback, to then give their own feedback to faculty on the extent to which it was timely and actionable – and indeed perceived as a fair judgement. To everyone's delight and amazement, a very high level of debate takes place from all sides, and the CyberSet has already evolved its own protocols for the process, including an assertive attitude towards service levels guaranteed and met. This type of interchange has led many senior faculty to conclude that the Internet offers a pattern for learning *superior* to many traditional tertiary educational models.

The use of faculty members as 'subject area experts' is most strongly felt in doctoral work, where the Associate is surely seeking to advance knowledge rather than find a helpful way around what is already known in whole or in part. We have developed no coherent measure for this element of quality on our programmes, since it is seldom possible to separate it out from the learning approach that suggests Associates should find out for themselves by searching the literature. Faculty members as subject area experts are expected rather to know how to help others find the specifics of a particular industry rather than have *ex-cathedra* knowledge to pass on. In this respect our embedded key-word searches from Anbar Management Intelligence and the Virtual Library support provided from Emerald and the British Library are incomparable (Sandelands, 1998).

Ironically, however, these seemingly satisfactory outcomes spurred further action and development as faculty development Sets were initiated in the wake of IMCA's joint ventures, first with the University of Surrey as described in Part 1 of this chapter, and then with Oxford Brookes University.

IMCA has, since its inception, insisted on faculty induction workshops to ensure that the specifics of action learning are understood and the Associates not left stranded. However, in a serious endeavour to share the nature of the university alliances that were being forged, and how they paradoxically had the potential to enrich but also the acute danger to dilute action learning, we resolved to convene faculty development workshops on a continuous basis. Effectively Faculty were formed into 'permanent' self-learning Sets, not driven by programmes they were formally delivering as a faculty team, but for the sake of learning together. Not surprisingly, the provision for them to take IMCA qualifications as a focus was also followed at Masters, Doctoral and Distinguished Professorial levels. Earlier attempts to focus simply on 'delivery effectiveness' had not been sustainable.

The faculty Sets met extensively face to face and explored issues such as improved coursewares and learning resources generally, and most recently using a CyberSet process globally to enhance research supervisory skills among senior faculty members. This latter proposition has been most vital for the growing demands at Doctoral level in the Orient, and will surely be shortly mirrored in the need for Virtual Tutors and Set Advisers for Cyber-Sets – especially via our colleagues at the Canadian School of Management which provides global SYSOPS for CyberSets. It grew from Ainslie's extension (1998) of her pioneering ISO 9002 activities on just such a faculty development Set.

No matter how well any Set or CyberSet relates with its given tutorial team – and we have empowered Sets to change tutors if they find them unsatisfactory after deliberate mutual attempts at improvement – there will always be a feeling that perhaps out there somewhere is a faculty member who could be better matched. To enable this, the Mk IV Registry and Faculty Database maintained by global EDI have been made partly searchable via Internet access. Associates and faculty can search to see what previous dissertations/theses have been written, what faculty members' CVs contain, what current research activities are in process, and, via the

Director (Published Learning), what new/grey literature is available on outcomes from IMCA's own graduates. These all use the same thesaurus as Anbar Management Intelligence for ease of access. Finally, IMCA sponsors, via MCB University Press, Anbar's publishers, and thereafter provides global access to numerous subject area and regional management Forums and to the Best Practice Club of enterprises willing to share and compare.

There is little room to doubt that the quantum leap in availability of knowledge, including grey literature, via the Internet from pioneering investors such as MCB University Press, has transformed and democratized the processes of learning. The quality of this resourcing is so clearly way beyond most of our previous experience that any cogent critique is almost non-existent. Whilst this will not continue for too long, it does enable attention to be focused more on the other elements of the learning dynamics discussed earlier.

Scope remains for continuous improvement, but what is most encouraging is the manner in which the search for and deployment of metrics within the learning processes has been welcomed by faculty and Associates alike, and applauded by sponsoring employers. The focus for research and continuous improvement can accordingly be summarized as:

- programme determinism;
- Associates' competence at learning how to action learn together;
- the engineering of a supportive workplace environment;
- the resourcefulness of Faculty services in support of Associates' learning;
- the accessibility and appropriateness of requisite library/knowledge services.

References

Ainslie, M. (1996) 'ISO 9002 Quality Charters', to be found at http://www.imc.org.uk/imc/news/iso9002/quality.htm.

Ainslie, M., (1998) 'Dynamic quality assurance in International Management Centres', Quality Management Program UK7, IMCA Buckingham, UK.

Asser, M. and Haines, J. (1995) 'A quest for the best', *International Journal of Public Sector Management*, Vol. 8 No. 7, pp. 6–14.

Atkinson, C., (1998) 'Set dynamics: the creation of a learning environment', 13th Annual Professional Congress of IMCA, Cape Town, April, IMCA Buckingham UK, can be found at http://www.imc.org.uk/imc/apc-1999/papers/cyril-atkinson-1.html.

Bacon, D. R., Stewart, K. A. and Giclas, H. (1996) *Journal of Management Education*, Vol. 20 No. 2, pp. 265–75.

Ball, C. (1991) 'Learning pays', *Education+ Training*, Vol. 33 No. 4, pp. 4–5.

Boaden, R. J. and Dale, B. G. (1993) 'Teamwork in services: quality circles by another name?', *International Journal of Service Industry Management,* Vol. 4 No. 1, pp. 5–24.

Campbell, J. (1996) 'From bricks and mortar to service excellence', *Business Quarterly,* Summer, pp. 65–9.

Cave, M., Harvey, S. and Henkel, M. (1995) 'Performance measurement in higher education – revisited', *Public Money and Management*, October/December, pp. 17–23.

Cleary, B. A. (1996) 'Relearning the learning process', *Quality Progress*, April, pp. 79–85.

CNAA (1992a) *Evaluating the Quality of the Student Experience,* February, CNAA, London.

CNAA (1992b) *Academic Quality in Higher Education: A Guide to Good Practice in Framing Regulations,* July, CNAA, London.

Collins, D., Cockburn, M. and MacRobert, I. (1991) 'Sandwell College: provider of quality assured education', *Quality Forum*, Vol. 17 No. 3, September, pp. 126–8.

Doherty, G. D. (1995) 'Accountability and excellence in education', *Total Quality Review,* January/February, pp. 37–44.

Farrugia, C. (1996) 'A continuing professional development model for quality assurance in higher education', *Quality Assurance in Education*, Vol. 4 No. 2, pp. 28–34.

Ghobadian, A. and Terry, A. J. (1995) 'How Alitalia improves service quality through quality function deployment', *Managing Service Quality*, Vol. 5 No. 5, pp. 25–30.

Goulden, C. (1996) 'Supervisory management and quality circle performance: an empirical study', *Benchmarking for Quality Management & Technology,* Vol. 2 No. 4, pp. 61–74.

Green, D. (1996) 'A case for Koalaty Kid', *Quality Progress,* August, pp. 97–9.

Hill, F. M. (1995) 'Managing service quality in higher education: the role of the student as primary consumer', *Quality Assurance in Education*, Vol. 3 No. 3, pp. 10–21.

Himmett, K. and Knight, P. (1996) 'Quality and assessment', *Quality Assurance in Education,* Vol. 4 No. 3, pp. 3–10.

Honey, P. and Mumford, A., (1986) 'Using your learning styles', Maidenhead, Honey; also Mumford, A., (1996) 'Effective learners in action learning sets', *Employee Counselling Today*, Vol. 8 No. 6.

Hosie, P. (1995) 'Promoting quality in higher education using human resource information systems', *Quality Assurance in Education,* Vol. 3 No. 1, pp. 30–5.

Idrus, N. (1996) 'Towards total quality management in academia', *Quality Assurance in Education,* Vol. 4 No. 3, pp. 34–40.

Kozubska, J. and Wills, G. (1992) 'Total quality assurance on IMC programmes', 4th IMCA Annual Professional Congress, @http://www.imc.org.k/imv/news/daproces/dap20.htm .

Lo, V. H. Y. and Sculli, D. (1996) 'An application of TQM concepts in education', *Training for Quality,* Vol. 4 No. 3, pp. 16–22.

McRobert, I. (1995) 'Hermeneutics and human relations', *Total Quality Review,* January/February, pp. 45–52.

Margerison, C. and McCann, D. (1985) 'How to lead a winning team', MCB University Press.

Marsh, P. (1991) 'Bounce in the showroom', *Times Higher Education Supplement,* 1 November.

Morgan, M. (1990) 'Quality circles: management accounting applications', *Management Accounting*, November, pp. 48–51.

Morgan, N. A. and Piercy, N. F. (1992) 'Market-led quality', *Industrial Marketing Management*, Vol. 21, pp. 111–18.

Muller, D. and Tonnell, V. (1993) 'Learner perceptions of quality and the learner career', *Quality Assurance in Education*, Vol. 1 No. 1, pp. 29–33.

Mumford, A. (1996) '5-year continuing review: progress to 1996', *Jubilee Fellowship Report*, @ http://www. imc.org.k/imc/news/occpaper/9apr96.htm .

Mumford, A. (ed.) (1997) *Action Learning at Work*, Aldershot, Gower Press, being an anthology of 30+ evaluative studies of IMC action learning activities since 1982.

Mumford, A. and Honey. P. (1986) *Using Your Learning Styles,* Maidenhead, Honey.

O'Neal, C. R. and LaFief, W. C. (1992) 'Marketing's lead role in total quality', *Industrial Marketing Management*, Vol. 21, pp. 133–43.

Peters, J. (1988) 'Customers first: the independent answer', *Business Education*, Vol. 9 No. 3/4, pp. 34–41.

Peters, J. (1995) 'Quality assessing the virtual business school', David Sutton Fellowship Report, @ http://www.imc.org.k/imc/news/occpaper/sutton.htm .

Peters, J. and Wills, G. (1996) 'ISO 9000 as a global educational accreditation structure', State Department Conference, Washington DC, for The Center for Quality Assurance in International Education, 9 May @http://www.imc.org.k/imc/news/occpaper/washingt.htm.

Pitman, G., Motwami, J., Ashok, K. and Chun, H. C. (1996) 'QFD application in an educational setting', *International Journal of Quality & Reliability Management,* Vol. 13 No. 4, pp. 99–108.

Revans, R. (1971) *Developing Effective Managers,* New York, Praeger.

Revans, R. (1982) *The Origins and Growth of Action Learning,* Bromley, Chartwell Bratt.

Rippin, A., White, J. and Marsh, P. (1994) 'Quality assessment to quality enhancement', *Quality Assurance in Education*, Vol. 2 No. 1, pp. 13–20.

Rosenthal, E. (1997) 'Social networks and the team performance', *Team Performance Management*, Vol. 3 No. 4.

Sandelands, E. (1998) 'Creating an online library to support a virtual learning community', *Internet Research,* Vol. 8 No. 1; reprinted as Chapter 16 in *The Virtual University*, Teare, R. *et al.* (1998) Cassell.

Schoengrund, C. (1996) 'Aristotle and total quality management', *Total Quality Management,* Vol. 7 No. 1, pp. 79–91.

Showalter, M. J. and Mulholland, J. A. (1992) 'Continuous improvement strategies for service organizations', *Business Horizons,* July/August, pp. 82–7.

Sommerville, A. K. (1996) 'Changing culture', *Quality Assurance in Education*, Vol. 4 No. 1, pp. 32–6.

Sutton, D. (1990) 'Action learning in search of P', *Industrial and Commercial Training,* Vol. 22 No. 1, @ http://www.imc.org.k/imc/news/daproces/dap16.htm .

Teare, R. (1996) 'The dynamic curriculum: a prospectus for organizational learning', IMC Joint Atherton & Sutton Fellowship Report, @ http://www.imc.org.k/imc/news/bulletins/fellow.htm.

Thomas, J. (1991) 'How IMC helps its associates learn how to learn', MPhil thesis, Buckingham, IMCA.

Thomas, J. (1993) 'Researching learning to learn', @ http://www.imc.org.k/imc/news/daproces/dap 13.htm.

Sandelands, E. (1999) *Cyber Tutoring and Learning: How to Facilitate Action Learning Online,* GAJAL Published Papers, Vol. 3 No. 2, http://www.free-press.com/journals/gajal/published-papers.htm.

Wills, G. and Oliver, C. (1996a) 'ROI, measuring the ROI from management action learning', *Management Development Review,* Vol. 9 No. 1, pp. 17–21, @ http://www.imc.org.k/imc/surrey.uni/papers/roi.htm.

Wills, G. and Oliver, C. (1996b) 'ROI in management development', *Management Development Review,* Vol. 9 No. 1; reprinted as Chapter 10 in *The Knowledge Game, op. cit.*; further reprinted as Chapter 30 in *Action Learning at Work*, A. Mumford (ed.) (1997) Gower Press (Chapter 13 in this book draws heavily on this article).

Wills, G. and Ainslie, M., (1997) 'Designing a quality action learning process for managers', 2nd ICIT @ Luton Hoo, England; reprinted in *Journal of Workplace Learning*, Vol. 9 No. 3; further reprinted as Chapter 10 in *The Knowledge Game, G.* Wills (ed.) (1998) Cassell (Part 2 of this chapter draws heavily on that article).

Chapter 13

Credit mapping

Validating work-based training using action learning outcomes

JULIAN WILLS

Credit mapping – learning frameworks in the UK

Credit is the currency of the academic system. Academic credit is a medium of exchange and is used to give a value to an amount of learning. Credits are awarded on the successful achievement of a set of clearly defined 'learning outcomes', regardless of the actual time involved or the mode of learning (Davies, 1998).

Credit has been used as a powerful tool for opening up access to learning opportunities by some innovative education providers (Robertson, 1994). This is increasingly the challenge facing all providers of higher education. The central proposition turns upon the need for a unified credit system containing accepted and agreed definitions of outcomes, units and credits, and which can lead to a 'credit framework'. A coherent credit framework permits recognition of learning that has not been formally recognized in the past. Credit also facilitates and encourages progression from level to level and permits transfer between institutions, thus widening student choice (Davies, 1998).

The learning outcomes model

A central strategy for the development of credit is the adoption of a learning outcomes model which specifies what each student is expected to know, understand or do as a result of the course of study. A learning outcome may be defined as something that a person would be expected to know, or to understand, or be able to do as the result of a specific learning experience (Davies, 1998). Once this is defined it is possible to assess the learning that has taken place. Learning outcomes are written in both general and specific terms and may focus upon academic knowledge and understanding, skills (often implicit rather than explicit) and personal development.

The aim of adopting this system is to encourage students to reflect both on what they know and what they can do as a result of their course. It also provides a method of assessing explicit achievements across the full range of subjects and disciplines and is a means of ensuring comparability of standards.

The trend towards the identification of learning outcomes shifts the focus of performance to the learner, who must be able to demonstrate the achievement of criteria that attest to successful learning, and away from the teacher's ability to provide the inputs to the process (Entwistle, 1992). As a result of this approach there exists an increased need for guidance and better information for students. It is also clear that there also needs to be a central referral point to which students and tutors can turn, during the life of a course, for advice and information (Davies and Nedderman, 1997).

Levels of achievement in academic and vocational learning

Mapping and planning the wider curriculum for adult learners is desirable yet problematic. The challenge is the development of a credit framework to enable and regulate learner mobility between academic and vocational domains (Davies and Nedderman, 1997).

In the past this process has proved difficult to achieve, as the British education system is not based on an explicit and rational framework of levels that systematically defines the progressive characteristics of learning and attainment. Rather it is based on a series of qualification frameworks whose relationship to level has not been unambiguously defined (SEEC, 1996a, 1996b). However, the development and use of CAT schemes (Credit Accumulation and Transfer) has led to a sharper focus on the matter of judging levels of intellectual development and attainment in programmes of study or experiential and work-based learning. It has also required institutions to make decisions about 'comparability' and relative values of prior experience and past attainment for entry and progression. Thus, we have gone from a situation where a few institutions have developed local CAT schemes to a situation in which most institutions have established and use a credit framework across all, or most, of their provision (Davies, 1998).

The main difficulty which remains to be resolved is the articulation of, first, academic, and second, vocational or workplace frameworks so that achievement in one framework can be recognized within the other. This is an important barrier to the development of dual accreditation of programmes in different awards frameworks.

Demand for dual accreditation stems from the growing area of partnership or client-negotiated programmes where a university designs and delivers, in partnership with an employer, a customized programme. Learning can involve mixtures of institution-based teaching, in-company research, work-based learning, distance learning and intensive residential study. Consequently, the accreditation of academic and vocational learning was a major issue on the agenda of higher education in the second half of the 1990s (Lloyd-Langton and Portwood, 1994).

In response to increasing demand for adaptive and responsive adult educational provision which is not restricted by the site of learning or the age of the student, the IMCA works with the providers of workplace and professional development programmes to develop credit maps based upon in-company training programmes. The credit mapping process applies the learning outcomes model as a means of comparing workplace learning outcomes with action learning-based qualifications. The aim of this approach is the development of highly workplace-relevant action learning awards. By validating existing training programmes, the site of learning remains within the organization, so broadening the scope and constituency of the learning process.

The approach which has been developed compares the learning outcomes of training courses with the postgraduate Action Learning Certificate in Management Studies (Action Learning CMS). Effectively this course equates to the first third of an MBA and is nominally allocated 60 'M' level (or Masters level) Degree Credits. A full MBA requires 180 'M' level Degree Credits. Experience has shown that the learning outcomes of this course are most closely aligned with those common to workplace or professional development programmes aimed at middle or senior managers. This is the current focus of IMCA credit mapping activity, for which the following process forms the basis for clear guidance on the assessment of learning outcomes.

It is acknowledged that the development of action learning CMS courses based upon existing training courses is an unorthodox approach to the validation of workplace learning. Generally the approach adopted in the higher education sector will grant credit for prior learning towards a university programme or deliver client-negotiated programmes, where a university designs a customized programme in partnership with an employer. In contrast, the IMCA approach places the emphasis upon the delivery of a customized programme, but not one which necessarily alters the tried and tested approaches already in place. Consequently, it is imperative that the rules by which credit can be accumulated and transferred towards an award must be clear, to facilitate coherent patterns of study for students and to safeguard academic standards.

To address this concern the approach to credit mapping which has been developed clearly defines the learning objectives required for the validation of an award, but also recognizes that:

1. tutors are integral to the process of course design and delivery and that students also need to be actively involved in the learning process if credit is to be an intrinsic part of their achievement; and
2. the importance of clear guidance arrangements if adult learners are to benefit from credit and use it for the purposes of access and progression.

To enable this process it is important that the organization facilitating the credit mapped course has a firm grasp of the principles of action learning and the outcomes which are required of Associates completing the courses. Therefore, in addition to providing clear guidance in relation to learning outcomes, the credit mapping process also aims to empower key staff from the training providers to deliver and eventually develop action learning courses. This objective is achieved through the induction of tutors and key members of staff from the training provider into the IMCA faculty.

The credit mapping process

The process of developing a credit map-based action learning CMS involves the consideration of the necessary learning outcomes in two distinct areas:

1. Core disciplines; and
2. Action learning requirements.

Part 1: Core disciplines

The action learning CMS requires understanding in two core disciplines, and the theories and principles underpinning these disciplines as they apply in organizational settings. The core disciplines comprise:

- financial management;
- human resource management;
- information management;
- marketing management;
- operations management.

Each of these areas has its own particular set of learning outcomes against which the learning outcomes of the training course must be compared. More generally, the study of core disciplines focuses upon:

- facilitating specification and/or measurement and control;
- addressing functional and strategic topics;
- the development of policy and new systems formulation;
- specialist support function work such as auditing and quality management.

The first part of the credit mapping process concentrates on achieving equivalence with the following core objectives of Action Learning CMS level study.

- Analytical and managerial competences appropriate to organizations and operations in a national setting and, where possible and appropriate, an international one.

- Transferable intellectual skills relevant to the study and practice of management in manufacturing and the service sector.
- The ability to define, investigate, analyse, evaluate and respond to the tactical and strategic issues of concern to organizations.

Part 2: Demonstrating the process of action learning
This part of the process involves the induction of key staff from the training provider into the IMCA. Inducted staff are thus empowered to carry the credit mapping process forward within IMCA protocols and to develop postgraduate action learning CMS programmes based on their existing training provision. The IMCA provides such additional support as may be necessary for this process.

This part of the credit mapping process is more subjective than the first, and therefore necessitates great attention to detail if a credit map is to be successfully developed. IMCA requires all Associates to follow an action learning approach. Consequently, there is a general requirement that programmes of study at action learning CMS level should enable Associates to:

- adapt and adjust to the systems, procedures and organizational culture in the Associate's own organization;
- contribute effectively to the tasks associated with managerial work at unit level.

These requirements relate to the following action learning objectives of action learning CMS level study:

- An understanding of the organizational and environmental context within which managers operate.
- The capacity of Associates to manage their own learning and self-development in the context of organizational change.

Equivalence with these requirements necessitates the demonstration of an understanding of the process of action learning and how it applies to the Associate's own workplace.

Facilitating action learning
The IMCA accomplishes the action learning objectives of CMS level study through the following assignments.

- Written analysis of the Associate's own organization and career development and of the interface relationships (integrative assignment) between management functions therein and the Associate's own department. This assignment (the OOM/CD) requires the Associate to reflect upon his or her position prior to the start of a course of learning.

- Evaluative assessment of management learning (EAML) and the quality achieved at the conclusion of the programme. This assignment is based upon on a Learning Log in which Associates are required to keep track of their learning process and specifically consider personal career development, the evaluative assessment of action taken and continuing management development issues.

These forms of assignment are important to the credit mapping process as they provide a vehicle by which Associates on credit mapped courses can be introduced to and take stock of their learning. It may be the case that a course to be credit mapped addresses these elements, especially if it has been developed specifically as an action learning-based course. Therefore, for longer professional development courses it may be possible to map learning outcomes directly against an award. However, where individuals take a number of short courses it may be necessary to require Associates to start the course of study with an additional assignment based upon the OOM/CD. They may then move on to a number of short courses or a single in-depth course, provided the core disciplines are covered. As such courses commonly have no form of assessment, Associates need to keep track of their learning. This can be accomplished through the requirement that Associates develop and implement action plans and reflect upon this process in a log book. This process is important as Associates *must* be able to demonstrate what they have gained from the core assignments in the form of an assignment that can be made available for external examination (the IMCA use the EAML assignment).

Figure 13.1 is an example of how the IMCA develops action learning CMS courses based upon the existing training provision of either an organization or upon the courses offered by a training provider. Faculty induction enables key staff to facilitate this process and ensure that the necessary learning outcomes are achieved. The credit mapped 'route' illustrated demonstrates how a number of short courses may be combined to provide the core disciplines required (see Part 1). The additional action learning assignments ensure that the Associate reflects upon the learning process and fulfils the action learning requirements of the action learning CMS (see Part 2).

Conclusion
In recent years the university sector has fundamentally altered the means by which qualifications are assessed. The development of modular and credit-based learning, and the accreditation of learning acquired outside the academic environment, is resulting in a reconceptualization of the mea-

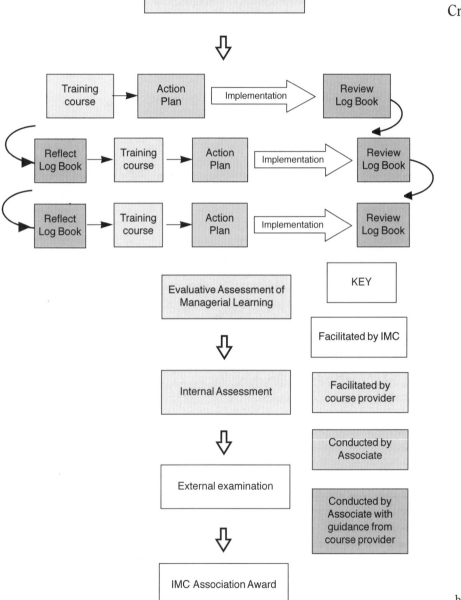

Figure 13.1
Example action
learning CMS-
based credit map

surement of academic achievement. The development of credit-based learning has prompted a move from a system which defines progression in terms of years to one in which progression is defined in terms of the changing characteristics of learning and attainment (Davies, 1998). Despite this progress, the means by which the academic and workplace learning frameworks may be articulated and compared remains confused.

In contrast to predominantly academic approaches to learning, action learning-based qualifications emphasise learning centred on the workplace. By facilitating a process by which workplace learning is conceptualized and placed in an academic context, action learning-based qualifications are well suited to provide a link between academic knowledge of the core managerial disciplines and the context within which skills are demonstrated. As the learning outcomes required by action learning-based courses relate directly to the Associate's place of work, the process of comparing the action learning credit framework with that present within the workplace is less problematic than if a more purely theoretical/academic framework is considered.

It is recognized that the rules and guidance by which credit can be accumulated and transferred towards an award are vitally important in order to facilitate understanding of the process, coherent patterns of study for students and to safeguard academic standards. Therefore, in addition to providing clear guidance in relation to learning outcomes, the credit mapping process also aims to empower key staff from the training providers to deliver and eventually develop action learning courses. This objective is achieved through the induction of tutors and key members of staff from the training provider into the IMCA faculty.

Inevitably this approach implies that some additional academic requirements may be required if a certificated award is to be gained. Specifically, it is likely that written assignments shall be imposed where in the past they may not have been a requirement of a training course. However, as the course may be based on existing training provision, it is possible to make the action learning elements of the course optional for those students who wish to gain a qualification – so enhancing student choice. This emphasises that the approach to credit mapping outlined in this chapter enables workplace and professional development courses to form the basis of certificated awards. The strength of the approach is that it addresses the demand for adaptive and responsive adult educational provision where it is needed and in a manner which is not restricted by the site of learning or the age or circumstances of the student. This approach has significant implications for organizations that recognize the benefits of workplace training but also perceive a need to make provision for higher awards on the basis of such training. Postgraduate certificate level qualifications provide a useful stepping stone not only to higher IMC awards but also to those offered by other institutions. Conversely, for the training provider, the ability to offer certificated awards to those who request it and on the basis of a selection of training courses adds value to the services they offer and 'thickens' their sales in the process.

References

Davies, D. (1995) *Credit Where It's Due,* Employment Department and University of Cambridge.

Davies, D. (1998) 'The virtual university: a learning university, Part 3: the learning framework', *Journal of Workplace Learning,* Vol. 10 No. 4, pp. 175–213.

Davies, D. and Nedderman, V. (1997) 'Information and on-course guidance to continuing education students', *Managing Guidance in Higher Education,* pp. 46–55, HEQC, London.

Entwistle, N. (1992) *The Impact of Teaching on Learning Outcomes in Higher Education,* London, CVCP.

Lloyd-Langton, M. and Portwood, D. (1994) 'Dual accreditation of work based learning: the relation of NVQs and academic credit', *Journal of Higher and Further Education,* Vol. 18 No. 2, Summer.

Otter, S. (1997) *An Abilities Curriculum,* Department for Education and Employment.

Robertson, D. (1994) *Choosing to Change: Extending Access, Choice and Mobility,* London, HEQC.

SEEC (1996a) *Credit Guidelines, Models and Protocols,* May.

SEEC (1996b) *Guidelines for Credit and Consortium General Credit Rating,* SEEC/DfEE.

Chapter 14

Measuring ROI from individual then organizational learning

GORDON PRESTOUNGRANGE AND CAROL OLIVER

Well-constructed management development and learning clearly presage a potential ROI (Return on Investment). The question at budget time each year has to be: How much? And over what timescale?

We are among the 'believers' that management development programmes are a good investment. We believe they are good for the people who participate. We believe we know from regular experience that they are good for the people who stay behind and who, by default, then get more scope to flex their muscles and brains when the favoured one is away. We believe that wise organizations will capture the learning by individuals into learnt systems and the cultural way we do things around here. But there are seemingly no analyses where such beliefs are systematically checked out with data of the hard programme ROI, at the end, then one year and five years later.

Between 1992 and 1999, we tracked what occurred when over £10 million was invested on MBA and doctoral programme fees to develop just under 1,000 managers, in fifteen countries around the world. Questionnaires were completed and their contents debated for six hours at graduation time in each of the years in question to explore their validity – at venues as globally distributed as London, Hong Kong, Cape Town, Curacao, Johannesburg, Helsinki, Oxford, Kuala Lumpur, Surfers Paradise, Buckingham, Harrogate and Amsterdam. The MBA and doctoral programmes were organized by the global International Management Centres Association, the leading action learning multinational professional institution, following the principles set down by Reg Revans over 50 years ago.

This study ($n = 280$) covers just one part of what has now, over eighteen years, become a £60+ million tranche of investment made for over 10,000 managers by more than 1,000 enterprises in 44 countries using the processes of action learning with the IMCA.

Best estimates indicate that the managers concerned spent 2,500+ hours each, some 2.5 million hours in total, talking with one another, with colleagues, sharing their managerial problems and challenges and helping one another to come to terms with actions which needed to be taken. IMCA faculty members, skilled and knowledgeable in their own areas, participated in their meetings, sometimes face to face and more recently via the Internet meeting places and forums, for all on such development programmes. Their role was to help the managers to be aware of what was already known in the areas they were seeking to improve, and to help them to discover new knowledge where necessary. The 10,000 managers in the overall programme spent an estimated eighteen million hours at the task. It is the largest-ever tranche of action learning programmes ever undertaken since Reg Revans originally formulated his propositions.

Just under half the 1,000 managers went on to implement most or all of their recommended courses of action with the support of their sponsoring organizations. These typically required investments which were well in excess of five times the programme fees and, on not infrequent occasions, in excess of £1 million. These investments in their turn yielded satisfactory returns, through major cost reductions and new revenues.

> My employer gave me full opportunity, responsibility and freedom to implement my projects.

> My employer invested £1.2 million to fully implement the project. We gained a threefold return in the first twelve months.

> Overheads fell by 18 million pounds per annum.

> . . . by three million pounds per annum.

> We stayed in business rather than making an undignified exit.

In addition, a wide range of non-financial benefits were cited. Human resource planning was improved, staff turnover rates reduced, market share increased, new distributors or suppliers found, and so forth.

This analysis suggests that the 1,000 managers triggered at least £30 million of investment to implement their action plans, with ROI expected of £150 million. Judgemental extrapolation suggests the 10,000 probably triggered over £300 million, with one and half a billion pounds ROI. Certainly some programmes!

This particular quantum of managerial development by action learning, *par excellence*, exemplifies the case for investing an enterprise's funds in such programmes regardless (and we say regardless advisedly) of whether the manager with an MBA or doctoral qualification stays with or leaves the sponsoring enterprise; and regardless of how much the individual *per se* may or may not have learned. This is not intended to belittle individual learning for a single moment. Our purpose here is to argue that soft benefits do not need to be educed to justify management development of the action learning variety. More and more of it should be done within any and every enterprise until the marginal hard ROI equates with other projects in hand. Educationists should cease being afraid of measuring and propagandizing the hard benefits they provide to enterprises.

Did the managers leave their organizations?

No: of course not. Most of them stayed put, relishing their new intellectual understanding and involvement in their enterprise. Would you leave an enterprise that has sponsored you on an MBA or doctoral programme that gave you the broader helicopter view of the business way beyond your previous experience, enhanced your self-confidence, presentation, listening, team and overall people skills, gave you better understanding in particular of financial issues, helped you to become more action-oriented on the critical issues affecting the enterprise, and more timely and objective in the conduct of your role? That is exactly what they reported had happened:

> We found the best solutions often came from those closest to the job. It was dangerous to have our own preconceived ideas or to think we knew best.

> As an action learner I was able to gather information more easily than as a manager; others wanted to help me – even commiserated with me.

> We gained confidence to talk to people at all levels in the enterprise.

> In developing our projects we learned what the other parts of the company did, their purpose and methods of working.

All this, it can be seen, was accomplished in the context of the organization itself, and their dissertation project and theses (while academically rigorous) had to be based on the key ingredients of the future strategies of the enterprise. The conclusions reached normally made their way directly to the boardroom. IMCA invariably involved top managers in the process as mentors, on Steering Committees and sometimes as adjunct faculty. IMCA ensured that bosses were fully aware at all stages of the action learning approach. Subordinates, colleagues and families who took up some of the manager's load while diverting 2,500+ hours to the programme were, by and large, grudgingly supportive too.

Over 90 per cent of the managers concerned were still with their

191

Measuring ROI
from individual
then
organizational
learning

employer at the end, and nearly half had been promoted during the 24-month programme.

The MBA dissertation project was seen as the runaway winner among all the assignments in terms of personal and organizational benefit. It also took the most sweat and tears to create. After that, the human resource or people management area was consistently most greatly valued across the decade, with all the specialist areas of management intelligence, corporate integration, finance, marketing and operations having their own following. These preferences were reassuringly based, first on usefulness to the enterprise and eye-opening potential, and only latterly on the faculty member's particular style and approach to supporting the learning processes. Very few were dismissive of any areas, but where there were regrets it was that the debate had not been vigorous enough.

Which learning resources were most valued?

All manner of resources are available to a work-based learner: yet the greatest contribution of all came from what Revans describes as 'comrades in adversity'. These are the fellow members of the small learning cell that action learning uses, known as the Set. On a semantic differential scale, it averaged 4.0 with a maximum score of 5 available. This pole position has been maintained across the decade: 'Feedback from the Set, the level of interaction and exchange of ideas were both fun and enlivening – as well as invaluable.'

The second greatest contribution came not from the subject area experts but the Set Adviser, or linker/facilitator, with a score of 3.9, which was followed by the tutors with the expertise at 3.8. During the decade these both improved perceptibly but remained behind the Set's own contributions one to another. Next came the course materials issued and found in support (3.8), bosses and mentors (3.2), colleagues at work (3.1), and finally library services with 3.0, with improvements across the decade for all but colleagues at work

One of the most valued but underestimated resources which managers use is feedback from tutors through the marked assignments that go towards the ultimate award of the MBA or doctorate. It is, of course, a crucial moment for faculty to make sure the measures of quality really do justice to the context in which the manager concerned works and seeks to act and improve performance. With programmes in 44 countries over eighteen years ranging from South Pacific islands and African homelands to the more mature Dutch, US, Canadian, UK or Australian economies, it is no small challenge. The verdict given by three-quarters of the managers (with considerable improvement over the decade) was that the process was 'good or very good':

After having done all nine assignments, the habit developed of going through the four learning stages is continuously with me.

Receiving my first A grade for an assignment was the greatest highlight.

I struggled with my Organizational Management assignment, but when I got a good grade it gave me confidence, it was a turning point. I knew I could do it.

How typical were these managers?

There are few ways in which we can assert that the managers who devoted 2,500 hours each to these IMCA programmes to gain the MBA, or even more to gain their doctorate, are normal: normal managers simply do not do this sort of thing. They do not seek and relish the intellectualization of their role as a manager. They live mainly off their wits and their hard-won successful experiences. And why not?

Action learners believe that wits and hard-won experience can be very considerably improved on when they are shared in a rigorous and disciplined way and developed with the benefits of rigorous analysis. Yet it would be erroneous to believe that IMCA's managers were a solely scholarly segment, although over 85 per cent did indeed have Bachelor-level university education (45 per cent) or its equivalent in a professional area (40 per cent). Twenty per cent were straight from their experience – often performing outstandingly on the programme as well as in their workplace.

At the end of the programme all were adamant that they had, for the first time in their lives, learned what learning was. It was continuous, of course, but, most excitingly, they had learned that all managers, all team members, have potentially got different styles and preferences for learning and for working. Unless each manager knows, understands and accommodates these differences, the workplace cannot hope to perform to its best. In this respect they believed they were henceforth and irrevocably a different sort of manager.

What did we do wrong?

If the whole action learning project across eighteen years sounds like an outstanding success, that is simply because it demonstrably has been. Our weaknesses at IMCA were mainly associated with faculty members who found it difficult to meet the expectations of demanding, action- and context-based managers. The second criticism was at the place of work, with top managers and colleagues giving less support than was hoped for. The third complaint was of IMCA's organizing skills for Sets around the globe. And finally, managers looked at themselves and criticized their own inabilities to

193

Measuring ROI
from individual
then
organizational
learning

manage their time effectively and to give enough attention to helping one another learn in Sets. In the new era of Internet Meeting Places and Forums for each Set, this feedback comes through even more clearly and receives the best attention all can give.

Our response to each of these recurring themes has been to empower managers to hire and fire their faculty, to provide boss mentoring development workshops and Steering Groups at work whenever possible, to evaluate and re-engineer our own support organization (leading us on to the Internet at http://www.imc.org.uk/imc/since 1995), and to introduce time management tutorial workshops at the beginning of all our programmes. These four themes of criticism would seem to be endemic to the process itself and are accordingly set to remain with us for ever. Forewarned thus, we have a continuing search to alleviate these complaints permanently on our managerial agenda. And we sensitize all incoming managers to the reality that these will be some of the key issues to live with and learn to manage.

One year and five years later

Since 1982 it has been a requirement of all the IMCA's graduates that they must renew their professional competences at least every five years and attest to what they have achieved. It is known as the Five Year Continuing Renewal. Experience has shown that five years after a major action learning project is normally too late to seek to evaluate its specific benefits. Events will have moved on, and almost always career promotion will have removed the individual concerned within or beyond the enterprise which sponsored participation on the programme.

After one year, however, where we introduced a progress audit option for graduates known as A+, we have had much greater success in seeing the extent to which their end-of-programme assessments have held up. They afford the supporting evidence we needed in the round, albeit with pluses and minuses present. For some, the hoped-for implementation did not happen: 'the organization is now focusing on alternative structures and the original idea has been discounted'. For others, the outcomes were better than expected: 'They actually implemented.'

Our conclusion must accordingly be that while soft benefits will continue to deliver well after the programme is over, through changed behaviours, growth in confidence and the like, most of the sensibly attributable hard ROI is realistically traceable by thorough, evaluative survey methods on completion and during the twelve months following a programme.

Training and development managers should, in our opinion, do a great deal more evaluative research to measure the organizational, and particularly the financial, impact of programmes. In this way, a budget-supportive culture can emerge to supplement the normal generalized feeling of goodwill towards development of staff.

Further reading

Bennett, R. (1990) 'Effective set advising in action learning', *Journal of European Industrial Training*, Vol. 14 No. 7.

Caie, B. (1988) 'Learning in style – reflections on an action learning MBA programme', *Business Education*, Vol. 9 No. 3/4.

Coates, J. (1988) 'An action learning approach to performance review and development', *Business Education,* Vol. 9 No. 3/4.

Cusins, P. (1995) 'Action learning revisited', *Industrial and Commercial Training*, Vol. 27 No. 4.

Espey, J. and Batchelor, P. (1988) 'Management by degrees: a case study in management development', *Business Education*, Vol. 9 No. 3/4.

Gore, L., Toledano, K. and Wills, G., (1994) 'Leading courageous managers on', *Empowerment in Organizations*, Vol. 2 No. 3.

Margerison, C. (1991) '1991 Revans Professorship Report', *Design & Process Newsletter*, Buckingham, International Management Centre.

Mumford, A. (1988) 'Developing managers for the board', *Business Education*, Vol. 9 No. 3/4.

Mumford, A. (1988) 'Effectiveness in management development', *Business Education*, Vol. 9 No. 3/4.

Mumford, A. (1991) 'Learning in action', *Personnel Management,* Vol. 23 No. 7.

Mumford, A. (1994) 'A review of action learning literature', *Management Bibliographies & Reviews*, Vol. 20 Nos 6/7.

Mumford, A. and Honey, P. (1988) 'Developing skills for matrix management', *Business Education*, Vol. 9 No. 3/4.

Peters, J. (1988) 'The new MBA – what it means for managers', *Business Education*, Vol. 9 No. 3/4.

Prideaux, G. (1991) 'Pan setting II', *Training & Management Development Methods*, Vol. 5.

Prideaux, G. (1992) 'Making action learning more effective', *Training & Management Development Methods,* Vol. 6.

Revans, R. (1986) *The Origins and Growth of Action Learning,* Bromley, Chartwell Bratt.

Revans, R. (1988) 'The learning equation: an introduction', *Business Education,* Vol. 9 No. 3/4.

Seekings, D. (1988) talks to Brian Wilson, 'Allied Irish Bank in Britain: organizational and business development through action learning', *Business Education,* Vol. 9 No. 3/4.

Smith, A. (1992) '1992 David Sutton Fellowship Report', *Design & Process Newsletter,* Buckingham, International Management Centres.

Sutton, D. (1988) 'The problems of developing managers in the small firm', *Business Education,* Vol. 9 No. 3/4.

Sutton, D. (1992) 'Action learning in search of P', *Industrial and Commercial Training,* Vol. 2 No. 1.

Thomas, J., 'Researching learning to learn', *Design & Process Newsletter,* Buckingham, International Management Centres.

'Total Quality Assurance' (1992) IMCA's 4th Annual Professional Congress, Buckingham, England, November.

Les Williams (1998) *Mirror Group Newspapers: First Steps to Quality,* GAJAL, Volume 2 Issue 1, can be found at – http://www.free-press.com/journals/gajal/published-papers.htm.

Wills, G. (1988) 'A radical alternative in management education', *Business Education*, Vol. 9 Nos 3/4.

Wills, G. (1988) 'The customer first – faculty last approach to excellence', *Business Education,* Vol. 9 Nos. 3/4.

Wills, G. (1988) 'Wealth creation through management development', *Business Education*, Vol. 9 No. 3/4.

Wills, G. (1991) 'Action learning pan setting', *Training & Management Development Methods*, Vol. 5.

Wills, G. (1993) *Your Enterprise School of Management*, Bradford, MCB University Press.

Zuber-Skerritt, O. and Howell, F. (1993) 'Evaluation of MBA and doctoral programs conducted in Pacific Region', report submitted to the International Management Centres, Pacific Region.

195

Measuring ROI
from individual
then
organizational
learning

Chapter 15

The knowledge harvest

Ensuring you reap what you sow

ANNE CHRISTIE AND ERIC SANDELANDS

The action learning route to knowledge management
Action learners generate new knowledge. With every new project, unique new insights are generated. Drucker (1995) tells us we are entering the knowledge society in which the basic economic resource will be knowledge. The evidence is there for our eyes to see and ears to hear. All those wishing to see their enterprise survive and thrive can hear a clarion call.

Systemize the action learning process in the design of your corporate university, and the new knowledge being created will be quite phenomenal. But if the enterprise as a whole does not earn from this knowledge, then only a partial benefit is gained. Each manager or supervisor will have made a real difference to his or her business area. Tangible results will have been obtained. Consider within your own organization the opportunity cost of being content only to tinker, not grasping the nettle and applying this knowledge enterprise-wide.

The IMCA, and its North American academic partner the Canadian School of Management (CSM), delivers action learning experiences, explained by IMCA's President Emeritus, Reg Revans (1998) as follows:

> We demand that each participant attacks a real-life task for which no course of treatment has yet been suggested, although efforts have already been made to do so. The problem may or may not be in the organization by which the participant is, at the time, employed, nor need it be in any professional field of their acquaintance. The programme is to help the manager develop *as a manager*, not as a business consultant, a staff adviser, a specialist in such-and-such a field or an expert in some other.

For organizations though, the breakthrough thinking came in 1993 when Gordon Wills published his *Enterprise School of Management* (ESM) model in which the generation and capture of new knowledge is built into the learnt systems of organizations, transforming the potential for organizational learning and profit from action learning outcomes. The first ESM was IMCA's official publisher, MCB University Press, a medium-sized enterprise based in the UK.

The second breakthrough emerged from the advances in publishing and communications technologies, particularly the Internet. Teare (1998a) and Sandelands (1998) were among those who developed the ESM model for the online learning age, developing methods of virtual resourcing and action learning programme delivery. All of which would have provided a neat round-up of recent evolutionary history, except that this work formed the foundations for the Internet-resourced and facilitated ESMs established in global organizations including Marriott, Bass, Whitbread and Granada group. The global acceleration in knowledge being created requires effective solutions for these organizations to experience something of the power of the knowledge being unleashed by their people.

Regarding...	Old thinking	New thinking
Resources	Only finite resources of materials available from earth's crust	Finite and potentially infinite resource of ideas created by human minds
Creation principle	No increase in actual sum total of material things	Increases actual sum total of knowledge and ideas
Employing law of...	... diminishing returns due to scarcity of resources resulting in increasing costs per unit	... increasing returns as replication of discoveries leads to falling costs per unit
Markets	Commodity markets based on same products and resources	Value-added markets based on distinctly different products
Ownership	Property rights of things in perpetuity	Limited-time property rights of patents
Goals	Goal is efficient production, extracting efficiencies from labour and machines	Goal is bolstering future discovery through development of human creativity and knowledge
Organization of labour	Division of labour	Peer-to-peer networks
Operative system	Tragedy of the commons when people share and deplete same resource	No diminishment of resource when ideas are shared
Value creation	Value chain of simple relationships	Value networks of complex, interdependent, dynamic relationships

Table 15.1
Evolution from industrial age to new economy

Table 15.1 (Allee, 1999) demonstrates the shift in thinking taking place as organizations reposition themselves for the knowledge economy. For organizations embracing the ESM model, the switch is taking place from industrial- to knowledge-based activity using a systemized approach to generating new knowledge from within, then capturing within learnt systems so that the next questions asked are based upon new ignorance, not the revisiting of old ignorance.

Questions in the action learning process

Many models of knowledge management, while being helpful visuals, miss the vital role of action learning completely. For example, Nonaka's model, which explores knowledge management as a knowledge creation process, categorizes it into discrete elements (Nonaka and Takeuchi, 1995). The 'tacit' knowledge is that which is unspoken, intuitive and unarticulated; the 'explicit' knowledge is that which is articulated – for example, in writing, drawings and computer programs.

	To	
	Tacit	Explicit
Tacit	Socialization	Externalization
Explicit	Internalization	Combination

Figure 15.1
The knowledge
creation process

Nonaka and
Takeuchi, 1995

Drawing upon the work of McLoughlin and Thorpe (1993), McAdam and McCreedy (1999) wonder how knowledge can be categorized like this.

Where does the concept of P and Q knowledge fit with this view, where P is programmed knowledge and Q is knowledge gained by questioning insight. Tacit knowledge does not exactly map onto Q, neither does explicit knowledge exactly map onto P. Thus P and Q represent a different categorization of knowledge. Therefore from a critical standpoint Nonaka's categorization of knowledge is perhaps limited or unidimensional.

The oft-cited formula used to explain action learning is that $L = P + Q$, i.e. learning equals programmed knowledge plus questioning insight. More satisfactory is when the equation is turned around so that the whole thing starts with the questions, because organizations do not just need knowledge, they need the knowledge that makes a difference enabling them to grow and compete. As Peters and Smith (1998) put it:

> . . . before taking medicine, it is very sensible indeed to understand what is wrong with you; that the question must come before the answer. Action learning is an educational methodology that encourages questioning insight, especially in groups, to work towards a deeper understanding. Then when action is taken, it is meaningful, based on a principle of understood causes and likely effect, rather than mythology or symbolism.

So an essential element of the action learning-based knowledge creation process requires a major focus on defining the questions to be undertaken. Does a manager's current workplace frustration matter? To whom does it matter? What is the precise nature of the problem? How does it fit with the stated aims of the organization? Support systems must be available within the organization to assist this questioning process (such as those in Figure 15.2). Where facilitators from the IMCA and CSM are delivering action learning programmes, and the team element is replaced by an action learning set, this is a critical stage in the process.

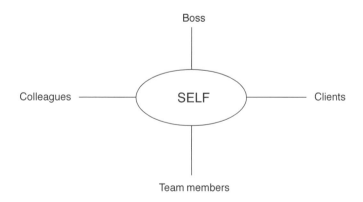

Figure 15.2
Sources of
personal skills
feedback

Margerison &
McCann, 1996

Knowledge management architecture
An action learning agenda and a knowledge management agenda can and must be combined within an organizational framework. Let us start by taking the seven key success factors suggested by Skyrme and Amidon (1997):

1. a strong link to a business imperative;
2. a compelling vision and architecture;
3. knowledge leadership;
4. a knowledge-creating and knowledge-sharing culture;
5. continuous learning;
6. a well-developed technology infrastructure;
7. a systematic organizational learning processes.

Figure 15.3
The concept and
vision of the
learning organiza-
tion

Teare, 1998b

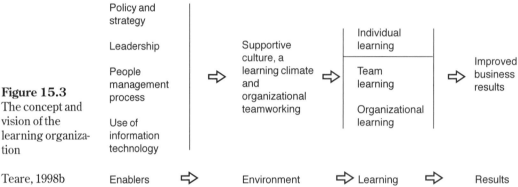

The shared agenda between this vision and the vision of a learning organization within BAA (formerly British Airports Authority) shown in Figure 15.3 is striking – the concentration on business imperatives and results, need for leadership, use of technology and so on. Within BAA the process used to keep the left to right momentum indicated by the arrows was and is action learning. The 'supportive culture, a learning climate and organizational teamworking' being transformed into simultaneously being a 'knowledge-creating and knowledge-sharing culture' by the introduction of Project Harvest.

Ever since IMCA began delivering action learning in-company in 1982 there have been efforts to cascade learning through encouraging participating managers to cascade knowledge to those around them in the organization (e.g. Bowerman and Peters, 1999). Some of this was achieved through analysis of programme outcomes and their effect on profit and loss within the enterprise. Public workshops within the organization have been held to impart knowledge and, of course, implementation plans generated from projects often included amendments or wholesale changes to organizational procedures. However, it was with the partnership to develop managers and facilitate organizational learning within BAA that the emerging knowledge management possibilities became a focus for serious study (Dealtry, 1998).

BAA is the world's largest airports operator with a dominant UK position and has internationalized its operations, notably in Pittsburgh, Indianapolis and Melbourne. In the first wave of action learning programmes, 47 managers were chosen to undertake an average of five projects each, supported by 180 other members of the enterprise as managers, mentors and contributors to the learning process. With the first wave of managers, around 235 new items of knowledge were generated resulting from tackling real business challenges – such as forecasting at Southampton Airport or managing the construction of the Heathrow Express rail service.

Clearly the projects as stand-alone activities created considerable new knowledge. However, the real challenge was to share this knowledge with those others within the organization who could act upon it in their own roles and in response to their own challenges. Project Harvest, as first envisaged, created a database of projects for access and distribution within the enterprise. As Peters *et al.* (1998) have observed: 'Knowledge databases are designed with library tools and must continue in an ever-simpler, more cost effective and more accessible manner.'

Databases are part of the solution, but not the whole solution. In the knowledge age, interpretation skills must come to the fore. Learning organizations building and delivering a global ESM model will generate many thousands of project outcomes directly relevant to organizational success. A database is an essential element, but within an IMCA and CSM designed ESM a macro-level analysis of what the summation of knowledge created means for the organization is a structural element of the knowledge management process. Each tutor and set adviser provides this analysis from the privileged position of having worked with the managers undertaking the projects. A marketing tutor on an in-company action learning MBA programme, for example, does not merely mark each individual's work and provide feedback, but provides a report for the action learning set and the executive team on what the generalizable themes are from all of the projects received.

Networked databases of projects, each with implementation plans that take account of the need to build results into learnt systems, is the first level of Project Harvest. Macro-level analysis and interpretation for use at the Set level and the corporate level is the second layer.

IMCA's Published Learning initiative
Being scholarly organizations, IMCA and CSM have developed substantial processes aimed at informing the community at large of new knowledge as it is developed, in addition to servicing a personal and a corporate need for knowledge and learning. In this process too, the transformation in access provided by the Internet has been crucially important, even if it may not have been universally welcomed, as Christie (1999) points out:

New technologies, and particularly the Internet, have revolutionized our lives. Even those who are wary of change and mistrust the intrusion of technology have been unable to avoid the transformation. Technology has crept up on us, seeping into everyday routine tasks such as shopping, banking and communication. The world really is a smaller place, as people from around the world link up to do business, share knowledge and build virtual communities using information that is more accessible, quick to retrieve and available 24 hours a day.

For IMCA, CSM and the enterprises they serve, in addition to proprietary knowledge benefiting the enterprise, there is an imperative to replenish and nourish the published knowledge pool from which they draw.

Action learning focuses on real challenges within the workplace. Outcomes are key to the learning process. For many years, IMCA action learning programmes have delivered tangible benefits to both individuals and their organizations. Real problems and challenges are tackled and actions taken to implement change and bring about improved services or processes. Dissertations and theses are written, action implemented, but what then?

IMCA believes that dissemination of knowledge is crucial that best practice is shared and information is easily accessed. Action Learning Harvest grew out of this commitment to sharing knowledge and best practice. As a strategy it focuses on publishing research, building archives of knowledge and opening up this knowledge to researchers, academics, scholars and practitioners. In effect, Associates are laying down foundations for future managers while utilizing existing knowledge to further their own research. Benefits from publishing research are many and impact upon the author, their organization and colleagues using the published knowledge. In an IMCA Published Learning Action Guide benefits are listed as:

- Dissemination of knowledge: access to research, practice and innovative thought.
- Organizational knowledge: lessons learned from worldwide best practice.
- Individual learning: concentrates the mind on important issues.
- Creation of archives: building a body of learning and experience.
- Research ranking: benefiting your institution.
- Career enhancement.
- Recognition from peers.
- Self-esteem: getting a buzz from seeing your work in print.

The Action Learning Harvest strategy, led by a full-time Director (Published Learning), drives forward the IMCA's commitment to disseminating learning and building accessible archives of knowledge. Associates undertaking Masters and Doctoral programmes are now required to publish a predetermined number of articles as they progress through their course. This normally consists of a literature review and a gestalt or summary paper. For in-company sets, a tutor-led paper is recommended to summarize main learning points of the Set as a whole. A system is in place to collect articles in a routine manner and house them in online journals. Management Literature in Review (MLR) was designed specifically to house literature reviews written by students from the IMCA and Canadian School of Management. Content is updated regularly and covers a range of management topics from around the globe. From the student perspective, MLR performs several functions:

- It acts as a central archive of management-related material.
- It provides good examples of how to write a literature review.
- It offers guidance and links to resources on how to get work published.

Journal users have access to current articles plus archived material. Visitors to the MLR website may be researchers, academics, practitioners or scholars. As the journal content appeals to an international audience, the work of authors and their organization will be open to a wide readership and networking opportunities.

At IMCA, Associates build on recorded knowledge, innovate, develop and implement solutions to real challenges within their own organization. They relate theory and best practice to actual problems. Publishing their outcomes and findings closes the loop, providing future researchers, managers and others with current best practice and knowledge. The process is continuous.

Publishing at IMCA is not just for the sake of it. Dissemination of knowledge is the main focus, but another element of the strategy is that Associates are encouraged to write about their work and get it published. For many, IMCA's online journals are a first step to publishing. Some may be daunted by the prospect of allowing others to comment on their research. Once Associates are required to publish in order to obtain degree credits, some are willing to take the plunge and submit work to journals of international publishers. It is part of the role of the Director (Published Learning) to facilitate a wider coverage of research, working with major publishers such as MCB University Press to achieve this aim.

At CSM an authors' club was set up to proactively develop writer skills and bring together a group of like-minded people who would help each other to find publishing routes. While interest areas cover a range of subjects, the desire to publish is a common thread which links Club members together. Within a few short months, progress was evident, with

several members having work accepted for publication. The Club looks set
to thrive.

To conclude

1. Action learning creates new knowledge. Organizations would be wise to
   realize the full potential of project outcomes by adopting a company-wide
   approach to the implementation of new ideas. A holistic view makes
   good sense.
2. New technologies are rapidly changing the way managers access information. Tapping into the latest international innovative thinking and
   practice is important if organizations are to stay ahead of the game.
3. Organizations seeking to discover the true potential of their employees
   are utilizing technology to develop new ways of learning. Enterprise
   Schools of Management or corporate universities are delivering
   powerful solutions for many companies.
4. Capturing knowledge in a systemized way and ensuring accessibility is a
   good way of making knowledge work. Publishing knowledge in a routine
   manner develops a culture where sharing best practice becomes second
   nature.
5. IMCA and CSM work with clients to understand theory and practice
   worldwide, apply this knowledge to solve real workplace issues and, in
   doing so, create new knowledge. The process is continuous and of
   benefit to individual scholars, organizations and future problem-solvers.

Optimizing learning outcomes goes beyond individual organizations. As
publishing opportunities increase, so the opportunities for networking and
collaborative actions improve. IMCA, CSM and their clients use technology
to leverage knowledge to their advantage while leaving a legacy of learning
for future scholars.

References

Allee, V. (1999) 'The art and practice of being a revolutionary', *Journal of Knowledge Management,* Vol. 3 No. 2.
Bowerman, J. and Peters, J. (1999) 'Design and evaluation of an action learning program –
a bilateral view', *Journal of Workplace Learning,* Vol. 11 No. 4.
Christie, A. (1999) 'Virtual universities and the publishing revolution: a publisher's view-
point', *Library Hi Tech,* Vol. 17 No. 1.
Dealtry, R. (1998) 'Engendering corporate scholarship: for top level management perfor-
mance', *Journal of Knowledge Management,* Vol. 1 No. 3, March, pp. 197–206.
Drucker, P. (1995) 'The information executives truly need', *Harvard Business Review,*
January–February, pp. 54–62.
McAdam, R. and McCreedy, S. (1999) 'A critical review of knowledge management
models', *The Learning Organization,* Vol. 6 No. 3.
McLoughlin, H. and Thorpe, R. (1993) 'Action learning – a paradigm in emergence: the
problems facing a challenge to traditional management education and development',

British Journal of Management, Vol. 4, pp. 19–27.

Margerison, C. and McCann, D. (1996) 'Five skills to improve performance', *Team Performance Management: an Internatonal Journal,* Vol. 2 No. 1.

Nonaka, I. and Takeuchi, K. (1995) *The Knowledge Creating Company: How Japanese Companies Create the Dynamics of Innovation,* Oxford, Oxford University Press

Peters, J. and Smith, P (1998) 'Learn to ask the right questions', *Journal of Workplace Learning,* Vol. 10 No. 3.

Peters, J., Wills, G. and Sandelands, E. (1998) 'Footsteps in the sand: A reflection on past and futures in our institutions of scholarship', *Virtual University Journal,* Vol. 1 No. 1, pp. 1–6.

Revans, R. (1998) *The ABC of Action Learning,* London, Lemos and Crane.

Sandelands, E. (1998) 'Developing a robust model of the virtual corporate university', *Journal of Knowledge Management,* Vol. 1 No. 3, March, pp.181–8.

Skyrme, D. and Amidon, D. (1997) *Creating the Knowledge-based Business,* London, Business Intelligence.

Teare, R. (1998a) 'Implementing virtual support for workplace learning', *The Journal of Workplace Learning,* Vol. 10 No. 2, pp 122–37.

Teare, R, (1998b) 'Developing a curriculum for organizational learning', *The Journal of Workplace Learning,* Vol. 10 No. 2, pp. 95–121.

Wills, G. (1993) *Your Enterprise School of Management: a Proposition and Action Lines,* Bradford, MCB.

Chapter 16

Learning renewal

A manifesto for career-long development

DAVID TOWLER

Introduction

There are two requirements for establishing career-long learning. One is the creation of a learning organization to provide the right environment; the other is providing a process or structure that will support individual learning over the longer term. The purpose of this chapter is to show how both a learning organization and career-long learning can be created and sustained.

Career-long learning lies at the very heart of a learning organization. It is essentially a partnership between the organization and the individual. Without the active involvement of the organization, the purpose and opportunity for individual career-long learning is simply not there. Unless individuals are positive about learning, it will simply not happen. Both sides of the partnership need to be actively and permanently engaged. career-long learning cannot be treated as a flavour of the month; it has to be worked at, nurtured and managed.

Most chief executives, directors and managers need something clear, specific, measurable and practicable that they can understand and do in order to create a learning organization. They also need it to fit on to a couple of sides of A4 and it needs to tell them:

- the features and benefits of being a learning organization;.
- how to become one;
- how to measure when they have become one.

Individuals also want something straightforward and structured. They want to be sure that any learning will be directly related to their own personal requirements and done at a pace and in a manner which suits them. They also need to know how to learn, how to make the best use of learning resources and how to relate off-the-job learning to on-the-job learning and *vice versa*.

In the following pages I will be exploring how these needs can be met by showing how some relatively complex theories and ideas can be brought together into a straightforward approach to developing learning organizations and career-long learning. This will include:

- An analysis of the reasons for becoming a learning organization.
- The key steps to understanding the learning organization and the essential processes which sustain it.
- The characteristics of a learning organization and what they look like in terms of management style and values.
- How to provide for and achieve career-long learning.

The case for becoming a learning organization

Organizations have gone through an extremely anti-people period over the last ten to fifteen years as they have tried to become more flexible and competitive (Leigh, 1997). This has generally been rationalized as a drive towards downsizing, delayering and decentralization. The theory behind it has emerged in the form of Handy's shamrock type of organization, where a core of permanent staff is supported by a fringe of contractors and casuals who are used as and when needed. This in turn has been further refined into what Handy calls the 'triple-I organization' (I = Intelligence, Information and Ideas) along with their flat, upside-down structures, strong customer focus and more bottom-up strategies (Handy, 1989).

The reality, however, is generally quite different. The main problem is that most organizations have simply got stuck in the drive for increased efficiency and have been very slow to identify and focus on new challenges. Downsizing and delayering have simply reminded people of just how vulnerable they are. They have also resulted in the loss of vast amounts of experience and talent. Business Process Re-engineering has been a corporate disaster. The concept that if you grow the person, you will also grow the organization, has become almost completely alien.

Evidence of this is the increasingly narrow focus on the contribution that training is expected to make to the bottom line. A good example is the relatively slow take-up of Investors in People in the UK, in which companies create and relate people strategies to their business plans. There is over-reliance on tightly defined company-specific competences which are very often poor imitations of nationally defined versions, particularly in the case of management standards. The abandonment of career planning in favour of self-development has been a recipe for favouritism and elitism. The introduction of individual performance-related pay has resulted in 75 per cent of employees feeling they have lost out.

Recent research by the American Society for Training and Development (ASTD) and Britain's Association of Management Education and Development (AMED) identifies a number of major trends in training and development. The ASTD argues that the major challenges facing companies will be:

- A continuing increase in demand for skills as a response to rapid technological change.
- An increasingly well-educated workforce.
- Personnel and training functions will reduce in size and will have to revolutionize the way in which learning and development are delivered.
- A continuing need to restructure to respond to changes in the business environment.
- A continuing shift in responsibility for training and development to line management.
- A much stronger focus in training and development on improving performance and human performance management.
- A growing evolution of companies into learning organizations.

AMED argues there are five key issues on which it feels management education and development should focus in order to meet these challenges:

1. Humanizing work.
2. Globalization.
3. Sustainable development.
4. Stakeholder relationships.
5. Ethics and values in development.

In other words, it is only those organizations which embrace individual and organizational learning as part of their structure, values and mission that are likely to survive. The case for the learning organization and career-long learning could not be clearer.

Action learning

In order to become a learning organization the first concept organizations need to understand is the Revansian concept of action learning. The reason for this is that action learning provides the underpinning process which drives all other forms of learning. Revans argues that unless an organization is able to learn at a faster rate than the changes taking place in its environment, it will very soon get into difficulties. He also argues that knowledge is not enough on its own to deal with change; it may even be a handicap if it is based on the past or dead events. The key to making knowledge relevant to real-life problems is by working in groups and through rigorous questioning. In other words, the key to generating collective learning within an organization is through working in teams on real, live business issues. For

Revans the group or 'Set' is the key to individual and organizational learning (Revans, 1984).

Five Core Disciplines
The second concept which needs to be understood is Senge's Five Core Disciplines (Senge, 1990). These are crucial to establishing the kind of learning outcomes individuals should be trying to achieve. They also complement and reinforce Revans' idea of Set working. Their primary role, however, is providing performance measures for individual development: in other words, a method of measuring the distance individuals travel in their development. They can also provide the basic building-blocks for individual development plans. Senge defines the Five Core Disciplines as:

1. *Systems thinking:* A way of thinking about, describing and understanding the forces and relationships that shape organizational behaviour.
2. *Personal mastery:* Learning to expand our personal capacity to create the results we most want, and creating an organizational environment that encourages all its members to develop themselves towards the goals and purposes they choose.
3. *Mental models:* Reflecting on, continually clarifying, and improving our internal pictures of the world, and seeing how they shape our decisions and actions.
4. *Shared vision:* Building a sense of commitment in a group, by developing shared images of the future and the principles and guiding practices of how to achieve it.
5. *Team thinking:* Transforming conversational and collective thinking skills, so that groups of people can reliably develop intelligence and ability greater than the sum of individual members' talents.

The essential question for the manager, however, is what do they mean in practice terms and how do they fit with Revans? The answer lies in a more detailed examination of what each of the Five Disciplines means.

Senge sees *systems thinking* as:

. . . a discipline for seeing wholes. It is a framework for seeing interrelationships rather than things, for seeing patterns of change rather than static 'snapshots'. It is a set of general principles distilled over the course of the twentieth century, spanning fields as diverse as the physical and social sciences, engineering, and management. It is also a set of specific tools and techniques originating in two threads: in 'feedback' concepts of cybernetics and in 'servo-mechanism' engineering theory dating back to the nineteenth century. During the last thirty years, these tools have been applied to understand a wide range of corporate, urban, regional, economic, political, ecological, and even physiological systems. And systems thinking is a sensibility for the subtle interconnectedness that gives living systems their unique character.

He sees its importance as follows:

> I call systems thinking the fifth discipline because it is the conceptual cornerstone that underlies all of the five learning disciplines of this book. All are concerned with a shift of mind from seeing parts to seeing wholes, from seeing people as helpless reactors to seeing them as active participants in shaping their reality, from reacting to the present to creating the future. Without systems thinking, there is neither the incentive nor the means to integrate the learning disciplines once they have come into practice. As the fifth discipline, systems thinking is the cornerstone of how learning organizations think about their world.

So essentially, what Senge is saying is that organizations need to develop the capacity of individuals to obtain, digest and make sense of vast amounts of information if they are to remain competitive. The problem they have in doing this is that it is impossible to divorce one part of the organization from the other. In other words, the organization is a system consisting of a series of interdependent parts, and a change to one part of the system will have implications for the rest. It is essential therefore that individuals are cultivated to see this.

The main question is how to ensure that organizational problems are considered from as wide a perspective as possible. There are two reasons for this. One is that a problem really is a problem and not just one form of perspective. As Senge says, 'Problems viewed from a systems point of view, as opposed to a single snapshot, can turn out not to be problems at all.' The second is that, having agreed there is a problem, all the necessary interests are brought together from across the organization to solve it.

This is where action learning comes in. Revans argues that the most effective way to bring people together to work on problems is by using the Set approach. He also argues that the combined input and learning of the Set will go some considerable way towards defining and solving the organization's problems in terms of the system as a whole. He acknowledges, of course, that the Set has to operate in the right conditions: namely that it has to have the backing of senior managers, and its members have to be prepared to put personal agendas aside to work for the common good.

Revans argues that the power to change and adapt is only effective in a Set environment. Senge argues that tackling problems in the broader context of the organization as a whole is the only effective way of responding to changes to the external environment. Therefore, by bringing the two approaches together the organization can optimize its ability to identify and respond to external pressure.

The next step is to ensure that individuals want to learn. Senge defines the importance of learning in the following terms:

> Organizations learn only through individuals who learn. Individual learning does not guarantee organizational learning. But without it no organizational learning occurs.

He sees the key to learning as *personal mastery* which he defines as:

> Personal mastery goes beyond competence and skills, though it is grounded in competence and skills. It goes beyond spiritual unfolding or opening, although it requires spiritual growth. It means approaching one's life as a creative work, living life from a creative as opposed to reactive viewpoint. As my long-time colleague Robert Fritz puts it: 'Throughout history) almost every culture has had art, music, dance, architecture, poetry, storytelling, pottery, and sculpture. The desire to create is not limited by beliefs, nationality, creed, educational background, or era. The urge resides in all of us . . . [it] is not limited to the arts, but can encompass all of life, from the mundane to the profound.'

What Revans offers is the way to implement the conditions laid down by Senge to achieve his concept of personal mastery. Revans argues there are two basic conditions for transforming individual learning into organizational learning. The first is that there must be a real organizational problem which needs to be tackled. The second is that each project must be something which senior managers are determined to do something about. He sees the role of the Set in this context as:

> . . . first, to understand the motivation of his client (a senior manager/managers) in order to secure the utmost of his confidence; second, to ensure that the client's confidence is expressed in the widest introductions of the participant throughout the enterprise: third, to classify the torrents of new facts, opinions, rumours, interpretations, doubts, misgivings and utter rubbish that will otherwise threaten to sweep him off his feet under three headings, or diagnostic questions. These are (and by the very nature of all intelligent achievement):

1. What are we (the firm, you, or even me, myself) trying to do?
2. What is stopping us (the firm, you, etc.) from getting it done?
3. What might we (the firm, etc.) be able to do about it?

It would be unrealistic to imagine that any single person, even the client, would have complete answers to these three questions.

In other words, Revans is providing the means by which individuals can achieve the kind of personal mastery which Senge describes. Set working provides the vehicle for bringing individuals together. Organizational issues or problems provide their focus. The involvement of senior managers as the Set clients provides the means by which individual and collective learning can be translated into organizational learning.

Having established what it is individuals need in order to learn, the next step is to create the *right climate for learning*. Senge sees each individual having:

> . . . an internal image of the world with deeply ingrained assumptions. Individuals will act according to the true mental model that they sub-consciously hold, not according to the theories which they claim to believe. If team members can constructively challenge each other's ideas and assumptions, they can begin to perceive mental models, and to challenge these to create a shared mental model for the team. This is important because ultimately it is the individual's mental model which will control what they think can or cannot be done.

In other words, within organizations there is a commonly held view that

> many of the best ideas never get put into practice. Brilliant strategies fail to get translated into action. Systematic insights never find their way into operating policies. A pilot experiment may prove to everyone's satisfaction that a new approach leads to better results, but widespread adoption of the approach never occurs.

Senge identifies the organizational constraints which lie behind this as 'the basic diseases of the hierarchy'. This means that too many organizations fall into the trap of always doing what they have always done, with the result that they always get what they already have. The objective, therefore, is to create a will and an urge to innovate, and Revans would see the Set as the basis for achieving it.

Senge describes the importance of *shared vision* in even more dramatic terms. He sees it in terms of a force in people's hearts, a force of impressive power. It may be inspired by an idea, but once it goes further – if it is compelling enough to acquire the support of more than one person – then it is no longer an abstraction. It is palpable. People begin to see it as if it exists. Few, if any, forces in human affairs are as powerful as shared vision.

He also sees it as vital to the organization

because it provides the focus and energy for learning. While adaptive learning is possible without vision, generative learning occurs only when people are striving to accomplish something that matters deeply to them. In fact, the whole idea of generative learning – 'expanding your ability to create' – will seem abstract and meaningless until people become excited about some vision they truly want to accomplish.

He goes on to say

Today, 'vision' is a familiar concept in corporate leadership. But when you look carefully you find that most 'visions' are one person's (or one group's) vision imposed on an organization. Such visions, at best, command compliance – not commitment. A shared vision is a vision that many people are truly committed to, because it reflects their own personal vision.

So how does action learning help? First of all, Set learning builds a strong sense of group commitment. Second, it facilitates and promotes the exchange of information. Third, it facilitates and promotes joint learning, thereby creating a more knowledgeable and effective workforce.

Having created the right climate, it is crucial to create the right approach to learning. Learning organizations are organizations in which individuals learn collectively. It is therefore a matter of first principle that learning has to be developed through a *team approach*. For Revans it is fundamental to the entire action learning process:

The power of adaptation to the unknown is the capacity to learn, which we call L. If we designate the rate of change as C, supposing it can be measured, then, if C is greater than L (if the world changes faster than the subject (institution) is able to learn) there will be trouble. The subject (institution) will be overwhelmed, as has happened since the Second World War to scores of British enterprises and organizations. On the other hand, if L is greater than C, the subject is able to adapt; change is welcomed since it offers a challenge that the quick-witted learner feels confident to accept. Since C will go on for a few years yet, we are not able to do much to modify it; the nature of L, on the other hand, must engage our most urgent attention.

Normally, those who feel it necessary to learn seek out some teacher with a book (often with two or more books) filled with knowledge, and then undertake to follow that teacher's instructions. And a student may even submit to taking so seriously what the teacher has to tell him that, after some time, the learner agrees to undergo examination and prove how much of the instruction has been remembered; all this is very common, and the university system turns upon it. But there is one snag. The knowledge of the teacher, especially if it has been printed in a book, must necessarily be rooted in something from the past; much higher education, indeed, is knowingly dedicated to the continuance of traditional argument, with great effort being made to ensure that the students remain proficient in the practices of yesterday. Sometimes this is more than desirable, as when degrees are awarded at Oxford and Cambridge to an accompaniment of mediaeval Latin, or visitors to Faneuil Hall start asking questions about Paul Revere. However, programmed knowledge, P, already set out in books or known to expert authorities, is quite insufficient for keeping on top of a world, like ours today, racked by change of every kind. Programmed knowledge must not only constantly be expanded: it must be supplemented by questioning insight, the capacity to identify useful and fresh lines of enquiry. This we may denote by Q, so that learning means not only supplementing P but developing Q as well. It is arguable which is the more important in 1984; the evidence is that a surfeit of P inhibits Q, and that experts, loaded with P, are the greatest menace to adaptation to change by questioning, Q. However this may be, our learning equation becomes:

$$L = P + Q$$

P is the concern of the traditional academy; Q is the field of action learning. Although the two terms on the right-hand side of this equation are implicit in the recommendation of 1945, it must be admitted that the explicit presentation of this simple identity has been made only in the past ten years or so. It is, all the same, a useful formula for comparing and contrasting action learning with the standard activities of the academy.

Senge defines team learning as:

Team learning is the process of aligning and developing the capacity of a team to create the results its members truly desire. It builds on the discipline of developing shared vision. It also builds on personal mastery, for talented teams are made up of talented individuals. But shared vision and talent are not enough. The world is full of teams of talented individuals who share a vision for a while, yet fail to learn. The great jazz ensemble has talent and a shared vision (even if they don't discuss it), but what really matters is that the musicians know how to play together.

He goes on to describe its importance as:

There has never been a greater need for mastering team learning in organizations than there is today. Whether they are management teams or product development teams or cross-functional task forces – teams, 'people who need one another to act', in the words of Arie de Geus, former co-ordinator of Group Planning at Royal Dutch/Shell, are becoming the key learning unit in organizations. This is so because almost all important decisions are now made in teams, either directly or through the need for teams to translate individual decisions into action. Individual learning, at some level, is irrelevant for organizational learning. Individuals learn all the time and yet there is no organizational learning. But if teams learn, they become a microcosm for learning throughout the organization. Insights gained are put into action. Skills developed can propagate to other individuals and to other teams (although there is no guarantee that they will propagate). The team's accomplishments can set the tone and establish a standard for learning together for the larger organization.

He outlines three main conditions for achieving effective team learning as:

Within organizations, team learning has three critical dimensions. First, there is the need to think insightfully about complex issues. Second, there is the need for innovative, coordinated action. Third, there is the role of team members on other teams.

Team learning also involves learning how to deal creatively with the powerful forces opposing productive dialogue and discussion in working teams. Chief among these are what Chris Argyris calls 'defensive routines', habitual ways of interacting that protect us and others from threat or embarrassment, but which also prevent us from learning. For example, faced with conflict, team members frequently either 'smooth over' differences or 'speak out' in a no-holds-barred, 'winner take all' free-for-all of opinion – what my colleague Bill Isaacs calls 'the abstraction wars'. Yet, the very defensive routines that thwart learning also hold great potential for fostering learning, if we can only learn how to unlock the energy they contain. The inquiry and reflection skills introduced in Chapter 10 begin to release this energy, which can then be focused in dialogue and discussion.

So what they are both saying is that in order to become a learning organization, organizations should establish group working across traditional boundaries on live business issues as a major feature of their operation. They should also establish self-managed learning as normal practice throughout the whole of their workforce. Senge defines what collective learning means and the essential conditions for achieving it. Revans shows how the process can be made to work.

Lifelong learning

The third concept organizations have to understand is lifelong learning. Basically this is creating a culture in which all employees accept the idea of continuous learning and development as the norm. Key features of this will include:

- Teaching people how to learn, helping them understand their own style and method of learning, and encouraging them to take responsibility for managing their future learning.
- Creating learning opportunities.
- Providing the resources for learning.
- Accreditation of Prior Experience and Learning.
- Continuing Professional Development.
- Encouraging and supporting personal development plans.
- Mentoring.
- Supporting self-managing learning groups or sets.

Triple loop learning

The fourth concept organizations have to understand is how to turn individual and collective learning into organizational learning. The way they do this is through triple loop learning (Swieringa and Wierdsma, 1993).

Single loop learning:

> Where collective learning in an organization brings about changes in the existing rules. This is usually applied at the level of improving quality, service and customer relations. In single loop learning the underlying rules of the organization are scarcely if ever questioned. No significant changes take place in strategy, structure, culture or

systems. Changes in rules and behaviour are more at the level of more of the same but better. Single loop learning can be described as improving within the existing organizational parameters.

Double loop learning:

Double loop learning is usually needed when external signals indicate that adjustment of the rules alone is no longer enough. It is also called for when internal signals suggest the rules are causing problems and friction; that people don't know what they are trying to achieve in a collective sense. Failure is often characterised by the avoidance of discussion and debate; doing nothing or running away from problems; apathy; and acceptance of collective incompetence; or, alternatively, unproductive action, i.e. rearranging deck chairs on the *Titanic* syndrome.

Triple loop learning:

This is when the essential principles on which the organization is founded come into discussion. When questions are raised about the position the company or section of the company wishes to adopt in the outside world. The role it aims to fulfil, the business it wants to be in and the identity it has. What kind of company, institution or department do we wish to be, and why? Triple loop learning can be described as development. It is the development of new principles with which an organization can move on to a new phase.

So essentially, the organization has to monitor and evaluate its performance against the requirements of its external environment, which will be in a constant state of change. It is crucial, therefore, that fresh thinking, new perspectives and insights are brought to bear to do this. It is crucial that all managers are fully involved and committed to taking the process forward. There has also got to be a willingness to change anything and everything from top to bottom.

Characteristics of a learning organization
The final concept organizations have to understand is what a learning organization actually looks like. Hitt compares and contrasts their key features with traditional organizations in the terms shown in Table 16.1 (Hitt, 1995).

Traditional	Learning
Efficiency	Shared values
Effectiveness	Excellence
	Organizational renewal
Working group	Team
	Synergistic team
	Strategy
Road map	Learning map
Structure	Dynamic networks
Hierarchy	
Staff	People who know
	People who learn
Adaptive learning	Skills
	Generative learning
Measurement system	Balanced scorecard
Financial reports	
Set objectives	Empowers staff – gives power to others to get things done
Evaluate performance	Develops a shared vision
Take corrective action	Provides the resources needed to achieve the vision
Retains authority	Delegates authority
Controller	Catalyst/facilitator

Table 16.1
Comparison of
key features of
traditional and
learning
organizations

Once the principles are understood, the next step organizations need to understand is how to implement them.

How to become a learning organization

Understanding the philosophy is one thing, but putting it into action is quite another. As with many theories, the answer is to turn the philosophy into a standard or series of practical actions which can be implemented and measured. The purpose of this is to provide a clear and straightforward statement of what is required to become a learning organization.

The learning organization standard

1. A learning organization makes a commitment from the top to create an environment of individual, team and organizational learning to achieve its business aims:

- The organization promotes learning by tracking its business environment.
- The organization ensures all employees are aware of and fully involved in developing its vision and aims.
- The organization ensures all employees at all levels work together to achieve individual and collective growth through learning.
- The organization ensures that individuals and teams are given every possible encouragement and support to grow and develop their level of responsibility, creativity and competence.

2. A learning organization promotes the exchange of information and joint learning between employees to create a more knowledgeable and effective workforce:
   - The organization establishes group working across traditional organizational boundaries on live business issues and problems as a major feature of its operation.
   - The organization achieves self-managed learning by groups and individuals as normal practice throughout the whole of its workforce.
   - The organization creates collective learning opportunities by bringing together individuals with a variety of skills, knowledge and technologies.

3. A learning organization takes action to create learning communities and to develop a culture of lifelong learning throughout their workforce.
   - The organization ensures that all employees are provided with incentives, resources and opportunities to continually develop their individual learning throughout their working lives.
   - The organization ensures all individuals develop themselves towards agreed goals.
   - The organization creates opportunities for individuals to work collectively to reflect on, clarify and improve their understanding of their working environment in order to improve their capability to take decisions and action.
   - The organization builds a sense of commitment by encouraging groups to develop shared visions and values for the future development of the organization.

4. A learning organization takes action to turn individual and group learning into organizational learning.
   - The organization evaluates its investment in learning to assess achievement and plan for future learning.
   - The organization evaluates the effect of learning on its culture, values, systems and performance.
   - The organization evaluates the effect of learning on its business strategy and its position in its business environment.

Achieving the standard

The next question is how to set about achieving the standard. The main steps would be:

1. The organization formally adopts the policy that it will work towards becoming a learning organization.
2. A 'health check' or audit is done with external help to establish how the organization measures up to the standard.
3. An action plan is drawn up and the organization formally commits itself to implementing the plan.
4. The organization takes action and collects and prepares evidence to show how it is meeting the standard.
5. When it is satisfied it meets the standard, the organization applies for recognition to IMC as a Learning Organization.
6. Assessment and verification of the evidence is done through site visits followed by a recommendation to IMC.
7. On receiving recognition, the organization draws up its plans for continuous improvement and renewal at three-year intervals.

Developing a career-long learning framework

The standard for employers is only one side of the equation. The other is the question of how to achieve career-long learning among individuals. There are five distinct stages forming an overall framework which we have developed at IMC in order to support career-long learning. These in turn are supported by virtual universities, credit mapping, Set-based learning, and self-managed learning. The stages are outlined in detail below.

During the start-up to all IMC programmes, Associates are introduced to action learning and learning to learn. This helps them to understand the learning process and to identify actual and potential blockages. It also helps them understand their own preferred, individual approach to learning; how to build on their strengths; overcome blockages; and to transfer learning from off-the-job to on-the-job and *vice versa*.

One of their first assignments is on 'Own Organization Monograph and Career Development' (OOMCD) in which Associates are asked to evaluate their career development in the context of their organization's requirements. This includes evaluating their past learning and identifying future learning aims. They are also required to develop specific learning objectives and create an action plan to achieve them.

Their final assignment, or 'Evaluative Assessment of own Management Learning' (EAML) takes the OOMCD a step further. The EAML is usually completed somewhere between eighteen months and two years after starting their programme. Associates are asked to assess progress against the action plan from their OOMCD. They are asked to evaluate how the off-the-job learning has been transferred to their work and *vice versa*. They are also asked to update their learning plans by producing a new set of learning objectives for the following twelve months.

Twelve months after they have completed their programmes they are invited to submit an A+ Enhancement. The purpose of this is very similar to the EAML, except they are also asked to show how the outcome of their main dissertation has resulted in new learning and action by their organization.

At the end of five years and in order to retain their membership of IMC, all graduates are asked to submit an evaluative assessment of their learning. This can take two forms. One is a full submission of between 3,000 and 7,000 words. On acceptance they receive full membership of the IMC and the title of Companion Member of IMC with the additional initials CintMC.

The second is by 'audit' in which members complete a questionnaire. The 'audit', however, is not considered sufficiently rigorous to entitle them to the full benefits of membership. Consequently they are not entitled to vote in the affairs of IMC, nor do they receive the title of Companion Member.

To complete the link between the standard and individual career-long learning we are also using Senge's Five Core Disciplines to define overall learning aims. In other words, from the beginning of the process Associates will work with their managers, their Set and others to identify specific learning targets which will improve:

- their way of thinking about, describing and understanding the forces and relationships which shape their environment, particularly their business environment;
- their personal capacity to create the results they want to achieve within that environment;
- the way in which they reflect on, clarify and improve their appreciation of their environment and the quality of their decision-making;
- the way in which they build a shared sense of commitment and vision with others of the way in which they wish to shape their future;
- the way in which they work with others to develop teams which create greater value than the sum of the individual members.

Figure 16.1 shows how this process works in practice.

This process or framework helps individuals to focus on their long-term learning aims. It also increases their commitment to the concept of career-long learning, particularly through action learning. It generates a much stronger contribution to their understanding of the organization's environment and development of its business strategy. It also fits in well with most appraisal and staff development systems.

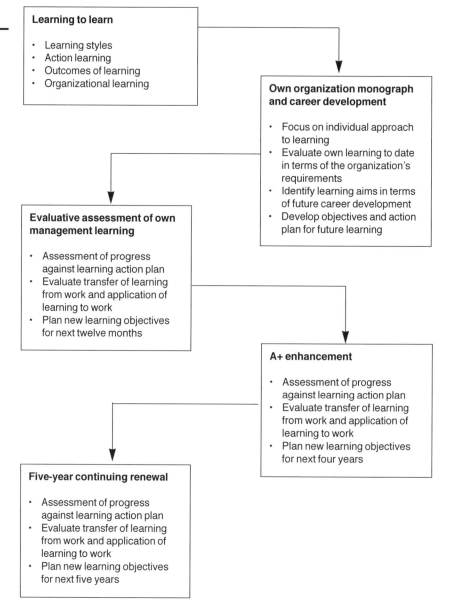

Figure 16.1
Learning targets

As I said at the beginning, career-long learning and learning organizations are two sides of the same coin. They can only be achieved through effective partnership between individuals and their employer. Each side of the partnership needs a structure or framework in order to deliver their part of the deal. The learning organization standard and the career-long learning framework meet that need.

References

Handy, C. (1989) *The Age of Unreason,* Business Books Ltd.

Hitt, W. D. (1995) 'The learning organization: some reflections on organizational renewal' *Leadership & Organizational Development Journal*, Vol. 16 No 8, pp. 17–25.

Leigh, A. (1997) 'Wake up to the end of the anti-people trends', *People Management,* 20 November, p. 49.

Revans, R. W. (1984) *The Sequence of Managerial Achievement*, MCB University Press.

Senge, P. M. (1990) *The Fifth Discipline,* Doubleday.

Swieringa, J. and Wierdsma, A. (1993) *Becoming a Learning Organization,* Reading, MA, Addison-Wesley.

Chapter 17

Building the campus for a university without walls

MATHEW WILLS

Introduction

IMCA has long been known for its action learning educational philosophy and, more recently, for the way in which it has aggressively embraced the online delivery of courseware, library resources and global discussion 'rooms' to support the programmes that it runs. Building from this position, IMCA has now resolved to move to a 'next generation' website solution, one that will facilitate and support the e-business models that it is now employing, one that holds content as a database and delivers multiple customer- and user-tailored web-based learning environments 'on the fly'. With content held this way, IMCA can create websites tailored to the specific needs of corporate customers and academic partners around the world. This we call Site 2000 – the IMCA content management architecture.

Site 2000 background

First, a bit of history.

IMCA is currently building its third-generation online campus. Generation 1 was a bulletin board system adopted in the early 1990s to deliver courseware and student interaction. Generation 2 (which is still currently in place – at www.i-m-c.org) is a 'traditional' website that has evolved and grown to match the requirements of IMCA. Now, a victim of its own success, it has arrived at the point where it is starting to become unmanageable! Generation 3 – Site 2000 – will draw on the learning, content and site structure that has evolved to date but will utilize the latest Internet technologies to deliver the multiple websites that IMCA now needs.

The IMCA website is actually a 'family' of interconnected websites. This website structure reflects the federal nature of IMCA which is made up of a group of partner institutions around the world. The initial IMCA website, like many others, has grown organically in recent years from a small, embryonic site to an unwieldy collection of more than 40 separate sites that makes collective use of the same pool of content (see Table 17.1).

Action Learning Harvest	http://www.imc.org.uk/imc/harvest
Action Learning Int.	http://www.imc.org.uk/imc/al-inter/
African Forum	http://www.mcb.co.uk/africa
Airport Bus. Forum	http://www.mcb.co.uk/imc/baa
Alumni Association	http://www.imc.org.uk/imc/alumni
APC '96	http://www.imc.org.uk/imc/apc-1996
APC '97	http://www.imc.org.uk/imc/apc-1997
APC '98	http://www.imc.org.uk/imc/apc-1998
APC '99	http://www.imc.org.uk/imc/apc-1999
Australia Forum	http://www.mcb.co.uk/pacific
Canadian Forum	http://www.mcb.co.uk/canada
Chairman's Homepages	http://www.imc.org.uk/imc/coursewa/chairmen/johnp.htm
	http://www.imc.org.uk/imc/coursewa/chairmen/mphilchp.htm
	http://www.imc.org.uk/imc/coursewa/chairmen/professional-hp.htm
	http://www.imc.org.uk/imc/doctoral/chairman/
Chinese Forum	http://www.mcb.co.uk/china
Continuing Education Forum	http://www.imc.org.uk/imc/surrey/ceforum.htm
CSM Newsletter	http://www.c-s-m.org/news/alumni/newsletter98.html
CSM	http://www.c-s-m.org
E-Postcards	http://www.imc.org.uk/imc/news/occpaper/postcards/postcd1.htm
Faculty 'website'	http://www.imc.org.uk/imc/faculty
GABAL	http://www.free-press.com/journals/gabal
GAJAL	http://www.free-press.com/journals/gajal
Global Doctorates	http://www.mcb.co.uk/imc/globaldox.htm
Graduation '96	http://www.imc.org.uk/imc/grad96/grad96.htm
Graduation '97	http://www.imc.org.uk/imc/grad97
Graduation '98	http://www.imc.org.uk/imc/grad98
Graduation '99	http://www.imc.org.uk/imc/graduation
IMCA	http://www.i-m-c.org
IMC/OBU	http://www.imc.org.uk/imc/obu
IMC/USQ	http://www.imc.org.uk/imc/usq
IMC Online Services	http://www.imc.org.uk/imc-online
Les Roches	http://www.mcb.co.uk/imc/les-roches
Marriott	http://www.imc.org.uk/mvu
MLR	http://www.free-press.com/journals/mlr
Petrochemical Industry Forum	http://www.mcb.co.uk/imc/fina
Revans University	http://www.imc.org.uk/imc/riu
Senior Partners	http://www.imc.org.uk/imc/partners/spab.htm
Surrey/IMC Authors	http://www.imc.org.uk/imc/surrey/literati
Surrey/IMC	http://www.imc.org.uk/imc/surrey
Uni. for Industry	http://www.mcb.co.uk/imc/ufi-hw/main.htm
VUP	http://www.openhouse.org.uk/virtual-university-press
WHATT	http://www.mcb.co.uk/htgf/whatt

Building the campus for a university without walls

Table 17.1
A family of interconnected websites that makes up the current IMCA 'website'

The admittedly unwieldy site structure and content reflects a great deal of learning that has been done in recent years as the second-generation IMCA website has evolved. The current site has much to commend it and is a testament to the action learning philosophy of IMCA being implemented. When building the third generation system – Site 2000 – we therefore have a great deal of high quality content, systems and structure to build on.

These strengths include:

- A system built around the action learning philosophy of IMCA – focusing on interaction and application of knowledge rather than 'learning facts'.
- IMCA's wealth of experience delivering in-company management education.
- Early adoption of Internet delivery (online since 1995) and a wealth of experience delivering online resourced tuition.
- Global partners and partnering delivering local support.
- Site structure developed over several years.
- IMCA courseware with links to the literature.
- Full regulatory documents online.
- Established online newsletter.
- Registry database with full student and faculty information (including all grades).
- Close links to publishers of online content libraries delivering access to more than 250,000 management articles (via the British Library post/fax service) and 25,000 online full-text articles from more than 100 management journals.

The team working within IMCA have recognized for some time that as the IMCA website has become ever larger and more complex there is a need to deliver and manage the site in a more 'professional' way. With many partners around the world, a federal structure of management centres and many exciting corporate university ventures being developed, the process of professionalizing the delivery of the IMCA website is an opportunity to do more than just deliver a better website. We resolved to deliver not just a better IMCA site but to reflect the current structure of the IMCA 'family of websites' and to deliver many similar websites in a better way. This is the essence of the Site 2000 concept. IMCA, global academic partners, institutions and corporate virtual university partners will, therefore, all get their own virtual university extranet solutions based on IMCA content but augmented by content added by themselves.

First a bit of background and some definitions. The Internet needs no introduction, but it is probably useful to explore the concept of extranets and how
they differ from intranets. Preston and McCrohan (1998) define intranets
and extranets thus:

> An intranet is a network of computers interacting in tandem through
> the use of a common software interface. The physical part of the
> system is linked together through a Local Area Network (LAN)
> and/or a Wide Area Network (WAN). A WAN is simply a collection of
> interconnected LANs. In the case of extranets the system is linked
> together through a LAN/WAN and standard Internet connections.
> Extranets are accessible from the World Wide Web, whereas intranets
> operate only within the LAN/WAN. The physical system is usually a
> client server running LAN and web-server software such as
> Microsoft's Internet Information Server or Netscape's Enterprise
> Server. The user-terminals or PCs utilize a shared Internet software
> platform. In most cases, the platform comprises a browser such as
> Netscape's Navigator or Microsoft's Internet Explorer. The browser
> allows the users of the system to exchange information with other
> system users. The type of user interaction allowed by intranet/
> extranets is multi-faceted. The applications are usually more focused
> and relevant to the needs of the users and allow instant interaction as
> well as feedback. Users can fill out surveys, take online tests, and view
> graphical and text-based material. One of the many advantages of an
> extranet is its ability to restrict the types of information that are
> exchanged. Unlike a LAN, the extranet facilitates the exchange of
> information through a user-friendly, WWW-based graphical interface.

While the current IMCA family of sites is open to all, the next-generation
sites will be a group of focused educational networks built around IMCA
partners and delivered over the Internet. They will be password-protected,
well-managed networked systems. They will be extranets.

Why build our own?
Why are IMCA building their own e-campus extranet solution? Couldn't
IMCA buy an educational extranet solution 'off the shelf'? The answer is
that they tried to find such a solution, but nothing was available that fitted
the bill in two key areas: delivering an action learning environment, and
making things easier for IMCA students and those who manage the system
that will deliver multiple educational extranets.

Driver No. 1: Action learning environment

Lifelong learning is, by definition, something done every day both in and away from the workplace – not occasionally in university lecture theatres. Valuable management development has to be focused on helping managers to 'learn how to learn' from what they come across in their job (and life!) as much as on learning important 'facts'. Any development programmes they undertake should really be based around action learning – the process of learning through doing.

Learning = Programmed Knowledge + Questioning

Traditional education programmes and associated online delivery systems tend to focus on teaching the established body of knowledge followed by a quiz to see how much students have remembered. The IMCA action learning philosophy delivers programmes built around the needs of individuals and their organization, that address the issues that their business is facing right now and will face in the future. The focus is on students learning how they learn and so better understanding how they can learn throughout their lives. Site 2000 is being built to deliver this rich action learning environment. IMCA want and will get an integrated action learning virtual university website solution. Our academic partners and corporate university clients want and will get customized virtual university extranets with an action learning bias.

How will Site 2000 be structured?
The new system will be made up of multiple educational extranets (online campuses) that feature some or all of the following features.

- Online library with 25,000+ articles online and ability to order 250,000 articles via the British Library.
- Online textbooks.
- Comprehensive courseware including links to recommended online articles and textbook chapters.
- Integrated searchable registry system.
- Individual user profiles for all faculty and students (including full academic history/grades with IMCA).
- Discussion areas and 'chat' rooms.
- Student, faculty and alumni newsletters.
- Recommended websites.
- Programme brochures and application forms.
- Campus 'tours'.
- Regulatory documents.
- All content fully searchable and indexed.
- Password/IP-based security (as required).

The aim of this system, along with IMCA accreditation processes, university partnering agreements and back-office administration systems is to create a comprehensive virtual and corporate university delivery system. It will also feature 'intelligent' content management. Where traditional website creation merges the processes of creating content, look and structure, Site 2000 will manage these separately. This will see the separation of website content (pages), appearance (style sheets) and structure (index/links), allowing the delivery of multiple focused 'extranet' sites, each with different 'look' and 'structure' but mostly sharing common content.

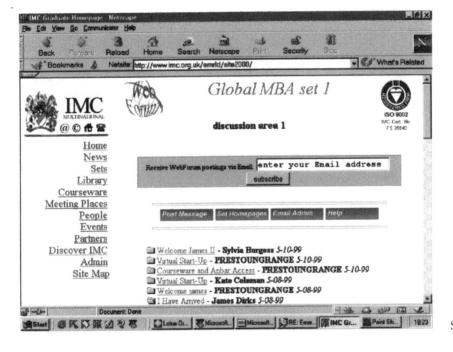

Figure 17.1
Site 2000 in action

Driver No. 2: Making things easier
Site 2000 needs to make things easier for IMCA students and faculty, academic and corporate partners around the world and the team who manage the site operationally.

For students and faculty, Site 2000 will be better in several ways – all the content on each of the Site 2000 sites will be searchable, grades and full personal information will be instantly (and securely) available online, the site will be simple to navigate, well organized, and interaction will be improved by using the latest Internet web conferencing and 'chat' technologies.

Corporate and academic partners will each, in effect, get their own university website to 'manage', the advantage being that almost all of the hard work will already have been done/be done for them on an ongoing basis – access management/guest access, sourcing and integrating the online library, high quality courseware, registry information, and conferencing systems will already be in place. The partner institutions can, however, add to this content and systems, re-organize how it is structured and give their website a different 'look' if they wish.

Perhaps most importantly, Site 2000 will make these ambitious objectives manageable from the centre, so allowing IMCA to deliver multiple IMCA-based websites tailored to our partners, faculty and students, and to split content origination and website creation and make both processes very much easier.

As a long-time deliverer of programmes online, IMCA is well aware of the importance of the Internet as a way of delivering better learning. Improved online content management systems are crucial as we deploy multiple extranet Corporate Virtual University (CVU) and Partner Virtual University (PVU) websites for our corporate university clients and academic partner organizations. IMCA and its customers need the extranets as soon as possible and can't get involved in anything that is complex to create or complex to manage (many of our partners have little Internet development experience). Under the 'traditional' HTML-based web system, IMCA website management has become increasingly problematic. With site design, construction and content all intermingled, the process of creating and managing sites is extremely difficult, complex and expensive. At the operational level, with content, structure and look all embedded into every page on the site, setting up a new website would have taken several months of work, and even making changes to the existing site requires several weeks of effort by the development team.

If it is to succeed, Site 2000 must (and will) reduce much of this complexity and streamline the process of website management.

Key operational points required
- Rapid deployment time when creating new partner websites.
- Ease of use for all IMCA and partner staff (i.e. minimize the need for Internet skills).
- Reduction in development and maintenance costs.
- Minimization of the need to create pages in HTML, allowing non-technical authors to originate and publish content online.
- Scalability (i.e. system needs to be able to handle thousands of users and many Site 2000 websites with minimal IMCA intervention).

The key to making Site 2000 manageable is the separation of site construction into three distinct 'phases':

1. Content (pages).
2. Look (style sheets).
3. Structure (index/links).

Each phase of development can then be dealt with individually by those best qualified to work on it. IMCA and partner organizations in the future might, for example, sub-contract site design (i.e. the 'look') to a website production company, leave site structure to the IMCA web team and pass content creation to the relevant members of IMCA faculty and the newsletter team. The system is being designed so that no Internet skills are required for adding content to any of the Site 2000 sites – creating new material or editing existing content will be a simple matter of filling in pre-formatted forms or creating content using Word (see Appendix 1). Once a Site 2000 extranet site is up and running, a process that should take less than a week, major modifications (e.g. a complete new 'look' for the site) should be possible within a matter of minutes.

IMCA students and partners also demand immediate access to their websites and the information therein whenever they require it. With this in mind, reliability and scalability are also essential parts of Site 2000 specification. The aim is to maximize availability, and as the number of extranets supported by Site 2000 grows, the system will need to allow capacity to grow seamlessly with no service interruptions.

Content for the IMCA website is currently contributed by partners from all around the world. The current centralized approach for maintaining and managing a site of this nature is complicated, time-consuming and runs counter to IMCA's 'Think global, act local' culture. To deliver the Site 2000 multiple extranet model using 'traditional' methods and technology would require a huge number of staff (webmasters, content authors, project managers and quality assurance staff). Site 2000 will significantly reduce the need for all these staff and functions, and create a much simpler system that can be run by the partners themselves. Using a system built around RTIS's Web Publishing Solution it will be possible for several partner staff to access their own site and make their own contributions. Content will then be released to their site once it has been passed for 'publication' by the relevant site editor. The workflow systems also check to ensure site integrity, style and structure and that content is passed to whoever needs to see it, ensuring that no stages in the standard publishing process are missed.

Delivering Site 2000 does, of course, require IMCA to strategically address how the new sites should look and how they should be structured. However, once the look and structure have been determined, the ongoing cost of maintenance will be minimal. Delivering complete new extranet sites will also be much faster – a matter of days rather than months. When IMCA last decided to give the website a completely new look and feel, it took a couple of months and the revision was more cosmetic than comprehensive – a normal approach/length of time in a traditional flat file environment. With Site 2000 a comprehensive revision of the entire site could be done in less than a week.

Implementation

As previously discussed, moving to 'next generation' website delivery requires a highly structured approach to site content, development and website management. Before the transition a thorough audit and classification of existing web content and a review of future system requirements of IMCA, academic and corporate partners is required. This audit and development process is currently being carried out by RTIS – an established Internet technology company – in association with IMCA staff, academic partners and corporate client organizations, to ensure that the system developed will reflect all of their requirements.

Moving to multiple websites delivered 'on the fly' from a database requires a much more structured approach to site content and website management than was the case in the past. The first stage of the Site 2000 project required an internal IMCA team to undertake a thorough audit of the existing website and the likely future requirements that IMCA, partners and corporate universities might have. This involved:

- a review of the document 'types' on the current site;
- consultation with all parties as to the document types that might be added;
- analysis of how the IMCA registry system could be integrated with Site 2000;
- an audit of Internet technologies employed on the current site (e.g. discussion forums and online submission of forms);
- a review of how the new site should be structured.

To achieve this review, IMCA started a dialogue both internally and with partner organizations and corporate customers to ensure that the system developed reflects the requirements of those partners and customers. Once the site structure and content were agreed, a mock-up of Site 2000 was created to help the developers and prospective users to visualize the concept. RTIS then created a specification document that outlined how the technology underpinning Site 2000 would work. Once this has been signed off by IMCA the system will then be built, tested (with selected academic and corporate partners) and then rolled out to all.

Conclusions

Site 2000 will deliver the 'family' of websites and educational extranets that IMCA deserves. IMCA is built around action learning, a federal structure of partner academic institutions, strong links to corporate customers and a focus on interactive online programme delivery – facilitating questioning in a way that traditional distance learning never can. Using 'traditional' Internet technology has meant that the IMCA site could never truly match the powerful learning philosophy, organizational culture and structure of IMCA. The new system will much better facilitate action learning and deliver many independent extranet websites that merge the best of IMCA's global resourcing and systems with local/corporate partner content.

Reference

Preston, P. and McCrohan, K. (1998) 'A strategy for extranet development for professional programs', *International Journal of Education Management*, Vol. 12 No. 4, pp. 154–62.

Appendix 1
RTIS' Web Publishing Solution

Site 2000 is being built in association with RTIS using the Reed Technology Web Publishing Solution (WPS). This system gives producers of timely information an easy-to-use, powerful system for publishing to the Web. Integrated with Microsoft Word, the WPS authoring environment offers a familiar interface, minimizing training and support requirements. Built-in functionality in Microsoft Word provides productivity-enhancing features, such as spell checking and visual table design. And since no knowledge of HTML is required, authors are free to focus on content, not format.

The WPS also provides a complete set of production tools for editors and administrators. An automated release and archive scheduling facility controls workflow and facilitates routine housekeeping tasks. Maintenance effort is also reduced, since the system is built on standard technology, not proprietary tools that require specialized training and knowledge to support.

The system ensures that none of the key quality control stages is missed. Automatic procedures provide audit control, version control, legal timing and can queue content items for the website to go live the moment they have been through all the necessary stages. If there is a need to add additional procedure, this can be done very easily, becoming another stage in the publishing workflow process. Similarly, access can easily be provided for additional individuals or groups of content reviewers who may wish to have access to the material prior to publication.

Appendix 2

Site 2000: Corporate and Partner Site Infrastructure

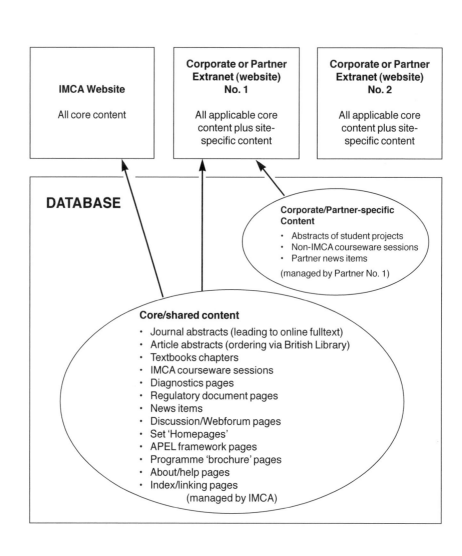

Appendix 3

The IMC Association

Twenty-first-century purpose, goals and structure of the Association of International Management Centres

http://www.imc.org.uk/imc

IMCA is the leading global professional association for career and management development through lifelong action learning, working in partnership with individuals and enterprise in Europe, the Americas, the Orient, the Pacific, and Africa. BAC and DETC accredited, ISO 9002 compliant and limited by guarantee of its Members.

The Association's purpose and goals

- The IMCA is committed to *advancing the professional and managerial careers* of its Members both directly and with the support of the organizations with which they work.
- The IMCA has exclusively espoused *action learning and action research* as the core processes for Member development. It is committed to *advance the understanding and dissemination of these processes* of professional and managerial career development on a global basis.
- The IMCA readily embraces all media for communicating and disseminating knowledge and learning, and is especially committed to remaining at the *forefront of new capabilities created by the Internet.*
- The IMCA is *inclusive* as a profession and makes provision to welcome and encourage new Members through the provision of open access to the Association's services to achieve the various degrees of membership.
- The IMCA believes that the twenty-first century will see a major growth in demand for *lifelong learning* to meet both unavoidable and deliberate career changes and that its Members will receive from the Association the significant support required in such transitions.
- The IMCA is *professionally independent* in order to serve the interests of its Members first and last but works whenever it can further advance its Members' interest with other organizations.

- The IMCA is a global and multinational professional institution and requires *affirmative action* from its Members on programmes of career development to improve the opportunities for the disadvantaged as well as moving forward with well-advantaged individuals and organizations.

The Association's professional structures
- The IMCA is made up of twelve Constituent Institutions and many associated organizations and partners around the world. Each is owned by its Members, being those who have been elected to degrees of membership. Each year at their Annual Assemblies the Members in each Constituent Institution elect their Council of Management which governs their business affairs.
- These Councils have acted in concert since 1988 when by *Their Common Agreement* they established a single *Common* Multinational Professional and Academic Board for the design, resourcing and conduct of all programmes of action learning and research to common globally accredited standards that they offer.
- They resolved further in 1988 that they would convene two *common* annual meetings together taking it in turns to host them. The first is the Annual Professional Congress held each northern Spring, and the second the Annual Congregation for the admission of new Members, held each southern Spring. Venues in recent years have included Australia's Gold Coast, Hong Kong, Kuala Lumpur, Cape Town, Johannesburg, Amsterdam, Helsinki, London, Oxford, Toronto and Curaçao.
- Under The Association's *Common* Ordinances 11, 13 and 22, Partnership Agreements provide financial resources for the development of the profession in addition to that arising from Members' annual subscriptions. These Partners ensure that research and development for the Internet and for career and management development are underwritten and that action learning and action research programmes for new Members are professionally conducted. The Association's Regional Professional and Academic Deans co-ordinate the work globally. The Association takes full advantage of its presence at the forefront on the Internet for electronic resourcing and real-time working. All the Association's programmes can be followed either exclusively via the Internet or resourced from the Internet but with substantial face-to-face workshops too.
- The IMCA's programmes are delivered with additional global accreditation from the British Accreditation Council (BAC) in London and the Distance Education & Training Commission (DETC) in Washington DC, within ISO 9002 Quality Assurance protocols for operational support.

How members benefit

1. *Professional recognition* – The IMCA acts at all times to represent the profession and the interests of its Members to all other parties. It played a major role since the 1960s in ensuring the growth and *development of global professional literature* through its Official Publisher, MCB University Press, and in support of the creation of the world class Virtual Library for practising managers in Anbar + Emerald.

2. *Access to professional services* – The IMCA has sponsored the major Career Development Internet Portal and provides within that Portal its own *Action Learning Institute (ALI)*. This, together with the Association's *credit mapping of prior experience and learning*, enables individuals to become *Affiliate Members* of the IMCA. They can then progress by action learning and action research to higher degrees of membership.

    Affiliates and Members receive continuous access to NewsNet and Virtual Professional Library services.

3. *Degree of Membership qualification programmes* – All Affiliates of the IMCA have the opportunity to advance their professional competence and their careers by taking appropriate qualification programmes. These are conducted around the world by and within the Constituent Institutions and the myriad associates and partners under the imprimatur and protocols of the Association. To develop this work further the Association has sponsored both *Revans University* and the *University of Action Learning* in the Pacific and the Americas. It also works in partnership in selected areas with Business School Nederlands (BSN), the Canadian School of Management (CSM), Southern Cross University in Australia, Surrey and Oxford Brookes Universities in the UK, Universidade Fernando Passoa in Portugal and Brazil and Asia International Open University in the Orient.

    The professional degree programmes are provided by the IMCA at North American and European credit equivalencies for undergraduate Certificate/Associate/Diploma/Bachelor and for postgraduate Certificate/Diploma/Master/Doctor.

4. *Lifelong learning support* – As well as the Professional Services provided, Members are offered A+ Enhancement Reviews and Five-year Continuing Professional Renewal services for Companion Membership. All Members receive *Scholarship assisted access to further programmes* of action learning and action research. *Virtual Conferences and Workshops* can be sponsored at the Action Learning Institute forums and *Member to Member communications* are enabled by the Association's Site 2000 facilities and Global Registry.

The IMCA beyond 2000

The Association's 36-year existence has already seen two major phases of professional growth and innovative development in which we take considerable pride. The third phase is already happening.

- *1964 was our Foundation Threshold.* The first cadre of mature professional practitioners who had completed the UK's new Diploma in Management Studies by evening classes at what are today the Universities of Portsmouth, Westminster, Thames Valley and The City resolved to launch a new association to be known as The Institute of Scientific Business. They held regular workshop meetings, annual congresses around Europe and established their own journal called *Scientific Business.* That journal went on to be the first of over 150 that the IMCA's Official Publisher, MCB University Press, has created and developed today.
- *1982 was our Action Learning Threshold.* It was the year that the Association became international, changing its name to IMC, and resolved to introduce its own professional qualification programmes. It did so because it believed that managers would be well served by a qualifying professional association that used the action learning and action research of Dr Reg Revans rather than traditional pedagogical approaches to career education. The IMCA's Council was immediately supported by five major enterprises – Dow Corning Europe, NatWest Bank, International Distillers & Vintners, Westpac and ICI Australia. From those beginnings we have assisted the career and management development of over 30,000 mid-career executives through the IMCA working on five continents in six languages, with a galaxy of enterprises, from South Pacific islands and Black African townships to major cities of Europe, Asia, Australia and the Americas. The IMCA is the first multinational institution of its type in the world. In 1994 it became the first such institution to be 100 per cent driven by the Internet giving access to every corner of the world. We have also attracted outstanding Honorary Members to our Multinational Court.
- *2000 is our Career & Management Development Threshold.* It is the year that the IMCA has sponsored the creation of the Internet's Career Development Portal. Within that portal, the IMCA's Action Learning Institute enables open access support of individuals' careers through Affiliate Membership to membership of the Association at higher levels and a comprehensive basis for global services. It is the threshold for provision of world class Corporate University resources matched to career appraisal requirements. The simultaneous establishment of the Association's University of Action Learning is the further assertion of the significant role action learning and action research play in Members' lifelong career and management development.

Presidents Emeriti
The Baroness Cox and Dr Reginald Revans

President: Action Learning Institute
Dr Charles Margerison

Principal: University of Action Learning & Revans Professor
Dr Richard Teare

Chairmen of Councils
Sir Robert Balchin, Dr James Kable and Marcel van der Ham

International Presidents
Dr Dick Gerdzen – Business School Nederlands
The Baron of Prestoungrange – Canadian School of Management

Registrar & Deputy Chairman
The Baron of Bombie

Global Marketer
Dr Clifford Ferguson

Partner and Accreditation Relations
Carol Oliver

Global Treasurer
Peter Watson

Director APEL and Credit Mapping
Dr Julian Wills

Dean of AR & Continuing Professional Development
Dr David Towler

Global Dean for CyberProgrammes
Dr Gordon Prestoungrange

Dean of Europe
Jo Denby

Dean of Africa
Dr Dick Gerdzen

Dean of the Americas
Dr Eric Sandelands

Dean of the Orient
Dr Leung Chee Koo

Dean of the Pacific
Dr Ortrun Zuber-Skerritt

All Multinational Resources & Enquiries via

http://www.imc.org.uk/imc

The Association of International Management Centres

Revans Action Learning Workshops
13 Castle Street, Buckingham, England MK18 1BP
Tel: (44) (0) 1280 817222 Fax: (44) (0) 1280 813297

Directorate for Partner Relations
21 Beaumont Street, Oxford, England OX1 2NH
Tel: (44) (0) 1865 207600 Fax: (44) (0) 1865 207601

International Management Centres Australia
16 Benson Street, Toowong, Queensland 4066
Tel: (61) (0) 73 870 0300 Fax: (61) (0) 73 8704013

Canadian School of Management
335 Bay Street, Toronto, Ontario M5H 2R3
Tel: (1) (416) 360 3805 Fax: (1) (416) 360 6863

The Court of Honorary Members of the Association of International Management Centres

The following Outstanding Career and Managerial Achievers have been elected to the Association's Court of Honorary Members in the years shown

Kenneth Adams, UK 1991
Digby Anderson, UK..................................1987
Kenneth Andrew, UK..................................1984
Professor Christopher Argyris, USA..........1987
Tan Sri Abdul Aziz Bin Abdul
  Rahman, Malaysia..................................1990
Tan Sri Dato Azman Hashim, Malaysia......1992
John Bamford, UK 1991
Pat Barrett, Ireland 1999
Michael Bett, UK.......................................1990
Sir Richard Branson, UK 1999
Denis Brosnan, Ireland..............................1990
Sir Adrian Cadbury, UK..............................1985
Tan Sri Osman Cassim, Malaysia 1985
Lui Chak-Wan, Macau................................1992
John C. C. Chan, Hong Kong......................1997
Jayantilal K. Chande, Tanzania 1995
Sir John Chandler, UK 1986
Sir Chio Ho Cheong Tommy, Hong Kong..1995
Sir John Collyear, UK.................................1987
Professor Anthony Cunningham,
  Ireland...1985
David Dand, Ireland...................................1988
Gaston Deurinck, Belgium.........................1988

Sir John Egan, UK.......................................1988
Nigel Farrow, UK..1991
John Foster, UK..1998
Hon John Freemantle, UK...........................1988
James Gulliver, UK......................................1989
Professor Charles Handy, UK.....................1991
Datuk Hassan Harun, Malaysia 1998
Sir John Harvey-Jones, UK..........................1990
Edward Haughey, UK 1992
Liam Healy, Ireland....................................1993
Noel Hepworth, UK....................................1987
Ho Mook-Lam William, Hong Kong..........1995
Sir Trevor Holdsworth, UK..........................1986
Sir Geoffrey Holland, UK 1988
Lord Peter Imbert, UK................................1989
Sir Antony Jay, UK......................................1988
Professor Ivor Kenny, Ireland 1987
Derek Keogh, Ireland.................................1996
Professor Malcolm Knowles, USA 1990
John Kerridge, UK......................................1993
Professor David Kolb, USA 1988
Professor George Korey, Canada 1985
Professor Phil Kotler, USA 1990
Professor John Kotter, USA........................1987

Georges Legros, Belgium	1999	Cliff Richards, Australia	1993
Hon Father Walter Lini, Vanuatu	1988	Gerry Robinson, UK	1996
Lo Yuk Sui, Hong Kong	1998	Gerald Scanlon, Ireland	1988
Linda McHugh, UK	1991	Hiroaki Seto, Japan	1986
Michael Marquardt, USA	1999	Mir Shahariman, Malaysia	1992
J. William Marriott Jnr, USA	1999	Lord Allen Sheppard, UK	1989
Lekgau Mathabathe, South Africa	1993	V. Steve Shirley, UK	1999
Phil Meddings, Australia	1990	Elizabeth Shiu Ching Sing, Hong Kong	1998
Boya Mohindar, Hong Kong	1986	Sir Brian Smith, UK	1989
Stephanie Monk, UK	1998	Dermot Smurfit, Ireland	1997
John Morris, UK	1985	Professor Gillian Stamp, UK	1992
Sir John Neill, UK	1989	Donald Stradling, UK	1987
Ng Kwan Wai, Hong Kong	1992	Sir Peter Thompson, UK	1988
Ng Siu-Chan, Hong Kong	1996	Erik Toivanen, Finland	1996
Edward O'Connor, Ireland	1991	Rev Canon George Tolley, UK	1987
Kevin O'Malley, Ireland	1998	William Venter, South Africa	1987
Anthony O'Reilly, Ireland	1994	Perween Warsi, UK	1999
Rai Bahadur Mohan Sing Oberoi, India	1988	Edward P. H. Woo, Hong Kong	1998
Alan Parker, UK	1997	Peter Wrighton, South Africa	1993
C. Northcote Parkinson, UK	1985	Tan Sri Nik Mohamed Yaacob, Malaysia	1998
Geoffrey Pitt, UK	1989	Yan Poh Soon, Singapore	1999
Joseph Prokopenko, Switzerland	1998	You Poh Seng, Singapore	1985
Sir John Read, UK	1989	Yeoh Tiong Yong, Australia	1996
Professor Reg Revans, UK	1984		

How to gain accredited recognition for Prior Individual Achievement & Learning from the IMCA

The IMCA has, since its foundation, admitted individuals to its Affiliate and Associate levels either partly, or wholly, on the basis of their individual achievements accomplished *prior* to application. The Association does so because it knows that much learning takes place in the world of work through action learning. The process (known officially as the Accreditation of Prior Experience & Learning or APEL) is based on two entry steps:

1. Individual applicants for IMCA membership can document their career to date and any formal programmes of learning followed, and with guidance from our Faculty reflect on their achieved learning.
2. Individual applicants can analyse and set down in a well-structured written or audio-video medium (which the Association calls a CaRD or Career Review Document) what that learning is, so that it can be assessed.

All applicants who submit a CaRD receive feedback from the Association's Dean of Continuing Professional Development that (i) gives a welcome to Affiliate Membership of the Association and (ii) outlines action learning options to improve their performance and enhance their qualifications via the IMCA's higher degrees of membership. In other words, the CaRD must show preparedness by prior individual achievement and learning for, say, entry to the Association's action learning Master of Science (MSc) or action learning Master of Business Administration (MBA) degree of membership with advanced standing credits up to the maximum available of one third; or with advanced standing credit towards the Association's Bachelor degree of membership up to the maximum of three quarters available. Every well-crafted CaRD always gives the opportunity for Affiliate Membership and access to and participation in a wide range of services offered by the IMCA.

Guidance is available online – Everything an applicant needs to know to create a successful CaRD is available online from the IMCA's Global Centre for APEL & credit mapping.

http://www.imc.co.uk/services/coursewa/apel/director.htm

Credit Mapping Services – The IMCA also accredits regular, well-docu-mented career and management development programmes conducted by other professional associations, by organizations in-house, and by training and educational institutions or consultancies. *All successful participants gain agreed levels of personal credit and the route forward to IMCA degrees of membership is set down.* This is achieved by mapping what the programme provides against what the IMCA requires – whence credit mapping. Programme providers may apply for this accreditation service from the IMC Association at any time. The staff involved on the programmes can normally also be accredited as Faculty Members of the IMCA.

Index